THE TWEEDMAKERS

LIBRARY OF TEXTILE HISTORY

General Editor: K. G. Ponting

Henson's History of Framework Knitters
  by Gravenor Henson

The Luddites
  by Malcolm I. Thomis

The Tweedmakers: A History of the Scottish Fancy Woollen Industry, 1600-1914
  by Clifford Gulvin, MA, PhD

The Spinning Mule
  by Harold Catling, BSc(Eng), PhD, CEng, FIMechE, FTI

The Textile Mill Engine, Volume 1
  by George Watkins, MSc

The Textile Mill Engine, Volume 2
  by George Watkins, MSc

DAVID & CHARLES LIBRARY OF TEXTILE HISTORY

The Tweedmakers

A History of the
Scottish Fancy Woollen Industry
1600-1914

Clifford Gulvin

David & Charles : Newton Abbot
Barnes & Noble Books : New York
(a division of Harper & Row Publishers, Inc.)

This edition first published in 1973
in Great Britain by
David & Charles (Holdings) Limited
Newton Abbot Devon
in the U.S.A. by
Harper & Row Publishers Inc
Barnes & Noble Import Division

0 7153 5973 8 (*Great Britain*)
06 492603 6 (*United States*)

Printed in Great Britain by
W J Holman Limited Dawlish

Contents

TO MY MOTHER AND FATHER

List of Illustrations

MAPS

List of Tables

Preface

This study is an attempt to explore one of the byways of British economic history. The Scottish woollen industry did not figure dramatically in the phenomenon known as the Industrial Revolution but it was part of a textile industry that did, and it was of great importance to the population of certain parts of Scotland. Thus the focus is a relatively narrow one, though it is hoped that by contributing to a growing number of regional studies of the nation's economy the book will play a role in permitting a greater degree of precision to be given to generalisations concerning the nature of its growth and development. Nonetheless it is not claimed that my subject has been covered exhaustively. The would-be researcher will, I trust, find his appetite sharpened rather than dulled.

The discussion has been necessarily limited to the mainland of Scotland partly due to the constraints of time, finance and space, but also because my aim has been to study the development of the factory-based industry. The Hebridean branch of the industry has recently attracted its own historian in Francis Thompson.

When dealing with industrial history one cannot ignore technical developments, but, in a conscious effort to get away from technique-based history, processes and machine improvements have only been considered when bearing on the wider issues under discussion.

The readers I have in mind are not only specialist students and teachers of economic history but the 'intelligent layman' who is anxious to ponder from his armchair on the way in which a few of

his forbears lived and worked, and why it is that Scottish
woollens, emanating from places whose whereabouts are still
something of a mystery to the average Sassenach, achieved for
themselves international fame and distinction.

I owe a great debt to many people who have helped me in the
writing of this book, some of whom are mentioned in the Acknow-
ledgements. Despite their valued assistance, however, I remain
entirely to blame for what follows.

ONE

Wool and Cloth in Scotland before the Industrial Revolution, 1600-1770

'We cannot reasonably expect that a piece of woollen cloth will be brought to perfection in a nation which is ignorant of astronomy or where ethics are neglected.' David Hume.

When James VI of Scotland crossed the border into England, following the death of Queen Elizabeth in 1603, he was about to mount the throne of a kingdom far superior economically to his homeland. England was a wealthy nation by Scottish standards. She was much engaged in international commerce; her agriculture was already undergoing those important organisational changes that were to be the prelude to industrialisation; and her woollen industry, though experiencing some difficulties, was large and well-established. Woollen and worsted products accounted for about 80 per cent of England's European trade and the government was much concerned in providing the industry with ample supplies of wool, and from the 1650s in keeping markets open in Europe and elsewhere by denying the foreigner access to her wool. The industry was further served by a pool of highly skilled labour and a well developed commercial and industrial organisation.[1]

By contrast, the state of woollen manufacture in Scotland was underdeveloped, faithfully reflecting the general backwardness of the economy; and, whereas in England the manufacture of wool

13

had become a most important export industry, and raw wool growing was reserved entirely for the benefit of native clothiers, Scotland continued to depend on the export of primary products, of which raw wool was one of the most significant, for most of her foreign revenue. Thus the manufacturing branch remained small and technically primitive. Although the bulk of the domestic market for woollen goods was supplied from home production and often a respectable surplus sent overseas, the demand for the home clip did not meet the supply for much of the century.[2] In addition, the demand by the merchants and gentlemen for higher-grade cloths was almost entirely met by imports from England and Holland.[3] The time-worn practice of heavily tarring sheep to prevent disease, and the general ignorance of sheep husbandry, were sufficient to keep the quality of home-produced wool low enough to make it difficult for any real improvement to be made in the standard of the manufactured product. The export of unimproved primary materials was recognised to be unsatisfactory, and the consistent, if sometimes blurred policy of Scotland in the seventeenth century was to achieve a shift in the structure and balance of the economy by stimulating the manufacture of woollen goods in general, and fine cloth in particular. In simple terms, Scotland's aim was to emulate the English cloth industry, which she saw as the secret of that country's wealth and greatness.[4]

Several factors combined to render the trade in raw wool important to Scotland. In the first place wool represented one of her few plentiful natural resources. The growing of wool in the Border counties was centuries old and favoured by contour and climate.

Secondly, wool was an invaluable commercial asset, providing a simple and speedy means of obtaining much needed currency to finance vital imports.[5] In Europe there was a great demand for wool, and, since supplies of English wool were unavailable, Scotland was well placed to conduct a fruitful trade not only in her own wool but in that smuggled over the English border, and also from Ireland. The progressive antagonism between England and Scotland, particularly towards the end of the century, caused the wool trade to become a political factor, an irritant to the English, and, at least in the eyes of some Scots, a method of gaining trading advantages from a neighbour who denied them access to the increasingly lucrative Atlantic markets.[6]

Reliable data regarding the size of the wool trade are lacking, the available estimates probably giving only a very approximate picture of the traffic. In 1614 the export of wool was said to be in the region of 10,000 stones, with 24lb equalling 1 stone. Annual exports to Baltic countries in the 1670s averaged about 820 stones and had increased to around 4,500 stones by 1700. It was stated in 1698 that 36,000 stones were exported annually to France. Estimates as to the value of the trade are likely to be equally unreliable. In 1614 the annual value of exported wool was said to exceed £50,000. In 1704 the estimates range from £20,000 to £45,000.[7] Decline set in at intervals, particularly after the Restoration, and between 1701 and 1704 when the export of wool was banned.[8] There is some evidence to suggest that trade had declined by 1700, before the prohibition on wool exports, when attention was drawn to the expensive English wool as well as Scottish wool lying 'for the most part unsold at the ports to which it was carried'.[9] Whatever its value, the wool trade certainly had a high relative significance, though the cattle trade was probably already more important by 1700.[10] The agricultural developments in the seventeenth century, though largely orientated towards grain and cattle production, are likely also to have included an increase in the number of sheep, at least in the Border counties. In 1708 there were over 81,000 sheep pastured in thirty Berwickshire parishes, producing enough coarse wool to fabricate more than 65,000 ells of cloth.[11] Writing later, in 1733, Sir John Clerk contended that 'the first and chief branch of the exportation of Scotland [in 1707] was wool'.[12] However, it must be remembered that because the wool trade had political implications it possibly received disproportionate attention from contemporary writers.

As we have said, considerable quantities of wool exported from Scotland were smuggled over the English border and a good deal came from Ireland. In 1698 Black estimated that 50 per cent of the wool exported to France was English, and in 1700 the value of imported English wool was reckoned at about £20,000, much of which, owing to the parlous state of fine-cloth manufacture, must have been exported from Scotland.[13] The strengthened English legislation of 1696, together with the Scottish Act of 1701, banning wool exports, doubtless reduced Scottish exporting at the end of the century. Again according to Black the flow of English wool over the Scottish border dropped from about 17,000 stones in 1698 to only 3,000 stones in 1704. Then, with the repeal of the ban on wool-exporting in Scotland, the volume probably rose again before the Union of 1707.[14]

Other evidence supports the view that the English content of Scottish wool exports was considerable. Government policy in England during the century aimed at maintaining ample and cheap supplies of wool for the manufacturers to ensure that cloth could be sold abroad at competitive prices. The English growers thus failed to exert such influence over policy as their Scottish counterparts and had every reason to run their wool abroad to gain a higher return. Repeated Acts of the English parliament endeavoured to stop the drain. In 1616 the English Merchant Adventurers drew attention to the leakage of English wool through Scottish ports which afforded help to rival woollen industries overseas. In 1622, and again in 1632, the export of wool and wool-fells to Scotland were prohibited by the English parliament, together with fullers-earth and wood-ashes. The importance of the trade from the English point of view is also indicated by her attempt in 1623 to control the destination of all wool from Scotland by buying the whole clip herself in return for a ban on wool exports 'that our neighbouring nations may not be furnished with wools . . . and thereby be enabled to hinder the vent of our cloth'.[15] This move was more an endeavour to remove the temptation to English farmers to smuggle their wool into Scotland, for it is unlikely that English cloth exports would have suffered very much from the export of Scottish coarse wool.

Towards the end of the seventeenth century the problem had again reached large enough proportions to provoke the English parliament into renewed and strengthened legislation, and an Act for 'the more effectual preventing the Exportation of Wooll' was passed declaring that 'the several inhabitants of the several Counties and Shires of this Realm next adjoining the kingdom of Scotland . . . do reap great Profit and Advantage by the Carrying out of Wooll . . . into the said kingdom of Scotland, and exporting them into France and other parts'.[16] Two years later stricter and more localised measures were deemed necessary. Within fifteen miles of the Scottish border owners of wool were required to submit details of all wool stocks and movements to the Riding Officers. Warships were also sent to patrol Scottish and Irish coastal waters to intercept wool shipments, and, on occasion, vessels carrying wool were seized. At the same time the inhabitants of Ripon were sufficiently worried about the running of local wool over the Scottish Border to fear for the survival of their market and petitioned the House of Commons. Despite these measures the smuggling continued and may have expanded, for in 1704 some Yorkshire woollen merchants and clothiers felt it was causing 'Great Decay' in their trading, adding that 'Ye offenders have grown so Bold that they come above 50 miles and carry Wooll off in Dispite all the Laws'. For their defence against 'ye insuelts of ye Smuglers' they advised the Riding Officers to carry firearms.[17]

Some of the English wool smuggled into Scotland was not re-exported but was used in the manufacture of fine cloth, particularly towards the end of the century when various fine-cloth works were being established. In 1700, for example, it was estimated that of 7,196 stones of wool imported into Scotland only 4,503 stones were exported.[18] Nonetheless, the real incentive to English growers was the demand emanating from overseas buyers, for the fine-cloth sector in Scotland remained undeveloped.

The export of wool from Scotland was consistently opposed by the woollen manufacturers there, both in the coarse woollen branch and by the makers of fine cloth. Their primary objection to the trade was that selling wool abroad inflated its price and led to increased costs of production, which neither branch was able to afford. 'If the Wooll masters design to export or if Merchants buy it for exportation, will any man get an ounce weight of it without paying double price . . . ' asked the manufacturers.[19] Scottish coarse woollens had little to commend them in overseas markets except their price, and in order to maintain that advantage in the face of higher costs further reductions in quality were imperative.[20] Moreover, it was claimed, the export of wool only served to encourage the establishment of rival industries abroad in the very countries where cloth was sold, so that the woollen trade declined. For 'When the merchant gets no price abroad [ie for

B

woollens] he cannot give a good price at home; when the poor industrious Manufacturer cannot reap half the value its impossible he can make goods sufficient, so the exportation of wool is the ruin of all.'[21]

The wool trade was also felt to endanger supplies to those Scottish manufacturers who used the choicer qualities that comprised the bulk of wool exports. The representatives of the northern counties and especially those for Aberdeen 'became very soon sensible that the exportation of wool in the Southern shires would in a very little time deprive them of the necessary supplys . . . and . . . utterly destroy their Manufactures.'[22] If the new Mills manufactory, established near Haddington in 1681, was typical, the fine-cloth manufacturers used mainly English and Spanish wool whose export threatened their supplies and drove up production costs, jeopardising their chances of obtaining a firm foothold in the home market for quality goods. Not surprisingly, they took vigorous action to prevent wool from going abroad.[23]

The counter-arguments of the wool-masters turned mainly on the fact that, since the home clip was too large for the purpose of the manufacturers, the export of surplus wool did not conflict with the latter's interests. Also such shipments were important sources of revenue; indeed it was alleged that earnings from the sale of wool exceeded those from cloth. Moreover, they argued, the fine-cloth manufacturers made little use of Scottish wool, preferring English and Spanish varieties; and discrimination against the home clip left them little choice but to export it.[24]

Because of this fundamental clash of interests within the wool textile industry, and in accordance with prevailing mercantilist sentiments the state sought to regulate the industry, as far as possible, in the interests of the manufacturing branch which would add to the value of the wool and also give employment to large numbers of the population. In this policy the Scottish government was hindered by three major factors: the strength of the wool-growers' lobby in parliament, the chronic shortage of foreign currency, and the weakness of the customs administration. Thus legislation tended to fluctuate between the interests of the growers and the manufacturers, and was in any case largely negatived by evasion. Hence wool textile legislation was commonly re-enacted during the century.

An Act prohibiting the export of wool was passed in 1602. Similar legislation was passed in 1614 and again in 1616. Despite an acknowledged surplus over requirements in 1620 and the rejection of the English offer to buy the Scottish clip, wool export was again banned in 1623.[25] The brief enforced union with England between 1654 and 1660 made English wool legislation applicable in Scotland, and the export of wool continued to be prohibited, except under Privy Council licence, at least until 1672.[26] The protective legislation of 1681 fell short of banning wool exports, but increasing pressure from the manufacturers, particularly those in the fine-cloth sector, found expression in the Act of 1701, which forbade the export of wool for a period of five years.[27] However the subsequent decline of wool prices and the presence of large unsold stocks on hand served to vindicate the arguments of the wool-masters and compromises were sought. A Committee of Trade, after investigating prevailing wool prices, suggested that export should only be forbidden when the price on the home market reached an allotted figure for each grade.[28] It was further noted that if the wool stocks could not be manufactured into cloth it would be 'a strange imposition on the proprietors to oblige them to run all their wool . . . into a Dunghill . . .'[29] The ability of the wool-masters speedily to bring some relief to the balance of payments problem swayed the Scottish parliament, and wool exports resumed once more in 1704.

The seventeenth-century Scottish woollen industry can be divided for convenience into (1) the coarse-cloth trade and (2) fine-cloth production. The former made use of local wool and native labour, and served the needs of the majority of the population. In addition considerable quantities were sold to the Continent, the Baltic countries and some even to the Plantations.[30] Production was organised domestically, the family carding and spinning its own wool and having it woven by the local weaver (webster). The raw material was poor, partly because the practice of daubing sheep with tar to protect them from the weather rendered the fleece almost useless for manufacturing purposes. Moreover the more sophisticated arts of dyeing and cropping (see Glossary p 191), the monopoly of the Royal Burghs at the start of the century, made only slow progress in rural areas. Even fulling mills were scarce though some lowland centres had one. In short, the Scots were ill equipped for textile manufacture, and it is not surprising that one contemporary observer described their coarse products as 'very nastily made'.[31] Nevertheless the goods were competitive on the home, and in some overseas, markets, mainly because of low production costs that 'balanced or even out-weighed the greater technical efficiency and superior organisation of the more advanced cloth-making countries'.[32]

Though domestic organisation gave the industry an ubiquitous character, the areas chiefly producing a surplus over local requirements were the central southern and south-western districts and Aberdeenshire, the latter being a sufficiently important centre for it to be regarded as a trade barometer for the whole country.[33] Goods for the market were sold at the local fairs to city merchants, who often travelled far to buy them, sometimes in sizeable amounts.

The foreign trade in coarse woollens was considerable for the greater part of the seventeenth century. In 1614 plaiding and cloth were said to be among the most important of Scottish exports. Discussion concerning the most suitable method of exposing plaiding for sale in the 1630s suggests that woollens still remained a significant item in foreign trade. The political upheavals of the 1640s and 1650s seem to have affected the trade to a lesser extent than others, over 73,000 ells leaving the port of Aberdeen in 1650-1 for Holland and the Baltic.[34] Towards the end of the century the large quantities of plaiding, fingrams and woollen hose formerly sent abroad from the north and from Stirlingshire were regarded with some nostalgia. Exports of 'Galloway Whites' were alleged at their height to have reached 600 sea-packs annually, and fingrams from the north about 600,000 ells annually. In 1668-9, 1669-70 and 1690-1 woollen exports from the city of Aberdeen totalled 138,000 ells to 168,000 ells annually.[35] Whatever credence can be given to these figures, it is clear that coarse-woollen goods occupied an important position in the Scottish export trade for much of the century.

From about 1685 onwards the coarse-woollen trade fell into serious decline. By the early eighteenth century exports of plaiding, fingrams, and stockings from the north were estimated to have fallen by nearly 75 per cent from their former heights. The Aberdeen trade was said to have declined to only 80,000 ells annually between 1694 and 1700, at greatly reduced prices. By 1706 the northern fingram trade was reckoned at only one-sixth of its former value, and that in 'Galloway Whites' was described as 'dead'. Reports were made of goods lying rotting in foreign ports.[36]

The reasons for this decline were partly economic, partly political. Although her union with England was not complete, Scotland was compromised by her neighbour's foreign policy. The Dutch wars of Charles II, the 1688 settlement with William III, and the ensuing French wars, all served to militate against Scotland's trade. At the same time France and Sweden were actively engaged in building up their own woollen industries, making good use of the wool imported from Scotland. The importation of Scottish cloth into France was eventually prohibited, and Sweden took more Scottish wool at the expense of her cloth.[37]

Once due allowance has been given to continued wool exporting and to the economic policies of Scotland's overseas customers for the state of her woollen industry, a third, and allied, factor must be added—the continued inferior nature of her products. Coarse woollens reflected the low level of technical ability in the body of the population, even in the basic processes of spinning and weaving. At the time of the Union most Scottish woollens were still being made from unsorted wool, and the finishing processes even in the fine-cloth trade were woefully inadequate.[38] Consequently it was not uncommon for consignments to be returned unsold from foreign ports.[39] In 1704 it was stated that 'the coarsest goods are the only goods exported as yet',[40] and in these circumstances even an infant woollen industry like that of Sweden was soon able to produce adequate substitutes for imported Scottish cloths.

The conditions necessary for substantial improvements in quality in the lower end of the trade were largely absent: per capita incomes remained abysmally low; the chronic practice of permitting the export of raw wool resulted in most of the better varieties leaving the country; and skilled labour was lacking. 'The unskilfulness of our awin people heirtoforr, togidder with the unwillingness to suffer ony strangeris to cum amangis thame, has bene ane of the caussis that hes hinderit the growth of woollen manufacturing, they being unhable, without the help of strangeris quha ar better acquent with that tred to attine to ony perfectioun in that work.'[41] As we shall see, some attempt was made to encourage foreign workers to settle in Scotland, but the financial considerations, social prejudices and not least the physical difficulty of injecting such labour into a domestically organised industry were usually sufficient to bar its entry.[42]

At the Union, therefore, the once thriving coarse-cloth trade was in an extremely parlous condition. Substitutes had begun to appear for plaiding and fingrams. Aberdeen turned her attention to hosiery, and a similar change was occurring in northern Ayrshire. More important, however, was the rapidly expanding linen industry, which was to replace wool as the main textile export during the coming century.[43]

The wealthier members of Scottish society in the seventeenth century not unnaturally disdained to attire themselves in ill-made home-produced goods. Instead English or French cloths 'of pale colour, or mingled with black and blue' were worn by merchants, while gentlemen dressed in 'English cloth and silks or light stuffs little or nothing adorned . . . '.[44] The French influence upon fashion was marked, at least at the beginning of the century. Throughout the century attempts were made by the Scottish parliament to found a fine-cloth industry in Scotland sufficiently furnished with labour, capital and manufacturing incentives to oust foreign cloths from the home market. Much legislation was enacted, and eventually, at least in theory, the fine-cloth manufacturers were given a remarkable degree of protection.

The encouragement of such an industry was one of James VI's favourite projects. He forbade the import of 'English claith' in 1597, only to rescind the Act in 1599 due to the low level of domestic production and lack of revenue from duties. Attempts had already been made to introduce skilled workmen into Scotland to teach the skills of manufacturing fine cloth to the native population: in 1582 legislative provision was made for a group of Flemings to instruct apprentices in the manufacture of serges, fustians, says and other fabrics. This venture was abortive, however, and in 1599 immigration was expressly forbidden—probably due to resistance from burgh craftsmen jealous of their own privileges.[45]

Nonetheless the condition of wool manufacturing in the country was still regarded as a matter of public concern, and after considering a petition from a native clothworker in 1600 calling attention to 'the grite abuisses and imperfectiounes of the claith maid ordinarily within this realm and the remedies thairof' a scheme was floated, this time with the acquiescence of the Royal burghs, to import better craftsmen from overseas. As an inducement they were to be offered naturalisation, the freedom of the burgh in which they resided, tax exemption for ten years and a suitably reformed minister to teach them the Word of God in their native tongue. They were to be distributed among several burghs in order to diffuse their skills more effectively among the native population.[46]

Eventually, after some difficulties, a number of Flemish workmen were brought over, but they refused to be split up among the burghs. Instead they settled as a group in Edinburgh, unimpressed by their new country and regarded with suspicion by the privilege-conscious burgh craftsmen. By 1609 most seemed to have returned home; the rest, having settled in the Canongate area of Edinburgh were said to be giving 'grite licht and knawledg' to the country-people.[47]

Little progress appears to have been made, however, for in 1623 a Standing Committee for Manufactures was set up, mainly to stimulate woollen manufacture. Nothing effective emerged from this body, but further attempts to meet the shortage of fine wool, skilled labour and investment capital were made in 1641 and 1645, when Acts were passed allowing for the free import of foreign wool, oil and dyestuffs. Any fine cloth made was to be free of taxation, while masters and men in the manufactories were exempted from military service and billeting duties. Masters were also given complete control over the employment of their workmen to prevent the poaching of this valuable asset by rival concerns. Subsequently enterprises for the fabrication of quality woollens were established in Edinburgh (Bonnington), Ayr and at New Mills near Haddington. Those at Bonnington and New Mills were reported to have met with some success, though the latter foundered when Haddington fell to General Monk in 1651.[48]

After the Restoration, further, more comprehensive legislation was enacted, the Act of 1661 re-enacting that of 1641 and offering naturalisation to foreign settlers. In a combined endeavour to avoid labour friction, restrictive trading practices, and the shortage of capital the Act encouraged the formation of joint-stock companies possessing full powers of incorporation, and the sole right to market their own products. Despite such encouragement the attempt to establish a fine-cloth industry continued to be unsuccessful, largely because the home market was not thought sufficiently protected; though some protection was afforded, in theory if not in fact, by Acts, or patents, of the Privy Council.

The continued importation of luxury cloths served only to worsen the already critical state of the Scottish exchequer. Consequently, by the Act for Encouraging Trade and Manufactures passed in 1681, a positive move was made to limit excessive expenditure on such commodities by prohibiting their importation into Scotland. At the same time further provisions were made to encourage native manufactures, especially fine-cloth works. Tax inducements were given to people with capital and technical skills to set up manufactories. Imported raw materials were to be free of duty and public dues.[49]

As a result of this Act and the more peaceable political scene several manufactories for the making of fine cloth were established, notably that at Haddington, the projection of which may have partly occasioned the legislation. Similar ventures were started at Glasgow and Edinburgh in 1683, and after the interruptions of the 'Glorious Revolution', at Aberdeen, Musselburgh. North Mills, Berwickshire, and Angus, in addition to two further concerns in Glasgow. The establishment of these firms enabled the manufacturers to increase their influence with the Scottish parliament in such a way that in 1701 not only was the wearing of foreign cloth prohibited once more but the export of wool was forbidden.[50]

Of the companies floated in the wake of the 1681 Act, that for manufacturing woollens at New Mills, Haddington was perhaps the most successful.[51] Taking advantage of the protection and extensive privileges afforded by current government policy, Robert

Blackwood, a prominent Edinburgh merchant, and Sir James Stanfield, owner of the premises of the earlier Haddington manufactory, found no difficulty in obtaining financial backing. With the aid of workmen and equipment imported from Yorkshire and the West of England the company ventured into the production of fine cloth and frame-knitted hosiery. The latter soon ceased, due mainly to labour problems, but, despite many difficulties, the manufacture of woollen cloth continued for some thirty years. All goods manufactured were sent to a warehouse in Edinburgh, whence they were retailed by the merchant stockholders or by other merchants whose benevolence the company valued. By 1683 the New Mills company was making a bid to secure contracts for providing military uniforms recently approved by the Privy Council 'to distinguish sojers from other skulking and vagrant persons'. It soon became apparent, however, that the company could not provide all the cloth that was needed, and none of it at a price competitive with cloth to be obtained in England. In the interests of economy, therefore, permission was soon being granted to Scottish regiments to import uniform cloths under special licence, thus seriously puncturing the hedge of protection enjoyed by New Mills under the Act of 1681. As a result of remonstrances and bribes from the Haddington company the Privy Council ceased granting licences in 1685 and extended to New Mills a practical monopoly in providing military cloth together with the right to search for and seize imported woollens.[51a] Under these arrangements the company prospered for some years.

The disturbances associated with the departure of James VII (II of England) after 1688, however, exacerbated the existing slackness in the Scottish customs and in 1696 the Haddington enterprise was still complaining about the import of foreign cloth to the 'great discouragement' of the company. Pressure to ban again manufactured imports, together with the export of wool, built up from the manufacturing interests and culminated in their being given complete protection under an Act of 1701. Foreign cloth was banned, and the export of wool was prohibited. This victory for the manufacturing interest was, however, short-lived. The laxity of the Scottish customs prevented the new law from becoming truly effective, though it provoked the wool-masters to wrath. Consequently skins with wool on them were permitted to be exported from specified ports as early as 1703 and the full resumption of wool exports was allowed in the following year. Some attempt was made to compensate the manufacturers by continuing the ban on cloth imports and renewing their exemption from export duties.

This chameleon-like policy of the Scottish government, coming as it did when Continental and Baltic markets were being progressively protected, helped to spell the doom of fine-woollen production in Scotland for a century. The New Mills company, which had had a degree of success, ran into trading and financial difficulties and was finally wound up in 1713. A few of the other manufactories, some only established after the protective legislation of 1701, also limped on beyond the Union but their demise was not long delayed.

The lack of success in establishing a quality woollen sector at this time cannot be wholly explained, however, in terms of government vacillation. Indeed it is easy to overestimate the significance of the investment in cloth manufactories after 1681. They were never more than a handful and the paucity of information concerning them may be indicative of their unimportance. It cannot be doubted that they failed to make a significant impression on the market, and for this several reasons may be offered. Firstly, the degree of protection afforded by the law was far greater in theory than in practice, since the policy of farming out the customs resulted in the Scottish government having little control over imports and exports. Furthermore the policy of the Privy Council in granting import licences at its leisure further undermined the effectiveness of the regulations.[52] Merchants, in the absence of a good example from the state, continued to flout the import regulations. For their part the upper classes continued to surrender to the 'Luxury and Itch' to wear foreign cloths and often returned from abroad 'stocked for several years'.[53] Even under complete protection after 1701 delegates of several wool and silk manufactories felt the need to petition Parliament to 'supply what yet may be remaining for curbing the excessive Vanity and Folly of wearing . . . Foreign Manufacture . . . to the Discredit of Public Order and the Ruine of the Kingdom'.[54] Wool, too, leaked abroad to the particular disadvantage of the fine-cloth makers. As a consequence enforcement of the law became the responsibility of the interested parties. In 1685 the New Mills company received the power to seize proscribed goods and to sue persons who contravened the Act of 1681, plus wide powers of search.[55]

In the second place, the scale of production of the manufactories was not sufficient to satisfy home demand. As late as 1700 promises that 'the Nation shall be . . . plentifully and cheap furnished with all manner of Woollen and Silk Manufactures made within this Kingdom as any of her Neighbours' were still related to the future.[56] The claim by the managers of New Mills in 1696 that they not only made woollen cloth 'as good as is made in any other nation [but also] in such quantities as may serve the kingdom and all ranks and degrees of persons within the same', is hard to accept. Another writer believed that in this period 'all the cloth we could make ourselves bore no Proportion to our Consumption'. This fact, again made for disregard of the import laws.[57]

In the third place Scottish fine cloth produced by the manufactories never became truly competitive in price or quality, as a result of which many complaints were made. Production costs were high for two reasons. Firstly, almost all the wool used by the fine-cloth makers (if the New Mills company was typical) was imported, either from England or from Spain. Spanish wool was in great demand from Dutch and Wiltshire fine-woollen manufacturers. Only the coarsest cloth was fabricated from Scottish wool. Thus the cost of obtaining the raw material for quality goods was high wherever it came from. The price of Galloway fine wool was itself driven up by the practice of exporting it and thus exposing it to international demand.

Perhaps more important, however, was the need to obtain skilled labour from either England or the Continent.[58] It is apparent that most, if not all, the manufactories depended heavily on imported skills: apart from that employed at New Mills, foreign labour began the manufacture of fine stuffs and bays at Bonnington early in the century; the similar project at Paul's Work, Edinburgh, was under the direction of foreign labour; William Black employed French workers at North Mills to make serges and imitation French products; and William Hogg of Harcarse in Berwickshire used English workers. High wages were necessary to tempt such labour into Scotland. Statistical evidence here is scant but it is probable that wages paid to immigrant workers were about 50 per cent higher than prevailing English rates, and nearer double those for Scottish labour.[59] James Lyell of Gardine complained that foreign workmen were 'very expensive' and planned to train his son to be works manager to save the 'dead Sallaries usually given . . . to Foreign Overseers'.[60] It is doubtful, however, if many such workers settled in Scotland. Certainly they possessed great scarcity value to the manufacturers, as is evidenced by the practice of poaching labour and the lengths to which masters went to recover runaway men. Moreover the efficiency of imported skilled labour was affected by internal squabblings with native labour and the management of the manufactories.[61]

These problems, together with the related questions of adverse exchange rates and difficulties in importing vital manufacturing equipment from England or the Continent, all served to prevent the fine-cloth industry from becoming truly competitive. Foreign cloth imports were not displaced and the looming commercial disaster immediately prior to the Union caused the government to abandon protection and permit once more the export of wool. The well-informed Scottish laird, Sir John Clerk of Penicuik, went so far as to argue that the extensive privileges offered to certain native manufactories 'served for little other purpose than to cover importations of the same commodities from England'.[62]

Thus the effort to establish an industry for the making of quality cloth in Scotland was seen to be a failure well before 1707. The Union merely guaranteed that it would not quickly revive.

The Scots were thus clearly unsuccessful in their bid to emulate England's cloth industry during the seventeenth century. In her retarded commercial and industrial condition, lacking markets, capital, technical skills, foreign currency and a thriving agricultural sector, Scotland had to rely on the export of commodities in which she was relatively well endowed or which could be easily obtained; wool figured prominently among these. Its export, however, was incompatible with the development of manufacturing and fine- and coarse-cloth manufacturers failed to compete successfully with the prior concerns of the economy. Moreover Scotland's trade was becoming increasingly slanted towards England by the 1690s, forcing the Scots to place more emphasis on commodities in which she had a comparative advantage, mainly linen and cattle. As far as textiles were concerned, therefore, the Union of 1707 between England and Scotland was of great importance to woollen interests north of the border.

Under the terms of the Union of 1707 Scotland became subject to the same commercial regulations as England. These included a ban on the export of wool in an endeavour to keep down the price to the manufacturer and stifle foreign competition. Insofar as wool played a part in the Union of the two countries, it was the wool trade rather than the (parlous) cloth trade that concerned the English negotiators. The regular export of wool from Scottish ports gave English growers an incentive to run their wool over the Border in order to obtain a price dictated by the demands of the international woollen industry, not merely the English. At a time when English clothiers were meeting real competition at the lower end of the market in northern Europe they were particularly concerned with the possibility of absolute shortages of wool leading to rising prices to the manufacturer and consumers. In addition the acquisition of English wool by foreign producers would in the long run only serve to strengthen foreign competitive ability. From a political standpoint the Scottish practice of sending wool to France, with whom England was at war at the end of the seventeenth century, was regarded as particularly iniquitous, threatening the revenues and manufactures of the country at a time of crisis.[63]

The Scots were correct, then, in making the loss of the export trade in raw wool rather than loss of protection the main basis of compensation to the industry at the time of union. Not only were the English very sensitive on the issue, but it represented a far more serious financial loss to the Scottish economy than did manufacturing. Scottish growers were seriously affected by the treaty. Smuggling wool abroad was hardly practicable as a long-term solution, though some growers nonetheless took advantage of lax customs administration and continued to export.[64] More realistic, however, was the possibility of exploiting the one remaining legal avenue for wool exports—the English market—even if here too the outlook was not hopeful in 1707, since growers almost certainly faced a substantial decline in prices. But there was little to suggest that such a switch to the English market would occur.

Admittedly, before 1660, North of England clothiers had taken part of the Scottish clip because of the inflated price of English fine wools.[65] Whether a demand continued into the second half of the seventeenth century it is not possible to say; but clearly Scottish growers in 1707 realised that they could not depend on this outlet, for they sought financial aid to stimulate native manufacturing. In any case it is likely that only the better grades of Scottish wool, found in Galloway, had sold much in the south. The bulk of the home clip was inferior and had little appeal to English manufacturers, who in any case were bent on quality improvement in order to combat competition from European producers.[66] In short the English were not so anxious to secure access to the Scottish clip as to remove one of the means whereby foreign producers obtained access to a proportion of their own clip, together with that of Scotland, to the detriment of the national economy.

If the outlook in 1707 was gloomy for the wool-masters, it was even bleaker for the manufacturers. An act of union would ensure that the dying fine-cloth sector could not be resuscitated, and would make things difficult for the coarse-woollen trade also. England was better endowed with resources and manufacturing skills. Scotland's overseas trade was not likely to expand without a marked increase in the standard of her product—at best a long term solution and one which had already proved elusive even in conditions of protection.

The Act of Union, therefore, was unfavourable to Scottish wool interests. Full union promised only reductions of trade and lowered prices. Though union made good sense for the economy as a whole it brought small comfort to those who lived by wool.

It is against these problems that the fifteenth article of union must be seen. Scottish wool-growers were successful in writing in this clause, which was designed to give them some measure of compensation for their loss of freedom to export wool. An annual sum of £2,000 for seven years was granted from public funds to stimulate the manufacture of coarse wool in those counties where it was grown in any significant quantity. It was not until twenty years after the Union, however, with the formation of the Board of Trustees for Manufactures that this money was applied to the needs of Scottish industry.

The Trustees' own general plan for wool, published in December 1727, made provision for the encouragement of manufacturing by offering premiums to persons who would contract with the Board to sort and manufacture coarse wool and who employed five or more persons in spinning it. The opinions of landowners were sought, but in the absence of any further ideas the Trustees proceeded 'to finish a particular plan for these ends from the best information they can have'.[67] Thus a period of twenty years' delay was ended in January 1728 with the publication of the Board's 'Particular Plan for Wool'.

An examination of the Board's records, however, soon shows that it was less than successful in promoting the manufacture of cloth. Centres in the wool-producing areas (mainly the southern counties) where official sorters had been established failed to become important for manufacturing. Neither were the Board's sorters successful in improving the marketing of wool that continued to be grown. In 1777 Sir James Anderson was still campaigning for experienced wool sorters; while in 1790 James Naismith claimed that 'a single stone of wool can hardly be bought in any of the ordinary wool markets of Scotland . . . which might not be sorted into half a dozen different parcels, no two of which ought properly to make a part of the same fabric'.[68] Inadequate sorting adversely affected the carding and combing processes, for wool of a uniform quality and grist could not be drawn from it to make an even yarn. Hence the final cloth remained of a low standard.

The real difficulties confronting the Scottish woollen producer after the Union could not be met adequately by a public body like the Board of Trustees, which had the added disadvantage of operating with very meagre resources. Growth in the woollen industry could only be achieved by fundamental changes in sheep-breeding and farm management, together with a buoyant home demand stimulated by increasing real income among the body of the Scottish people. These desiderata were largely absent in the first half of the eighteenth century.

Nonetheless, despite the prognostications of the wool-masters in 1707 and although the economic conditions were not favourable to growth, it would be wrong to conclude that the Union witnessed the demise of woollen manufacturing in Scotland.

It was claimed by a group of Scottish merchants and linen-manufacturers in 1719 that competition from England had 'totally sunk' the woollen sector in Scotland.[69] Much later it was argued that the fashion for English products after the Union had brought native industry into 'disrepute'.[70] But the consumption of English goods was nothing new in Scotland, and it would appear that local woollen manufacturing was not in fact 'totally sunk', or did not remain so for long. It has already been argued that fine-cloth manufacturing was in decline well before the Union and that the events of 1707 did no more than put the lid on its coffin. The coarse-cloth sector was not so likely to be overwhelmed by English competition. The home market for coarse woollens remained largely in Scottish rather than English hands. Of course, most of the nation's clothing needs in rural areas continued to be met by household manufacture employing wool from the family sheep and the services of the local litster and 'custom' weaver. The Union made little difference to this subsistence-type manufacturing. It was the trade in cloth made for the open market that was particularly vulnerable to increased English competition after 1707. Yet there is sufficient evidence that a coarse trade did continue. A Swedish traveller to the country in 1720 noted that locally woven wool goods were a prominent feature of regular markets held at Dunfermline, Inverkeithing, Dunblane, Lanark, Maybole, Dumfries, Thornhill, Kilmarnock and Stirling.[71] In 1733 Patrick Lindsay admitted that Kilmarnock, Stirling, Aberdeen and Edinburgh were not unimportant centres of woollen manufacture and that Musselburgh and Galashiels were also manufacturing for the open market.[72] By the 1760s Postlethwayt found 'many hundreds' of looms at work in the Stirling area and a number around Alloa. By then woollens were also expanding at Edinburgh and in the Lothians. At Aberdeen woollens were declining relative to linens, but the old cloths were still made 'to a great amount' and the stocking trade was thriving.[73]

Production was not confined to the home market. An exact breakdown between home and foreign sales is not possible, but it appears that some goods were still being exported in the first half of the eighteenth century. Kilmarnock sent quantities of 'Exeter' serges to Holland, while the famous bonnet trade had recovered by the 1730s. Holland also continued to provide an outlet for Stirling products, and additional markets were found in the West Indies and North America. Cheap Musselburgh stuffs found a ready sale in the southern states.[74] There was of course no *a priori* reason why Scotland's coarse-woollen export trade should suffer as a result of the Union, since she had been competing with England in international markets throughout the seventeenth century. After 1707 it would appear that the weakening markets of northern Europe were balanced by a rise in the Atlantic trade in cheap wool fabrics. How complete that compensation was it is impossible to say on present evidence; but it is clear that, insofar as Scotland in the eighteenth century could legally exploit the colonial markets, the Union conferred an advantage rather than a disadvantage on the woollen industry.

That Scottish manufacturers were able to meet some of the demand from the New World was due mainly to two developments: the first was the expansion of negro labour on the plantations, and the second was the emphasis on the manufacture of light worsted fabrics in Scotland. Negro-owning planters required cheap and light garments to clothe them. Quality did not matter, but price did, and in this Scotland possessed advantages over England. These new exported cloths were different from those that had given Scotland a lively export trade in the previous century, and comprised fabrics that may roughly be described as 'new draperies'. These had already become established in southern European markets in the early seventeenth century and had gradually penetrated colder climes. By 1705 even Scotsmen were being advised to wear them to encourage native manufacturers.[75] Insufficient is known about home demand to say whether they responded to this advice. It is likely that they did not, owing to the climate and the strength of household manufacturing. It is clear, however, that urban clothiers did turn to these products, presumably in response to the growing colonial market. Camlets, light stuffs, bays and serges all figured prominently in the output of the chief woollen centres.[76] This relative shift in the nature of production as a result of a geographical switch in the market suggests that entrepreneurial ability was not entirely lacking among Scottish woollen manufacturers, despite Cockburn's complaints in 1744 that they

C

acted 'like blind men in a mine'.[77]

The question remains how the woollen sector was able to continue to compete with English products at home as well as abroad in the free-trade conditions of union. There is little evidence to go on, but there were a number of factors conducive to the industry's survival if not expansion. In the first place manufacturers could produce cheaply, since they benefited from what the wool-masters feared most as a consequence of union—a steep fall in wool prices. Wool revenue, on which many of the southern proprietors depended for their rents, was said to have declined by as much as 50 per cent following the Union.[78] Extant price data suggest that a fall certainly occurred in the price of coarser wools compared with the years immediately prior to the Union, but to a lesser extent than that claimed by the growers. Blackface was selling for between 5s and 6s a stone in 1700 and was quoted at 4s in 1720.[79] The growers' loss, however, was the manufacturers' gain; a long-term rise in the price of wool was to have to await changes in supply and demand during the second half of the century. Meanwhile the fall in the price of wool extended the market for cheap woollens, and there is no reason to suppose that the Scottish manufacturers did not profit thereby.

Prime costs were also kept down by the low earnings of Scottish labour, whose rates of pay were generally regarded as being well below those in English manufacturing districts.[80] In rural areas servants and farmworkers were often given yarn-spinning or hand-knitting assignments by their employers while being paid for other work such as tending cattle and sheep. Such labour was virtually 'free', and although productivity in Scotland probably trailed behind that of English wool-workers, it remains likely that labour costs north of the Border were lower than in England.

On the English side the nature of the goods produced and the difficulties of transportation reduced English ability to compete on price with domestic products in Scotland. Much of the output of the English woollen districts was of a superior quality and was aimed at a higher but smaller market in Scotland. Most English woollens were not direct substitutes for Scottish cloths. While it is true that the West Riding was growing in importance as a centre of cheap worsted manufacture in this period, communications in that area remained poor, serving to keep markets fragmented. The high relative cost of transporting and merchanting low-grade cloths under these conditions gave the Scottish manufacturer a price advantage in his own country in this quality range.[81]

The inferior cloths produced in Scotland were often different from low-priced Yorkshires, which further strengthened the Scottish manufacturer's ability to withstand English competition. Scottish cloths aimed at the home market were normally densely fabricated carded goods and twilled in the weave. Indeed the word 'tweel' was often used as a synonym for yarn. It was no accident that plaiding, worn by shepherds and Highland folk in general, and Scotch blankets, were thick, twilled fabrics to protect users against wind and damp. The rigours of the climate caused Scots of all ranks to prefer, for some purposes at least, the products of their native looms. Some clergy, who could presumably have afforded better, were often content to wear the coarsest of materials for this reason, and Sir John Sinclair declared that in the late eighteenth century men at work or appearing at kirk or market usually wore home-produced cloth 'which they thought warmer and more comfortable' than the English products.[82]

The Scottish woollen trade after 1707 remained in its traditional manufacturing areas, not the Border counties, which were the main concern of the Board of Trustees. Nonetheless influences in the economy enabled the population even in these remote counties to salvage something from the Union. The growers of the finer wool in the south-west continued to find outlets both with English and West of Scotland manufacturers. According to Adam Smith wool-producers in this region amply made up for falling wool prices by the rising price of mutton in the first half of the century.[83] But what of the producers of coarse tarred wool in the border counties, who were potentially the greatest sufferers by the Union? The continued manufacture of coarse woollens and the increased use of the longer fibres of the native Dunface sheep in cheap worsted production was in their interest. So was the flourishing Aberdeen stocking trade, for this was partly based on supplies of wool from the southern counties. In addition, however, border wool-farmers found help from an unexpected quarter—a growing demand for coarse wools in England. This development was due to the growing importance of the West Riding as a producer of cheap worsteds, and in time a substantial wool trade grew up between the border counties of Scotland and the north of England textile centres. In 1738 Sir John Clerk bemoaned the fact that 'large quantities of our worst tarred wool' were used at Leeds to the detriment of home manufacturing. Cockburn was of the same opinion.[84] In 1759 Roxburghshire wool-masters, in claiming that their county produced over 20 per cent of Scotland's wool clip, stated that 95 per cent of their production had to be sent to England or the 'north country' (presumably Aberdeen) for manufacture.[85] The situation in the Borders, therefore, in the early decades after the Union was not so materially different from the pre-1707 period. Wool continued to be exported, though at lower prices, as the market was narrower. In one respect, however, the border economy slowly changed. As the north of England section of the woollen industry expanded, so northern cloth producers began to recruit labour in the border counties as outworkers to spin yarn for worsteds. As early as 1734 the Hawick justices successfully petitioned the Board Trustee for funds to set up a spinning school there in order to employ idle people as spinners for English worsted manufacturers. A wool-comber was also provided.[86] By the third quarter of the eighteenth century it was claimed (maybe with some exaggeration) that waggonloads of combed wool arrived daily in the main border centres from the north of England to be spun. By this time a few weavers were also working on commission for English clothiers.[87] After the Union, therefore, the southern counties of Scotland gradually became integrated more closely with the economy of the north of England than with that of Scotland itself.

Woollen manufacturing for the open market thus survived in Scotland under the competitive conditions of Union. English manufacturers were for the most part unable to undersell domestic producers. Moroever the export trade to the Continent continued, though it was probably less important than in the previous century. One compensation of the Union was the opening of a legal Scottish trade with the plantations in North America, and there is evidence that the Scots placed more emphasis after 1707 on goods suitable for that market.

Scotland, however, in the later eighteenth century still lacked much sign of that quality cloth industry for which she subsequently became renowned. It is to the formation of this that we must now turn.

TWO

The Formative Years,
1770-1830

'Too thin does not please, too stout does not pay. Galashiels cloths
has the appearance of going out of fashion.' Henry Brown, manufacturer, 1828

The fundamental economic changes that began in Britain in the
latter part of the eighteenth century have been correctly associated
with the meteoric rise of the cotton textile industry. The woollen
branch, for long the doyen of manufacturing industry, swiftly lost
its pride of place. Nonetheless the manufacture of wool products
expanded rapidly in this period, raw wool imports growing in
Britain from 3.9 million lb per annum in 1792-4 to 21.3 million lb
in 1822-4 at a time when the re-export of wool was negligible and
when the domestic clip was also expanding.[1] Between 1770-5 and
1815-20 the annual production of broadcloth in the West Riding of
Yorkshire rose from 100,000 pieces to 330,000.[2] These figures may
reflect the increasing tendency of Yorkshire to gain at the expense
of older centres of production such as East Anglia and the West
of England, but absolute expansion in the industry is confirmed by
the raw wool imports.

One region not declining relative to Yorkshire, however, was
Scotland, which in these years laid the foundation of its modern
woollen industry. In the previous chapter it was suggested that,
while attempts were made over extensive periods of time to en-

38

courage the growth of woollen manufacture in Scotland, a dearth of skill, poor wool, administrative laxity and restricted markets prevented any real progress being made. During the final decades of the eighteenth century, however, clear signs of expansion appeared in the industry. By the 1820s, though still small by Yorkshire standards, the industry had grown, quality of wool and finishing had been improved, and the organisation of manufacturing had undergone a radical transformation. Furthermore, woollen production had largely moved to the Border counties.

The annual reports of the Board of Trustees in Edinburgh, long silent concerning the fortunes of the industry, began to sound a note of cautious optimism in the last two decades of the eighteenth century. In 1784 the Board noted that the 'methods of manufacturing the coarse wool have received considerable improvement' though progress was admitted to be slow.[3] In 1791 there was every reason to hope that the industry would be of no small importance in the economy.[4] By 1814 the Trustees claimed that superfine cloth was being made in Aberdeen 'equal in quality to any of the kind manufactured in Britain'.[5] By the turn of the century the hosiery industry and cloth making were employing about 7,000 persons, and about one-third of the population of Aberdeen was said to be dependent in one way or another on the manufacture of wool.[6]

Expansion was also occurring in the Border counties. In 1790 it was noted that woollen mills had been erected at Hawick and Galashiels 'notwithstanding the great obstruction . . . arising from the scarcity of fuel . . .'.[7] The Wordsworths, passing through Galashiels in 1803, noted (without sympathy) the 'townish bustle' and the 'ugly stones houses' that were taking the place of the brown-roofed thatched cottages.[8] In 1815 another observer found the town in a state of 'great animation, the woollen manufacture being uncommonly busy' and noted the 'rapid advancement' that had lately been achieved.[9] Earlier, in the 1790s it was considered that investments in the Galashiels woollen industry had been a major factor in the decline of linen-weaving in the Melrose area, since the woollen manufacturers were paying higher wages to spinners than the linen trade could afford.[10] The success of clothiers in the Galashiels area in competing for the premiums offered by the Board of

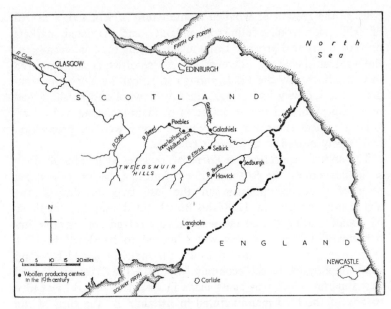

The Border Woollen District

Trustees is further testimony to the activity of the industry there. Between 1791 and 1829 the Board distributed £4,744 to Scottish manufacturers, Galashiels clothiers taking £3,803, and the Borders as a whole £4,021.[11]

Unfortunately no official statistics of production were kept at this time, so it is impossible to measure its precise expansion. From unofficial fragmentary data, however, one may estimate the growth in the industry. In Galashiels, for example, the number of employers rose from ten in 1778 to thirty-five in 1825. The amount of wool consumed grew from about 17,000lb in 1774 to over 500,000lb in 1825. Only about thirty handlooms were in regular use in the 1770s but 175 were employed in 1828. It was estimated that the town's output of woven goods increased in value from about £5,500 in 1790 to almost £58,000 in 1825[12] made up of mainly 'blues' and 'drabs' but also striped cloths and checks.

Though the burgh did not figure in the prizes for cloth offered by the Board of Trustees, industrial expansion was also marked by the early nineteenth century in Hawick. This burgh was larger than Galashiels and, lying as it did on a main thoroughfare between England and central Scotland, had built up a strong commercial tradition. Yarn-spinning for English worsted manufacturers began there in the 1730s and lasted well into the nineteenth century. But, unlike Galashiels, the manufacture of woollen cloth only became significant in the local economy after the French Wars, and more particularly from the 1830s. In the latter part of the eighteenth century Hawick began to concentrate on hosiery and carpet production, the latter industry being introduced about 1750 by members of the local gentry in association with a Dunfermline weaver, who used the local coarse Blackface wool and gave it out from a central storehouse to local women to be spun into yarn. The venture succeeded for a while, in 1798 it being estimated that the Hawick carpet factory consumed over half of the manufactured wool of the county.[13]

Hosiery-making was to be the main arm of the local economy, however, at least down to the 1830s. Baillie Hardie introduced frame-knitting to Hawick in 1771 for the manufacture of stockings and woollen underwear, perhaps because of the success of Aberdeen's hand-knitting industry and perhaps in an effort to enlarge the market by introducing mechanical means of manufacture to cut production costs. Hawick rapidly became the dominant frame-knitting centre in Scotland, Aberdeen being still bereft of frames in 1794. Whatever his intentions Hardie himself performed little but local 'customer work' and in 1780 relinquished the trade to John Nixon, who was soon making quantities of worsted hose for the open market. As fashion gradually shifted from coarse worsted hosiery to soft woollen varieties, Hawick, with about 8,000 sheep bearing good clothing wool in the vicinity, was well placed to exploit the new demand.[14] Individual firms grew to considerable stature. William Wilson produced 50,000 pairs of hose and 47,000lb of yarn in 1813 and there were several like him.[15] The yarn itself was also growing in the hands of local and English weaving and knitting concerns. By the mid-1820s yarn output in the burgh was estimated in excess of 1 million lb per annum.[16]

By contrast, cloth weaving in Hawick made only slow progress at this time, the number of looms in regular use hardly increasing between 1775 and 1825. Nonetheless the 1780s saw the beginnings of a regular trade in cloth as opposed to the traditional customer weaving. Narrow fabrics, dyed with woad or indigo, and doubtless similar to the Galashiels 'blues' that were becoming famous in Scotland, were introduced to Hawick and sold in the fishing towns of the north and east. Less than 3,000lb of wool annually were used for these products in the 1780s but this had grown to about 30,000lb annually by the turn of the century. It was only after the Battle of Waterloo in 1815, however, that Hawick manufacturers turned seriously to woven goods, for about that time the yarn trade faltered, due, it was claimed, to the fact that much Leicestershire labour was being subsidised from the poor rates, thus reducing production costs among hosiers there. By 1825 Hawick firms were engaged in making blankets as well as plaiding and flannel. The total value of Hawick's hosiery, yarn and cloth trade in 1825, a boom year, was estimated at £88,000.[17]

Compared with the development in Hawick and Galashiels expansion elsewhere in the Borders was less marked. The Board of Trustees paid intermittent premiums to Jedburgh clothiers, who, with nearby Kelso, were building up a reputation for blankets and imitation Welsh flannel. Jedburgh could only boast two clothmakers in 1826, however, and had fewer weaving looms in 1828 than in the 1770s.[18] By the early nineteenth century Jedburgh like Hawick, came to concentrate on hosiery products. Many makers were small producers and may well have been employed by larger Hawick concerns. Further east, Kelso was the scene of some activity during this period, manufacturing linen and cotton goods as well as wool, and possessing seventy looms in 1828.[19] Though a little carding and spinning machinery was installed, the fertility of the local farmland meant that local capital was channelled more readily into agriculture than into manufacturing. Little development occurred in the burgh of Selkirk. It was claimed that severe burgh restrictions remaining in force here hampered industrial development until later. A contemporary observer considered that the burgh had never possessed any manufactury worthy of the name 'save the highly estimated one of manufacturing the fourth part of a member of parliament'.[20] Only one woollen manufacturer was listed in the town in 1825-6, he being a native of Galashiels and employing only a handful of people.

At Innerleithen in the valley of the Tweed a woollen mill was erected in the 1780s as a magnanimous gesture by a former local blacksmith, Alexander Brodie, who had made a fortune in the Shropshire iron trade. Costing an estimated £3,000 to build and equip, the four-storied mill housed carding and spinning machinery driven by water. It is possible that Brodie, apart from building himself a local monument, was seeking to expand the local yarn trade with the north of England, but by the early nineteenth century the enterprise was in serious financial difficulties and appears to have been used mainly by local 'customer' weavers for their personal yarn production until taken over in the late 1820s by a Galashiels firm of tweed manufacturers.[21] Already by the early nineteenth century the later dominance of this region by the Ballantyne family was foreshadowed in the partnership of Ballantyne & Dobson operating in the village. Nonetheless the scale of operations remained small, only ten looms being employed there in 1828, some of them on cottons.[22] A similar situation prevailed in Peebles where, James Dickson was the sole clothier manufacturing for the market.[23]

The upper Tweed valley was a remote area well removed from the main routes through the Borders to Edinburgh and the Forth, and south into England. Langholm, on the other hand, not far north of Carlisle, seemed better situated for industrial development, and here the cotton and thread industries of the West of Scotland maintained an outpost. Woollen manufacturing remained for long on a small scale. In 1794 the local minister could complain that 'considering all the advantages which Langholm enjoys, it is a matter of surprise that a woollen manufacture, upon an extensive scale, has not long ago been established'.[24] Somewhat later a small check and candlewick business was started in the town, but Langholm woollens did not develop much beyond the country-work stage till the 1830s, hand-knitted worsted hose and thread-making being the main employment of the residents until then.

Before the 1830s, therefore, the woollen industry in the Border region had mainly expanded in Galashiels and Hawick. Developments elsewhere were by no means so significant. Though evidence is slight it would appear that the attitude of the local landlord or of the burgh authorities was a determining factor in the extension of manufacturing. The Duke of Buccleuch was not regarded as the most liberal patron of industry and his miserly attitude to the feuing of land at Langholm and Hawick in particular came in for criticism. In 1825 a Hawick burgh official, Robert Wilson, drew attention to the amount of unused water power surrounding the town and added

> ... for a few years some of these [falls of water] were not comeatable owing to a whim of the late Duke of Buccleuch. His Grace seemed to have forgotten that the manufacturers and their workers were the principal consumers of the produce of his land. Should the present Duke ... be disposed to grant feus of the water-falls on his property in the vicinity of this town he might make it a principal seat of the the woollen manufacture in Scotland ... The other principal proprietor of waterfalls in this neighbourhood is Mr. Douglas of Cavers, whose property ... is well-adapted for the erection of mills of powerful magnitude. Were this gentleman to learn how essentially it might contribute to the manufacturing enterprise ... his known generosity and public spirit are guarantees that these water-falls would not long be withheld and that the price required would not be exorbitant.[25]

While Wilson was prodding the local Roxburghshire aristocracy as forcibly as etiquette and tact allowed, the Scotts of Gala were setting a better example. Feuing does not appear to have been a problem in Galashiels and neighbourhood possibly because its landlord, of lesser stock than Buccleuch, needed to augment his income in this marginal agricultural area as much as possible. Wilson felt able to contrast Scott of Gala with Douglas and Buccleuch. 'Mr. Scott of Gala, and his father, whose views seem to have been equally sound and liberal, have raised a town (Galashiels) which is likely ... to become the Leeds of Scotland.'[26]

The emergence of the Borders as the principal seat of wool-manufacturing in Scotland between 1780 and 1830 requires explanation. Since the seventeenth century the chief manufacturing centres had been towns with distinct geographical advantages: Stirling, Haddington, and Musselburgh had good access to local wool and to water communication on the Forth; Kilmarnock was well situated in respect both of Galloway wool and markets in Ireland and on the Continent; and Aberdeen's trading connections and access to local labour had made the city a natural centre for woollen manufacture and merchanting, and wool was obtainable by sea from the southern counties of Scotland. Agriculture or fishing provided the principal employments in and around these towns but the somewhat seasonal nature of these activities enabled earnings to be augmented by the manufacture of cheap woollen articles for sale in local or more distant markets.

Towards the close of the eighteenth century this ancient pattern of industry was changing. The importance of the traditional centres of woollen manufacture was declining. Thus it was stated of Haddington in 1793 that 'the number of weavers employed in [coarse wool manufacture] is greatly diminished of late'.[27] No woollen company any longer remained in the burgh. By 1845 there was said to be 'no manufacturers in the town', though it remained an important wool market.[28] By the 1790s the manufacture of stuffs at Musselburgh had long been superseded by cheap cotton articles. These in turn had succumbed to those manufactured in the western districts, which were still cheaper. Though one sizeable woollen mill survived in the town in the 1790s, it was reported that 'none very considerable' manufactures had been established 'owing to their having been at all times carriers and furnishers of various kinds of provisions for the capital, which employed them in a manner more agreeable to them than the sendentary lives of manufacturers could have been'.[29]

Similarly the nature of Kilmarnock's economy was changing: by 1792 carpets made from local Ayrshire wool were increasing in importance, as were footwear manufacture and the cotton industry. Various types of woollen cloth, however, accounted for little more than 5 per cent of the value of the burgh's manufactures.[30] Woollen cloth production also ceased to be significant in Edinburgh, none being mentioned in connection with the city in 1845. Instead local producers concentrated on the fashion trade in decorated shawls and fancy linens.[31] At Stirling, though the manufacture of shalloons in 1793 was said to be 'considerably revived', carpet-making was growing, several companies having been started for that purpose. But increasing numbers of people were being employed as out-workers for the Glasgow cotton manufacturers, about 260 looms in the area being engaged on muslins.[32]

In the absence of documentary evidence accounting for changes in the structure of these local economies one can only surmise what had happened. It seems clear that in some cases, notably at Kilmarnock, better employment and investment opportunities were offering themselves in the rapidly expanding cotton industry. Other centres found that poor local wool was better employed in carpet-making rather than in cloth, whose standards were improving. Alternatively, traditional centres were not suitable geographically for the textile machinery. The lack of a good fall on the River Forth was stated to be the reason why woollen mills had not been considered at Stirling in the 1790s. Similar factors may have operated at Haddington and Musselburgh. The proximity of Edinburgh to these burghs also, with its growing demand for a range of provision from the countryside, tended to stimulate agricultural employment and its associated activities.

The tendency for woollen manufacturing to concentrate in the Border counties, though similar efforts had failed in the eighteenth century, cannot be explained simply in terms of the decline of other areas. In many ways the Borders remained as unlikely an area of industrial growth as previously. For example, they lacked fuel, and even before the coming of steam power manufacturers required considerable quantities of coal. Large amounts of hot water were needed in dyeing the cloth, and coal-fired stoves were used to dry it. The small partnership of J. & H. Brown of Galashiels, with an annual turnover of only about £1,300 in 1828, consumed half a ton of coal per week.[33] The coal consumption at Hawick in the 1820s was considered to be 'almost incredible for a place so limited in size', and 30 miles from a mine.[34] Similarly coal supplies had to be transported over poor roads to Galashiels from Middleton, a distance of more than 20 miles. Jedburgh was considered to be at a considerable disadvantage from a manufacturing point of view in having to obtain coal from the Lothians. Border woollen clothiers, therefore, faced heavy fuel costs: prices were often higher than those ruling in the Lothians; and in the 1820s Hawick coal prices were at times double those ruling nearer to the pits, though coal prices in Jedburgh were kept down somewhat by the carriers obtaining a return load of grain to Dalkeith.[35]

Supplies also were irregular, due partly to the bad state of the roads in winter and partly to the seasonal nature of the carrying trade, the carters spending some of the year tending land, and driving lime for the farmers.[36] Communications in the Borders were poor. Galashiels was not on the main route to Edinburgh, which was constructed in the mid-eighteenth century via Selkirk, Clovenfords, and Stow; and no road connection with Selkirk existed till 1833. The Hawick-Selkirk road, the main north-to-south route through the Borders, was described as 'execrable' in 1826; and to another contemporary its line appeared 'palpably objectional' as if its designers had 'intended to punish the horse species for some original transgression'.[37] The bad state of communications in this area had enabled Hawick traders to appeal successfully against a trade tax.[38] These local conditions led Sir Walter Scott to support a proposal to construct a tram road between Dalkeith and St Boswells in 1821, with a depot at Galashiels, for the carriage of coal and limes.[39] The road to Edinburgh from Galashiels was so bad that carriers sometimes had to walk their ponies up the bed of the Gala Water instead. It is true that many road improvements were carried out in the Borders during the eighteenth century, especially in Roxburghshire, but they had little influence on the main manufacturing districts, and, therefore, served little to obviate the region's high carriage costs and the inaccessible markets.

Not only was the Border region isolated geographically, it was also remote psychologically. The manufacturing towns lacked other nearby industries that could act as spurs to change and investment, as, for example, existed among the West Riding manufacturers. In some places, it is true, there was a degree of overlapping between woollens, linen and cottons, but where this did occur—at Langholm, Peebles, and Melrose—these alternative industries were either themselves in decline or were not large enough to exert much influence on woollens. In fact the Borders developed as a 'single industry' area, and little attempt was made to find alternatives and encourage an influx of labour from elsewhere.

Nonetheless, despite these apparent disadvantages, the Border counties did possess many of the prerequisites for a woollen-manufacturing area. The district possessed an abundance of suitable water for power and for the scouring, milling and dyeing processes. Adequate falls of water could be found on most of the rivers to encourage the erection of water-driven scribbling and spinning mills. The settlement pattern of the region already reflected the presence of water. The fulling mills had been located, naturally, on the rivers, and villages had tended to grow up around them. Galashiels, for example, had been a fulling centre since the Middle Ages and had three waulkmills by the end of the eighteenth century. The limited amount of labour that the Borders did possess, therefore, tended to be localised in those parts well suited for the growth of factory industry.

Agricultural advances in Scotland in the eighteenth century, especially in the southern counties, made large quantities of improved wool available to manufacturers, and helped to overcome one of the oldest drawbacks to the successful establishment of a woollen industry in the area. An ignorance of, or unwillingness to promote, sound breeding, lack of good pasture land, deficiencies of fodder for winter feeding and harmful traditions such as daubing sheep with tar, had ensured that wool appeared on the market in a coarse and dirty condition that made it unfit for any but the most inferior products. Also the loose, informal organisation of an industry where the family unit predominated precluded much change to better imported varieties of wool, though this did occur to some extent in larger towns. The relationship between the growth of the Scottish Border woollen industry and contemporary changes in agriculture cannot be too firmly stressed.

Border farmers and landowners figured prominently in encouraging improved methods of sheep husbandry and the introduction of better breeds.[40] No development could have been more propitious for the nascent local industry than the introduction over a wide area of the Cheviot sheep, which appears to have evolved from the native Dunface.[41] The Cheviot in time dislodged the traditional Blackface from the Border Uplands, except in the highest districts, and eventually penetrated the Highlands. The Blackface breed possessed a fleece of very coarse and open fibres, long in the staple and containing a large proportion of 'dead' hairs and kemp, which militated against its successful manufacture. Thus only the coarsest of homespuns, rough carpets, and worsted hose from the longer fibres were manufactured from it, while much was sold to English clothiers either in the raw or as yarn. The wool of the Blackface proved capable of little improvement, but eventually the crossing of the Blackface ewe with the Border Leicester did lead to an ideal type of wool for 'tweed' cloths later in the nineteenth century from which the famous crossbred qualities arose.

It was the Cheviot sheep, however, which was to have the most marked effect upon the Scottish and English woollen industries. Its hardiness allowed it to thrive on the lower grounds of the Southern Uplands, while it carried a heavy fleece, supplying large quantities of wool for manufacturing. Moreover the fibres were short and even and of a finer texture than the Blackface's while the fleece was bright and lustrous and possessed good felting properties suitable for the currently fashionable dense heavy cloths. The shortness of the fibres made the wool suitable for carding, and thus for the woollen rather than the worsted process of manufacture. It was the ideal sheep for the manufacturing skills of large numbers of the population in England and Scotland.

The excellence of the breed and its large economic potential soon led to its superseding the Blackface in the Border pasture lands. In 1791 it was reported that 'so much convinced are the farmers of Ettrick Forest, of Tweeddale and Liddlesdale of their superior excellence that they are now converting their flocks as quickly as possible into the Cheviot breed'.[42]

Lord Napier of Ettrick stated that the Blackface sheep had been driven from the Southern Uplands by 1828, and Southey could remark in 1851 that 'the change most remarkable in Scotland is the decrease of the Blackfaced sheep accompanied by the substitution of the Cheviot'.[43] Moreover experiments were made to improve the Cheviot itself, notably by crossing the ewe with the Leicester ram, the result being the Border Leicester, which possessed a sound fleece, finer and shorter in the staple than the Midlands ram though lacking some of the lustre of the Cheviot itself. Also the New Leicester or Dishley breed found some acceptance on the lower grounds, particularly in Berwickshire, where its soft heavy fleece supplied wool for the hosiery industry.

Scottish woollen manufacturers and hoisiers benefited greatly from these developments, obtaining their supplies almost exclusively from local sources, and using little foreign wool before 1830. Surviving business records of this period illustrate the wool-buying habits of the local manufacturers. David Ballantyne of

D

Innerleithen bought most of his wool from nearby farms in the late 1820s; and J. & H. Brown of Galashiels obtained their wool in the same way, buying often from the same farmers a year's supply at 'wool time'.[44] Ure stated in 1794 that the local woollen manufacturers consumed 'a great quantity of wool, chiefly the product of the store-farms in the neighbourhood'.[45] This constituted no departure from custom, but by the last quarter of the eighteenth century the wool offered for sale in this way was of a higher quality and marketed in a superior condition than formerly. As a consequence the standard of woollen goods improved and product differentiation increased. Thus the founding of the modern Scottish woollen industry is inextricably, though not exclusively, associated with the contemporary changes in agriculture; the availability of improved wool encouraged investment in woollen manufacture and helped the industry to achieve an initial quality 'breakthrough', which in the shorter term enabled part of the growing demand for woollen clothing to be met by home (ie Scottish) producers, and which in the longer term may be viewed as the harbinger of the second quality 'breakthrough' associated with the foundation of the 'Tweed' industry in the 1830s.

While the supply of good wool led to the expansion of local woollen manufacture, the main impetuses to sheep-farming in Scotland at this time were the growing demand for mutton (in relation to which wool was merely a profitable by-product) and the demands of the large Yorkshire woollen industry. It has already been noted that subsequent to the Union a regular export trade in wool to England from Scotland expanded as the century proceeded.[46] Yorkshire dominance continued into the 1820s. Her staplers were the main buyers and price leaders at the great Border wool sales despite the growth of local woollen manufacturing. 'At Melrose fair yesterday' wrote a Galashiels manufacturer in 1828, 'there was almost no wool sold . . . it is somewhat remarkable that we have not heard of any Englishman that have bought a single parcel yet, who but never opened the market till this year'.[47] In the same year Lord Napier of Ettrick emphasised the dependence of the Scottish grower on the English manufacturer when he claimed that in the post-war years 'when the Yorkshire woolstaplers came in one would give an offer which was not accepted;

next came another who underbid him; and next came another who underbid him and therefore we were generally very glad to get what the first man bid . . . '.[48] Nonetheless, despite the fact that the supply of wool in the Borders was largely orientated towards, and dominated by English needs, which were by no means always in the interest of the Scottish manufacturer, the provision of better quality clothing wools in increasing quantities benefited the local woollen industry,

The presence of local wool supplies is not a sufficient reason in itself, however, to explain the success of woollen manufacture in the area. The weaving of woollen cloth has traditionally been widespread both in Scotland and England, and the lack of local wool supplies has not always precluded its successful manufacture. The sizeable trade in woollen cloth associated with Aberdeen in the seventeenth century was mainly founded on wool brought from the south of Scotland. or even England. English manufacturers bought wool from the extremities of both kingdoms, not confining themselves to the finer and thus more valuable varieties. Wool, being valuable in relation to weight and bulk, is able to bear considerable freight costs, making the industry 'footloose' in character. Later in the nineteenth century, when the Borders imported the vast majority of the wool consumed, the established location pattern was in no way affected. 'Being near the raw material is of very little consequence . . . ' wrote a northern manufacturer at that time.[49] Nevertheless, the use of local Scotch wool was of fundamental importance to the Scottish industry, and in the 1830s it was the specific characteristics of Cheviot wool that gave the industry its distinctive 'tweed' products.

A further necessity in the successful establishment of woollen manufacture in the Borders was an adequate supply of labour. It has been observed that its lack was a prime reason for the backwardness of the area in previous times. However, by the last quarter of the eighteenth-century changes in the labour market were benefiting the woollen industry. The concurrent reorganisation of agriculture was tending to undermine the ancient dualism of the rural economy. In the sheep-rearing districts in particular there was a tendency for small tenants to be displaced by enclosures, despite the resettlement of some in the extended cultivated area.[50] In the upland grazing areas, such as Selkirkshire and parts of Roxburgh, the nature of the terrain did not permit much re-allotment, and some tenants moved to villages where advantage could be taken of their alternative skills of spinning and weaving. Thus agricultural labour and woollen manufacture slowly 'became more distinct, and a complete separation [eventually] took place between them'.[51] The gradual evolution of a permanent work-force in the woollen industry was a prerequisite for expansion of production and a higher standard of product. Available population statistics suggest a drift from country areas to nearby industrial centres, coupled with a relatively slow increase in total population. The number of people in the counties of Roxburgh, Selkirk and Peebles rose from an estimated 47,600 in 1755 to 61,000 in 1831. Galashiels increased its population by about 50 per cent between 1801 and 1831, while Hawick's numbers rose from 2,798 to 4,970 over the same period.[52]

In addition to employing many of these extra hands manufacturers made greater and more regular use of existing capacity. The decline of the linen industry in favour of woollens released workers and looms particularly in the neighbourhood of Melrose, for wool-cloth manufacture. Perhaps more important, investment in power-driven teasing, carding and spinning machinery allowed considerable increases in production without a proportionate expansion in the labour supply. Even so labour was sometimes short, present-day difficulties in this regard not being new. Weaving long remained a seasonal trade when production was very largely geared to heavy cloths for men's winter wear. Workers would initially be reluctant to commit themselves wholly to the industry when opportunity for agricultural work still existed. At harvest time the chance of supplementary earnings would not often go begging.[53] As output grew, however, and production became more centralised, full-time employment could often be given at wages well up to agricultural standards.

The emergence of the Border counties as the foremost woollen manufacturing area in Scotland also presupposes an adequate supply of men willing to develop it. Here the nature of the terrain was not without importance. The large physiographic unit termed the Tweed basin is surrounded on all sides by upland areas often over 1,000ft high—poor land with a high rainfall, capable of little agricultural development compared with the valleys. The same was true of upper Teviotdale, where Hawick is situated. Sheep-farming was the mainstay of these higher regions, and the inhabitants of the villages naturally turned to woollen manufacture in the absence of any profitable alternative.

The success of the local entrepreneurs, however, was not simply due to their geographical and economic position. There is evidence, for example, that qualities of energy and bold enterprise were to be found among the Border population long accustomed to living at the margin of subsistence. David Loch found the inhabitants of Hawick in the 1770s very industrious and deserving of public notice. He also commended the villagers of Galashiels for their industry when he found them to be more prosperous than they had been previously. He upbraided Jedburgh, however, for indulging in petty political squabbles that sapped the industrial vigour of the inhabitants. Selkirk was likewise condemned.[54] But in the important cloth and hosiery towns leaders of industry were prominent. The pioneering spirit of the Galashiels clothiers is seen in the way the town dominated the competitions held by the Trustees in Edinburgh from 1780 onwards, and by requests to the Board for aid to study manufacturing techniques in England.[55] Their single-mindedness was noticed by the agent of Scott of Gala, the local landowner. 'The parks and fields proposed to be let to the inhabitants,' he noted in 1797, 'seem to be sufficient . . . as most of them are (to their credit) so intent on their own business that they have not great desire to be farmers . . .'.[56] In their enterprise the leaders of Border industry appear to have had the backing of the Church, which may have played a part in the conditioning of the local population to the disciplines necessary for industrial expansion. The minister of Galashiels, Dr Douglas, encouraged the local inhabitants in their endeavours to the extent of making a long loan to the clothiers of £1,000 for a cloth hall. Encouragement was also obtained from local landlords like Scott of Gala and Sir Walter himself.[57]

Here then in the Border counties existed a community of rural dwellers, pushing and hardworking, who by dint of changing economic circumstances successfully began to exploit the growing commercial possibilities of crafts they had long practised in a minor way as an adjunct to an agricultural way of life.

The gradual expansion of production that took place in the Border counties in the sixty years after 1770 poses the question as to how it was actually achieved. Clearly where workers' attention was divided between agriculture and handicrafts the possibility of greatly expanded production together with quality improvement was slim. Thus the growth we have noted suggests fundamental changes in manufacturing techniques and organisation. Men and women left the soil for the factory, or at least the loom-shop, becoming wage-earners dependent on capitalist producers who had somehow emerged to found factories and workshops equipped with the latest textile machinery. We may presume, too, that these decisions had been made in response to an increase in demand for Scottish woollen products. How then did these developments take place? Who were these capitalists and whence came their capital? What circumstances were producing a greater demand for products from Scottish looms?

On one level of explanation the growth of woollen production in Scotland can be accounted for by the way in which the new textile technology, pioneered in England, was applied to the industry, especially in the wool-preparation and spinning processes. Scribbling and carding machines that disentangled and then blended the wool fibres were extensively applied in several areas from the late eighteenth century, thus reducing dependence on hand labour and increasing the supply of prepared wool to the spinners. In the later processes of production, however, increasing demand was met at first by greater use of capacity within the confines of the existing technology. Thus more intensive use was made of single-thread spinning wheels and handlooms, and more of these units were added to the capital stock. Minor technological changes were not long delayed, however, in response to growing demand for products old and new. For example, as the customary narrow cloths failed to meet the entire demand, the fly-shuttle loom was adopted to facilitate the manufacture of broadcloth and blankets.[58] By the 1790s, however, and more particularly in the early nineteenth century, spinning began to be mechanised, first by the introduction of hand-jennies and later by water-driven semi-automatic 'mule' jennies. The weaving process did not at this time lend itself to mechanisation. For mainly technical reasons power-operated looms were not to be the norm in the industry until after 1850. Rather the increased production of yarn made possible by carding and spinning machinery led to a greater demand for handloom weavers, who by the early nineteenth century were beginning to become full-time 'industrial' workers.

The new machines were adopted in many parts of Scotland. In Aberdeen Charles Baird, a silk dyer, introduced carding machinery in 1789, and he was soon followed by Alexander Haddon, who by 1814 possessed twenty steam-driven carding sets.[59] Spinning 'jennies' figure in the records of another Aberdeenshire firm, the Kilgours, in 1788.[60] Carding machinery was installed in the Hillfoot towns of Alloa and Tillicoultry from the 1790s.[61] Most of the investment in textile machinery, however, occurred in the Border counties of Roxburgh, Selkirk and Peebles. Hand-operated scribblers were bought by a group of four Galashiels clothiers in 1785 and the first water-driven carding engines were probably erected there in 1791. Spinning 'jennies' appeared in Galashiels and Jedburgh in 1790, and in Peebles in the following year. Buildings to house the machines (where they were not rented) were erected by groups of clothiers. Six mills were founded in Galashiels between 1780 and 1805.[62]

On the strength of present knowledge we cannot be sure of the precise economic and social conditions that were forcing manufacturers to make fundamental changes in their traditional production methods. It is possible that labour costs were rising, especially in the Borders where the demand for female labour at least is shown by the employment there of possibly several thousand women yarn spinners by north of England worsted manufacturers.[63] This absorption of Scottish labour into the English domestic system may well have raised costs to the home producer or created bottlenecks in the preparation of wool for weaving that could only be overcome by technological change. Furthermore wool prices rose steeply during the French wars which added to production costs and gave a further incentive to clothiers to innovate.

Alternatively growing competition in Scotland from Yorkshire producers towards the end of the eighteenth century may have forced new techniques on native manufacturers in order to lower costs and prices and to enhance the quality of their products. There is evidence that Scottish consumers who had hitherto been content with cheap, low-grade homespuns were turning to Yorkshire blue cloth as incomes rose.[64] What is clear, if only from the frequent visits of Scottish manufacturers to the West Riding to study production and finishing techniques, is that the main stimulus to innovation stemmed from that quarter rather than from the Scottish cotton industry.

The mechanisation of carding and spinning led to the desired increase in productivity and the cutting of unit costs. Once given a modest degree of capital equipment, a worker was able to produce a good deal more yarn in a given time than formerly. In 1798 Dr Douglas, the paternal minister at Galashiels, stated that his parishioners were able to make 'a much greater quantity of cloth on a shorter notice' than before, and of better quality. Costs had meanwhile been reduced. Weft yarn spun on the 'jenny' was reckoned to cost about 4d per 'slip' in 1798 as opposed to 6d on the handwheel.[65] As the jennies became larger, the cost differential between machine-spun and hand-produced yarn doubtless increased. The productivity gain made possible by these early simple machines should not be underestimated. In the early nineteenth century a hand-carder could prepare about 1½lb of wool per day, whereas an early carding 'set' produced anything between 48 and 72lb daily. Similarly, whereas a hand-spinner would take about a month to spin enough yarn to produce a piece of cloth 30yd in length and 30lb in weight, an early jenny of thirty-six spindles could produce it in about eight hours.[66] Admittedly early jenny yarn was only suitable for weft, but soon 'mules' enabled strong warp yarns also to be spun mechanically.

The level of output in the industry, therefore, began to be raised from the late eighteenth century by the application of new highly productive forms of technology which required little in the way of new skills and which were readily grafted on to small-scale industrial activities such as domestic woollen production. But technological innovation of this kind presumes the existence of a class of entrepreneurs with sufficient capital and commercial intelligence to go well beyond the bounds of domestic manufacturing and to lay the basis of a factory-oriented industry. Who were these men? If they were lowly, how did they accumulate sufficient capital to raise themselves from among their equals to become masters? We have seen that before the second half of the eighteenth century few of the economic desiderata for open-market trading in woollen goods existed in the Border counties. As the bulk of woollens produced was for domestic or local consumption, the organisation of production was necessarily simple. No expensive capital equipment could be carried nor a fully dependent labour force employed. Thus the home was the natural basis of organisation; the family provided its own wool and also much of the labour as and when required. If the husband was a weaver, the manufacturing equipment was also provided; if not, a local 'custom' weaver and tailor provided their specialist services. The finishing processes were often dispensed with altogether, but, if not, the weaver took the web to the fulling mill and to the litster (dyer) for completion. Such an organisational pattern was only relevant to conditions of low output and technological stability. The growth of demand and the new textile machinery made the family manufacture of woollen goods increasingly uneconomic. As demand grew, a state of disequilibrium arose as hand methods of carding and spinning proved insufficient, especially so when weavers began to realise the need for wider and more elaborate looms. Thus by the late eighteenth century conditions were ripe for the application of capital and changes in the organisation of production.

The most likely leaders of industrial reorganisation and growth were merchants seeking outlets for commercial profits and landlords looking for productive forms of investment for the rents from their land and ways of increasing estate revenue. On the whole, however, landed proprietors were not prone to invest directly in manufacturing pursuits. Though many Scottish landlords encouraged the growth of manufacturing indirectly by granting feus for building, others actively opposed industrialisation from a keen sense of the social pressures such changes would produce.[67] Neither was the application of merchant capital prominent in the southern counties, though it did figure in the development of other areas.

Glasgow merchants employed many Hillfoot tartan weavers well into the nineteenth century, though it is not clear whether they supplied any of the fixed capital that was needed. Aberdeen had a long tradition of merchant-organised woollen manufacture, which did not end with the coming of machinery. James Knowles, partner in the firm of Crombie, Knowles & Co, formed in 1805 and forerunner of J. & J. Crombie of Grandholm, came from an Aberdeen merchant family long engaged in wool-selling, corn-dealing and the marketing of hosiery products. When based at Rotterdam for a while, he leased an Aberdeen mill and took Crombie. a local weaver, as a partner to manage the mill and manufacture high-grade cloth for sale through his Dutch connections. Later Knowles and Crombie were joined in the firm by Alexander Rhind, an Aberdeen merchant with interests in shipping and real estate, who, by means of a circumspect marriage became heir to a large West Indian fortune.[68] Further north at Elgin the present firm of James Johnston & Co was also started in the late eighteenth century from general merchanting activities. The founder, Alexander Johnston, had a hand in most of the business opportunities that presented themselves in the district—he dealt in oatmeal, fish, whisky, snuff, tobacco and beer as well as English cloths, and sold flannels on commission for a Rochdale firm, hats for a Manchester business, cloth for Prest's of Leeds, crockery and, for a while, insurance. Alongside these ventures he dealt in local wool, made cloth on his own account, and, after installing carding machinery in a grain mill, began to prepare wool for the local population. Not content with this Johnston took a financial interest in a local iron foundry and, in conjuction with a local timber concern, chartered vessels to sail to the Americas in search of timber and rare wools like alpaca and vicuna. Later, the firm was able to specialise in high quality products made from them.[69]

In the Border counties, however, merchant capital in the growing woollen industry appears to have been non-existent. In fact, the situation was reversed. Small-time manufacturers had long since marketed their products themselves, embarking on 'journeys' at intervals during the year, selling cloth from the backs of ponies or carts at local fairs and markets. An employing class arose from among the woollen workers themselves, and what evidence there is points to the fullers and dyers as providing the focus round which the industry came to be organised. As unmilled undyed cloth became rarer in the latter half of the eighteenth century, the services of the fulling mill and the dyehouse were in growing demand. Indigo dyeing became firmly established in the Galashiels area by the 1780s (as evidenced by the formation of a Dyers Corporation in 1789), the local 'greys' giving way to 'blues'. Indigo dyeing not only required particular skills, which not all weavers possessed, but also access to sufficient capital to purchase cases of the dye from the importers.[70]

For technical reasons it was fitting for dyeing to be allied to fulling in the woollen industry. Both processes came in the final stages of production, for most cloths at this time were dyed in the piece rather than in the wool. Similarly, both dyeing and fulling needed covered premises of some kind other than a dwelling house. More important, both crafts necessitated the presence of large quantities of running water ·for boiling in the dye-vats, to scour and mill the cloth, and to drive the fulling stocks. It is not surprising, therefore, that a close link developed between the two occupations. In time dyeing and fulling came to be practised by one man, or a group of men, under the same roof. Members of the Dyers Corporation in Galashiels in the 1790s were also tenants of the local fulling (waulk) mills, and the same connection can be seen elsewhere.[71]

The dyer-fuller, therefore, was in a convenient position to become an organiser of production as well as perform specialised services for other clothiers. He handled, in the main, completed webs passed to him by weavers; he owned or leased premises capable of housing dye-vats and the new water-driven carding and spinning machinery. It was but a short step for the dyer-fullers to begin to purchase wool on credit or with savings from their previous services, and to distribute it for manufacturing before finishing it and marketing the final product themselves. Gradually local weavers and spinners lost their independence and became bound up with the entrepreneurial activities of the dyer-fullers in the neighbourhood. The process may also have been hastened by the steep rise in wool prices that occurred during the Napoleonic wars. Thus in 1797 weavers in the Galashiels area were said to have few webs in their looms that did not belong to local clothiers.[72] The latter may well have included non-fullers or dyers among their ranks—men who were the most successful and ambitious weavers—but wherever possible these men erected or rented premises for housing manufacturing and finishing equipment and combined with others who could conduct fulling and dyeing operations.

Given the low level of woollen production in the Borders during the eighteenth century, it is surprising that dyer-fullers could find sufficient capital to finance fixed plant and machinery, together with the processes of production, without external assistance, even though the independent domestic worker found it increasingly difficult to bypass their services. On the other hand one should not overstate the amount of capital needed to set up in business at this time. Buildings could often be rented. Galashiels already had several fulling-mills. Grain mills were sometimes converted to house woollen machinery. Some early 'factories' were primitive in the extreme: four stout posts and a thatched roof sufficed for a late eighteenth-century Galashiels fulling mill, though most were stone structures. Early machinery, too, was relatively inexpensive. The breakthrough in textile technology at this time was made possible by marginal improvements to old methods of production at first. The new machines were designed to relieve bottlenecks in yarn production, not to bring about an industrial revolution. That they helped to do so was largely because the potential of initially marginal improvements proved to be enormous. One would expect, therefore, that early machinery would bear some resemblance to existing equipment both in design and cost, and this does seem to have been the case.

Six spinning jennies and a warping mill were insured in 1805 for only £45 by a larger than average Jedburgh clothier.[73] A fly-shuttle broadloom cost about £12 to mount in 1795 and could be made fully operational for around £20.[74] Early insurance records suggest that the entire fixed capital of a Scottish woollen firm in the early nineteenth century averaged between £200 and £300.[75] Circulating capital to finance the actual production of cloth was of greater importance. An inventory book for 1777 of an Aberdeenshire firm shows nearly £2,000 invested in yarn, wool, dyestuffs and customers' credit, whereas manufacturing utensils and premises were valued at only £156. By 1788 working capital had grown to £4,400 but fixed assets to only £250, despite the acquisition of some spinning machinery.[76] Capital calculations based on insurance policies between 1790 and 1800 show that in that time thirty Scottish firms took out total insurance of £58,199, making an average of £1,940.[77] If the figure of £300 suggested above for fixed assets is correct, the ratio of working to fixed capital requirements seem to have been about six to one. Wool was expensive relative to other fibres; in addition other raw materials, such as oil and dyestuffs, had to be bought, and rent and wages had to be paid. Often several months passed before wool was actually turned into cloth for sale. In these days before wool-stapling and broking facilities were available, when communications were poor, and when few banks existed in the remoter manufacturing areas, working capital must have comprised a considerable problem.

The organisation of the Scottish woollen industry long reflected the fact that many individuals were unable to afford to enter into business without much sharing of equipment or common ownership. In the Borders the Galashiels Manufacturers' Corporation was formed in 1777 by a group of local weavers who shared a stock of reeds for their looms and other apparatus. Well into the nineteenth century a guild-like atmosphere prevailed in the Borders. Weavers continued to hold common stocks of reeds for their looms when steel replaced cane for reed-making to avoid breakage by the fly-shuttle. The new 'machinery mills' were usually jointly owned or rented by a number of clothiers who shared the use of machinery and their equipment. ('Our turn with the stove today' states a contemporary account book.) Men like Richard Lees of Galashiels, who owned a summerhouse, a private bridge over Gala Water and a goldfish pond were exceptional. Most woollen men in this period were like James and Henry Brown of Galashiels who rented their father's fourth share of a mill building and shared their machines with others, or like William Nixon of Hawick, who began his career with a seventh share in a gig-mill.

Often money was tied up for long periods because the taking of credit by customers forced many clothiers to take it in turn from farmers and other suppliers. Credit was a mixed blessing. It enabled firms of slender resources to set up in business and to acquire working capital by borrowing more on credit than they allowed. In time the banks played an important role by injecting credit into the system by discounting bills of exchange. However, banks seem to have played only a small part in the Scottish woollen industry before the 1820s, and often clothiers had to wait patiently for their money or try to collect it when going on their marketing trips. In 1812 Alexander Johnston of Elgin informed a Fraserburgh customer that his account was 'shamefully overdue . . . some part of it two years'. He advised a southern firm trading in the north to add something to the price of some customers' goods as 'we question whether they will pay regularly at 6 months'. Later he asked an English firm trading in Caithness to allow four customers 'another year's credit'.[78] It is doubtful whether conditions were much different in the south of Scotland. In any case many Border manufacturers themselves traded in the north.

Consequently the clothiers often found themselves very short of cash. In 1789 Galashiels weavers petitioned the Board of Trustees in Edinburgh for financial help because they were indebted to tradesmen supplying equipment for broadlooms. In the 1790s Dr Douglas of Galashiels stated that local clothiers were obliged 'to purchase on credit . . . and to sell the produce instantly at whatever ready money it will fetch'.[79] Alexander Johnston in Elgin had to sell his few banking and insurance shares in 1812 to meet current needs, and when involved with bankrupt firms invariably exhorted other creditors to settle quickly for what they could get. Manufacturers in the Borders often borrowed among themselves. Henry Brown in Galashiels lent a total of £540 to local colleagues between March 1828 and December 1829 in seventy or so amounts ranging from a few shillings to £40. Over the same period he borrowed about £340 in the same way. All debts were paid promptly a week or two later, and no interest was charged. By this time bills of exchange also circulated there as freely as money, often covered in endorsements.[80]

Though most of the financial needs of the growing woollen industry were met from personal savings of men engaged in it, there were occasions when outside help was given. Dr Douglas, as we have said, invested £1,000 of his own in erecting a Cloth Hall there in 1791 in an attempt to make the town a marketing centre. The venture failed in a few years, but while it lasted clothiers were able to obtain part of the price of their cloth from a fund on its lodgement in the Hall, the remainder being paid on its sale.[81] After the Leith merchant and ardent supporter of woollen manufacture, David Loch, had reported on the favourable state of the industry in the mid-1770s the Board of Trustees began to take an increasing financial interest in the industry. Grants were made to manufacturers, especially in the Borders, to purchase looms, dye-vats and carding and spinning machinery. Travel grants were also given to enable clothiers to travel to Yorkshire to study finishing techniques. The aid offered by this public body, however, should not be overstressed. Between 1775 and 1825 annual grants made to woollen manufacturing averaged only £400. Between 1775 and 1833 the average sum paid annually to Border clothiers was only £85. Over the same period Hawick and Galashiels, where, as we have seen, most activity was taking place, received an annual average sum of only £23 and £25 respectively from the board.[82] Funds of this nature, therefore, seem to have been just a useful supplement to investment. The bulk of capital requirement, in the southern counties at least, came from the meagre savings of ordinary men. Those who invested about £3,000 in the Galashiels woollen industry in the 1790s were described as 'poor people who began business without any capital', raising themselves 'by their own energy and enterprise',[83] and religiously ploughing back any profit that accrued—men like James and Henry Brown, who in the relatively prosperous 1820s took 15s each from their business once a fortnight.

So much for investment in the supply of woollen goods. What of demand? One reason for expansion in the woollen industry was the growth in the number of people needing to be clothed. The Scottish population rose from about 1¼ million in 1755 to more than 2 million by 1821, increasing the number of potential customers by about two thirds. Moreover this population growth was accompanied by rising living standards among the body of the people, especially between 1760 and the 1790s. Though rising consumption standards often took the form of wearing English, especially Yorkshire, cloth, the rising quality of Scottish woollens and their dense nature allowed native manufacturers a share of the expanding market. Overseas sales began to grow also. Between the 1760s and the 1780s woollen exports from Scottish ports averaged about £20,000 per annum (official prices). After the French wars the average annual figure rose to around £50,000 down to the late 1820s.[84] Though this increase reflected growing carpet sales from the West of Scotland, it also included larger exports of druggets, tartans and other cloths.

By the 1820s the Scottish woollen industry had developed considerably from its position half a century earlier. Output had increased, quality had been enhanced, the Borders had become the focus of cloth manufacture despite growth in Aberdeen, the Hillfoots, and the West of Scotland while organisational changes were transferring woollen manufacture from a domestic, often subsistence-type industry to one based on factory methods, at least in carding and spinning. Some mills were at a transitional stage, like those of David Ballantyne at Innerleithen or Alexander Johnston at Elgin, where carding and/or spinning for country people still continued alongside manufacturing for the open market. In larger centres like Aberdeen, Galashiels and Hawick little 'servicing' appears to have survived by the 1820s. Here the firms were wholly engaged in manufacturing for the market. Even weavers had been affected by factory methods. In 1828 most Galashiels looms were described as 'factory' looms, suggesting that in the interests of managerial efficiency weavers had been grouped together into loom-shops and that the domestic weaver was declining.[85]

Despite these developments factors were at work by the 1820s that threatened to undermine the progress that had been made. In the first place Cheviot wool, whose use had helped to bridge the quality gap between English and Scottish woollens, was progressively deteriorating and becoming unsuitable for the manufacture of fine cloth. Sheep farmers were more concerned with breeding mutton stock than good wool, and intensive fattening was leading to increasing length of wool fibre and poorer quality. The longer fibres were suited to combed worsted goods, but few were made north of the border now that carding had been mechanised. Moreover the continued cross-breeding of sheep gradually blurred the distinction between those bearing combing and those producing clothing wool. This was not always in the interest of the manufacturer, who preferred to be able to distinguish between manufac-

Page 65. The original ingredient of the tweed trade: the black and white checked plaid of the border shepherd.

Page 66. *Hawick Roxburghshire, in 1960.* The woollen mills can be seen clustered in the centre of the town alongside the River Teviot, which once provided their power. Workers' houses are dotted among the mills, and have been forced to spread up the sides of the valley. Manufacturers' houses, tastefully sited on the far hillside, look down paternally. The friendly conglomeration of Hawick reflects vividly the laissez-faire attitude to town planning in the last century.

turing wools to facilitate sorting and blending. In 1830 an Edinburgh wool merchant complained that the introduction of numerous breeds of sheep into Scotland had made it impossible to manufacture decent cloth from native wool.[86] Similarly many English staplers had ceased to purchase Cheviot wool, considering it unfit any more to make a good grade of cloth. The changing nature of Scottish wool, together with the gradual return to stable trading conditions after 1815, led to increased use of imported wools, especially from Germany. The amount of foreign wool imported for consumption within the United Kingdom increased from 7.5 million lb in 1816 to 32.3 million lb in 1830. Yorkshire manufacturers in particular turned to foreign wools and began to produce lighter and better quality 'blues' than their Scottish counterparts. A Galashiels firm noted in 1828 that its English rivals were now able to send cloths into Scotland 'which entirely cut up the finer cloth made from Cheviot wool'. Demand for Border cloth fell away and prices slumped from 6s 6d per yard in 1818 to only 4s in 1827, though falling wool prices helped to offset loss of revenue.[87]

The logical course for the Scottish producer was to try and adjust himself to these new market conditions, and turn to Spanish merino and German wools. Such a switch posed considerable problems, however. The industry was young and equipped with new plant geared mainly to making coarser goods from the lower qualities of Cheviot. Any large-scale changeover to finer foreign wools entailed adaptations to existing, fully operable plant. In particular card 'clothing' would need to be replaced. Furthermore many manufacturers regarded themselves as insufficiently skilled in the manipulation of the finer wools to compete successfully with Yorkshire goods. Wool dyeing was hardly practised and recent attention to finishing had not destroyed Yorkshire's traditional lead in this field. Some Border manufacturers also considered that any attempt to change from long established products would meet with the prejudice of city merchants in Edinburgh and Glasgow. There were organisational difficulties, too—no facilities for wool stapling, and, since premises and machinery were jointly owned and wool and dyestuffs often bought communally, production changes had to be agreed by several parties. For these reasons many Galashiels

E

manufacturers decided at a special meeting in 1828 that they could not 'adopt the making of fine cloth', and attention was concentrated on the lower qualities in the hope that their cheapness would minimise competition from the south. They cut back on their better grades of Cheviots and turned more to stocking yarn for the Hawick hosiery trade, cheap plaiding and duffles.[88]

With hindsight it is clear that Border manufacturers at this time were flying in the face of fashion, for by the 1820s public taste was demanding something lighter and more colourful than the traditional, densely made blues and drabs, the predilection for lighter finer Yorkshire blues being an early indication of this trend in Scotland. Current changes in fashion, however, affected many small Yorkshire manufacturers adversely as well, and it is hard to avoid the conclusion that the troubles that afflicted Scottish woollen producers in 1828-30, when many went bankrupt, were not wholly the result of the general economic depression in the country. Vision and enterprising management also appear to have been lacking.

There were, nonetheless, a few progressive Scottish firms that reacted positively to competition and changing fashion. As early as 1815 some firms began to invest in fine-toothed carders and to buy foreign wool. A petition was sent from Border clothiers to the House of Lords in 1819 declaring their hostility to any tax on foreign wool, though this may have aimed merely at keeping down the price of the home clip.[89] (Cheviot wool had jumped from 21s to 35s per stone between 1817 and 1818.) Although foreign wool for flannel manufacture was first used in Hawick in 1826 and a few Galashiels firms were steadily increasing their consumption in the 1820s, only about 5 per cent of the town's annual consumption was imported in 1829.[90]

The collapse of many Border firms in 1829 should not blind us to the existence of some that were to became renowned in the woollen trade in subsequent years. Nonetheless the outlook for the Scottish woollen industry looked bleak. Fashion frowned on its products and threatened its future. Yet the fashion cloud proved to have a silver lining; changes in social habits, in particular a growing interest in tourism, stemming from new wealth and better communications, were helping to put Scotland on the map. Its history, literature and topography were of increasing interest to the middle-class Englishman. Fashion was soon to reflect this new affection—to the lasting benefit of the Scottish woollen producer.

THREE

The Origins and Growth
of the Tweed Trade
from 1830

'About the origins of the tweed trade there is little to be said.' Adam
Cochrane, 1863

It is tempting to see the year 1829 as a rigid dividing line in the
history of the Scottish woollen industry. Despite the economic
dislocation of that year, and the collapse of the market for the
traditional blue cloth it witnessed the introduction to the London
market of the products to be known later as tweeds, which were to
give the Scottish woollen industry its main claim to fame. In a
real sense 1829 did mark the end of an era for the trade. Old goods
were progressively discarded, new markets were opened. Horizons
widened. Yet different though the new products were from the
older cloths, they nevertheless constituted an evolution rather than
a revolution in cloth design. The fancy trade on which the name
of the industry was built during the nineteenth century was rooted
in the products of the pre-tweed era, and in one product in particular—the black and white checked plaid used by Border shepherds.
  This garment had long been manufactured in the district. It was
made of local wool, and was often undyed, the black and white
effect being obtained by the natural colouring of the wool. The
white was sometimes improved by the use of sulphur, so that the

plaid usually possessed a dirty or smokey hue. Its length was customarily about 4yd and its width 6 quarters or about 1½yd. By the 1820s the growing number of tourists were welcoming these plaids as travelling wraps.[1] The plaid's ability to withstand the rigours of journeying 'outside' on the stagecoach did not escape the attention of passengers who 'found that to roam through different and changeable climates at such great speed they needed something warmer than "a light heart and a thin pair of breeches" '.[2] The plaid, therefore, though traditionally associated with humbler folk, became an adornment of the travelling aristocracy.

A taste for tartan cloths similar to the traditional garb of the Highlands also developed after the ban on the wearing of male Highland dress, which had been imposed after the Jacobite rebellion of 1745, was lifted in 1780. Tartans quickly became fashionable with both sexes, and a lady's costume was not considered complete without a tartan plaid or shawl with borders and fringes. Manufacturers in the Borders and Hillfoots gradually turned to these goods, finding a large market among Glasgow wholesalers.

By the middle of the 1820s the more restrained designs were being adopted as men's wear also. Historically, however, the Borders did not possess a tartan, this omission being filled by the shepherd-check pattern, which was adopted by Sir Walter Scott (a friend of shepherds) as the 'tartan' of the clan Scott.[3] This fusion of the shepherd-check with the growing popularity of tartans was the kernel from which the Scottish fancy woollen trade grew.

These developments did not in themselves constitute a revolution in the industry, however. As we have seen, these years were difficult for the trade. Fancy products occupied but a minor part of the manufacturer's output. The old blues, greys and drabs still predominated in 1830. The fashionable had not yet replaced the customary, and the clothes-conscious young bourgeois had not yet become the typical customer. The step that changed the pace and direction of the Scottish branch of the wool-textile industry came when the shepherd-check design was adopted as a trouser cloth. Around 1826 Sir Walter Scott ordered a pair of trousers from such material, and the idea caught on in the upper ranks of society. Scottish merchants rather than manufacturers exploited the new fashion. One such merchant, Alexander Craig of Edinburgh, who had London connections, first noticed the design being worn as a trouser cloth in Glasgow in 1829—the bold light check design standing out conspicuously among the blues and drabs—and deduced that the original material was a 'smoked' shawl or plaid. Soon afterwards similar garb was to be seen on occasion in Edinburgh, and must also have reached London, for about the same time a Scottish-born tailor, James Locke, with a business in Covent Garden asked Craig for patterns of a 'coarse woollen cloth black and white checked stuff, expected to be wanted for trousers'.[4] Since patterns of the material were unknown, Craig snipped a corner from a checked cloak and forwarded it to Locke, who immediately ordered six pieces. These were woven in Peebles. Further orders followed and were supplied in Peebles and Bannockburn. By late 1830 Galashiels manufacturers, too, were engaging in the trade, but had to be convinced that the material was not wanted for plaids, with the usual borders and fringes, but for trouserings. Thus Scottish-made shepherd-checks vigorously promoted in Scotland by Craig and others and in London by Locke (who with consummate vision moved from Covent Garden to Regent Street) rapidly took hold among the 'avant garde' of the middle and upper classes.

Not without some sagacity Scottish manufacturers had not in general yet warmed to the trade in trouser cloths, since they considered it might be ephemeral, a fleeting whim of the idle rich. This was equally clearly perceived by the trade's merchant promoters, who soon realised that variations on the theme were necessary if the 'music' was to continue. The arrangement of the shepherd-check pattern in different sets and colours, which gave further scope for a variety of styles, quickly supplied this need. The black and white check was dipped (perhaps accidently) in brown dye, producing a black and brown check, which proved equally popular; and blue and black, and green and black followed, plus broken and larger checks in all the former colourings. Many of them were given topical names such as 'railway' and 'Victoria'.[5]

About the mid-1830s a happy accident led to the coining of an exceedingly appropriate collective name for these twilled products. Locke, on receipt of some goods from a Hawick firm, gave the invoicing to a clerk who is said to have misread the word 'tweel' (the

Scottish form of 'twill') as 'tweed', he knowing that the cloths originated in the south of Scotland. The commercial advantage of such a trade name was quickly realised and the term 'tweeds' was generally adopted.[6] About the same time the practice of twisting together yarns of different colours was adopted in the industry, possibly first in Jedburgh, and this gave a new impetus to design.

Alongside the growing demand for checks, tartans and coloured shawls continued to prove equally popular with people of taste. To stimulate the trade even further London merchants, particularly Locke, devised new tartans. On the occasion of the Queen's first visit to Scotland, Locke took the large 'Murray' tartan and incorporated it with the 'Victoria', from which came nearly all the 'Dress Clan' patterns in shawls.[7] All kinds of vagaries were produced in tartans bearing little or no resemblance to true clan designs, but popular demand was not discriminating. 'If a young gentleman can show his smart plaided stockings or cap, or if a young gentleman of large growth can procure a plaid waistcoat or trousers, he forthwith dubs himself a highlander, and thinks of Rhoderick dhu or Rob Roy, without stopping to enquire whether it be or not a recognised tartan.'[8] Thus designers showing great freedom and boldness in experiment produced a large variety of 'unauthentic' tartans for cloths and shawls.

The vogue for fancy shawls lasted until the late 1840s, when demand for at least the Scottish-made products began to wane; but until about 1850 the trade in these goods in some markets far outstripped the demand for other types of cloth. In that year, for example, Henry Ballantyne of Galashiels sold £7,250 worth of goods to London buyers of which £5,300 was in plaids and shawls.[9] By 1852, however, an Innerleithen manufacturer could write that 'few or no orders for wool shawls' were given and most factories hitherto mainly employed upon them were changing to tweed production. 'The wool-shawl trade in the mean time seems to be done,' wrote the manufacturer, 'year after year only bringing disappointment and great loss of money to those who have clung to it.'[10] Though shawls continued to be made until the 1870s, in fine and heavy qualities, cheaper Yorkshire-made mixed-yarn goods were competing successfully with them by the 1850s in the highly volatile ladies' trade. The Cobden-Chevalier commercial treaty with

France in 1860 also hastened the end of the quality shawl in that it led to the increased import of French merino dress fabrics. By the early 1850s many of the manufacturers in the Hillfoots specialising in the Glasgow fancy trade, and particularly in shawls, were turning to tweeds.[11]

The early preoccupation with tartans and the shepherd-checks was gradually modified by economic developments. Many estates in the Highlands were bought up by Lowland or English gentlemen for shooting and fishing, and sheep and shepherds were often displaced by the formation of deer forests and grouse moors. It was not unnatural for the new owners to regard themselves in some way as the new Highland chiefs, and to wish to clothe their 'retainers' in some form of tartan uniform. These 'retainers', however, had non-military functions and comprised, in the main, ghillies, keepers and foresters. Thus their uniforms required to be distinctive but capable also of merging with the scenery in order to camouflage the wearer when out hunting or shooting. So the Border shepherd-check was modified to provide the foundation for these 'District Checks', as they became known, and such modification was made easier by the fact that the Border plaid had been taken north by shepherds towards the end of the eighteenth century with the extension of sheep-farming in the Highlands. The District Checks, therefore, arose from a social and economic revolution and were not directly related to the traditional clan tartans.[12]

The 'Glenurquart' check, which still provides the basis for many fancy cloth designs, was adopted by the Countess of Seafield on her Glen Urquart estates, and was worn by all her tenants, factors, gamekeepers and the like from the 1840s onwards. The influence of the Border plaid is also clearly visible in the 'Glenfeshie', which by the addition of a red overcheck, became an almost invisible clothing when merging with the red and grey granites of the glen. Other checks reflecting the influence of the shepherd-check were the 'Ing', the 'Ballindalloch' of Strathspey, the 'Ardtornish' of the west coast, the 'Glenquioch' of the north-west, and the 'Coigach' in black and brown check, later to be adopted in America by shooting clubs and renamed the 'Gun-Club'. New ground in the evolution of protective colourings was later broken by the intricately woven 'Balmoral', attributed to the Prince Consort for use on the royal estate there. Similar distinctive designs were developed by Lord Lovat, who, by experimenting with primroses and bluebells, produced the 'Lovat Mixture'.[13] Not unnaturally the protective principle was applied to the uniforms of Scottish regiments, the 'Elcho mixture', for example, becoming associated with the London Scottish Rifle Corps. It was but a short step forward to the wearing of khaki cloths or field greys instead of the highly coloured uniforms formerly used. Though the origins of many of these estate cloths are unknown, their manufacture was an important element in the trade of northern merchants and manufacturers like Mcdougall of Inverness and Johnston of Elgin.

The significance of the district checks to the Scottish woollen industry was their adoption for informal men's wear, by which means they became part of the staple output of many Lowland manufacturers. The Shepherd, Glenurquart and Coigach checks 'dominated the designing of the vast bulk of ordinary checked woollen cloths'. The Glenurquart was of particular importance because it was capable of an infinite range of variations, which was especially valuable to the industry when demand for the more traditional tartan cloths eventually went into decline. The Lovat, too, by skilful selection and blending of bright colours opened up to the designer a whole range of new territory. The 'Districts', therefore, added an important dimension to the fancy woollen trade of Scotland and came to form the bulk of the designs exported to the large north American market.[14]

The products of Scottish woollen looms after 1830 were identifiable by three design characteristics—skilful use of colour, employment of pure virgin wools, and uniqueness of texture. These factors, combined in a carded cloth, gave tweed its quality and distinctive appearance. The colour effects of the early tweeds were often obtained by copying leaves, heather or even stones from the countryside, and these colours gave the cloth its appeal. Thereafter the skilful blending of colour to produce natural ground effects and bold patterns was perhaps the chief aim of the designer. Nothing that was not effectively and artfully coloured would sell, irrespective of pattern or price. For some time tweed patterns used large areas of broad colour to give a bright solid effect, but in the second

half of the nineteenth century there was a transition to softer
patterns and more mellow colour effects. Colour novelty was increasingly obtained by fancy weave patterns that made effective
use of twist yarns to distribute the colours in the material. Without
the use of such yarns it would have been impossible to mix bright
and strongly contrasted colours and at the same time avoid a harsh
broad effect not always to the public taste. Increasingly soft
broken effects were achieved by various 'mixtures'. By the 1890s
the trend to softer colouring gave way to a distinct lessening of
colour altogether; district checks resumed their popularity and
coloured weave effects were largely superseded by greys and slates.
Colour quality and purity remained important nonetheless.[15]

Good colouring necessitated the use of good wool, and strict
attention to wool quality distinguished Scottish tweeds from those
of other areas. (Yorkshire 'tweeds', for instance, made much use of
shoddy and mungo.) In order to show off colour to the best advantage the wool fibres needed to be spun fine enough to manufacture
a cloth of the desired weight or thickness but not so fine that the
eye could not discern the individual fibres carrying the colouring.
Wool of a good natural colour displayed the dyes more pleasingly
than dull wool, and wool possessing a natural lustre reflected the
light more satisfactorily. All these desirable characteristics could
be found best in Cheviot and colonial cross-bred wools, and the
success of the tweed trade was largely dependent on the choice of
such material. Thus in making use of broader-fibred wools such as
Cheviot the old tradition of manufacturing coarse cloth was maintained. The advent of tweed cloths was, at first, more a new departure in pattern and colour design than in the textural composition
of the cloth. Despite this, reference to contemporary pattern
books makes it clear that the early tweed designers also made use
of finer wools.[16]

The growing use of imported fine wools in the 1820s has been
noted above, and Saxony and Australasian varieties were increasingly employed. Cloth made from such wool was finer and softer
in texture, but, because the fibres were narrower and because of
the cloth's sensitivity to the milling process, it could not match
the brilliant colourings of the Cheviot. As fashion drifted towards
lighter and less highly coloured products, however, 'Saxony' cloths

became increasingly popular, while the coarser 'Cheviot' was blended more with colonial cross-bred wools. When worsteds were in demand manufacturers turned more to Saxonies, because the finest grades closely resembled worsteds in finish and handling.[17] The diminished need for strong colours, however, did not lessen the need for pure wool, which was regarded as a prerequisite of good colouring whether bold or subdued. The introduction of impure wools was resisted by the trade with some resolution. In 1851 Galashiels manufacturers, through their local corporation which still existed, agreed not to sell waste in the town but to employ a 'reputable agent' in Huddersfield.[18] That some waste was consumed locally, however, is implied in a resolution of 1860 that 'waste of every description will only be sold to such parties as will at once send it to Yorkshire', and a committee of mill employees was formed to prevent local dealing in waste.[19] The interest of the industry in virgin wools was neatly summarised by a Hawick manufacturer in 1855. 'Spare no expense on your wools . . . your dyestuffs . . . aim at excellency of fabrics . . . and beauty of design; repel every attempt to compromise.'[20]

The Scottish tweed industry thus became synonymous with quality. 'Quality is our only fort', announced Henry Ballantyne of Walkerburn in 1856, after flirting with cotton warps in the 1840s.[21] He thereafter vigorously refused to reduce his standards in dull times. For their part the merchants were constantly corresponding with the mills about faults in the goods received and not infrequently returned goods on the slightest pretext, which could result in serious loss to the manufacturer who had made them exclusively for particular merchant houses. Surviving letter books are preoccupied with complaints and queries by merchants dissatisfied with the yarn or the colour or even with the smell of the cloth, or because the design did not quite match the pattern ordered. Such complaints were often used as a lever to exact better terms from the producers.

The quality of materials used in their production and the care exercised in manufacture gave Scotch tweeds a different texture from other cloths. It was of basic importance to make a fabric that was weather-resisting, but possessed style and colour. It had to be sufficiently dense to keep out the cold but the individual nature of the fibres had to be preserved in order to obtain good colour effects. Thus tweeds were twilled in the weave, for in crossing threads two under two and simultaneously moving forward to the right or the left a denser result was obtained than in the plain weave without losing the individuality of the fibres.[22]

It followed that tweeds required less milling to obtain a satisfactory degree of density when the thicker-fibred wools were employed. They were 'made-in-the-loom' rather than 'in-the-finishing'. This lack of heavy milling helped to preserve the full bloom of the colours, even in winter weights, and gave the texture elasticity and comfort with durability. This factor made Scotch tweeds particularly suited to leisurely pursuits, in contrast in the 1830s and 1840s to Yorkshire's tightly woven, heavily milled, inflexible cassimeres. The use of twist yarns, as well as improving colouring, also helped to achieve this distinctive texture. The warp and weft threads in Scotch tweeds were spun equally firmly, but inflexibility, which might have been expected, was avoided because twist yarns added strength and equalised the fabric both lengthwise and crosswise. In this way firmness and closeness were combined with flexibility and elasticity.[23]

From its preoccupation with coarse inferior homespuns for local country wear and fisherfolk Scottish woollen manufacturing after 1830 evolved into the most aristocratic branch of the British wool-textile industry. The impetus behind this radical change of emphasis was largely fashion. Fashion shifts are difficult to account for but not entirely capricious, and a number of reasons for their occurrence are discernable in the early decades of the nineteenth century.

With the fall of the ancien régime in France and the successful British prosecution of the war against Napoleon, western European fashion moved its centre from Paris to London. Men's fashion in particular adopted the English mode of unostentatious elegance, indicative of a nation proud of its superior military and economic performance. One manifestation of this movement towards informality was the supersession of the traditional breeches by trousers. Moreover status and prestige were increasingly to be gained in British society by demonstrating one's access to leisure and the wealth that permitted it. In an age increasingly symbolised by toiling masses incarcerated in ugly industrial towns the ability to live among green fields and to pursue rural pleasures lost none of its attraction and prestige. One's superior status in nineteenth-century society was assured if one hunted or travelled for pleasure, for only the moneyed classes possessed the time and wealth to indulge in such a way of life.

The cult of the carefree existence was well expressed at the English court by the Prince Regent, though it was the more respectable side of his nature that unwittingly helped to pour some of the prevailing fashion trends into a Scottish mould. The Regent admired the writings of Scott, and developed a taste for Scottish things, illustrated in 1822 when he visited Edinburgh dressed in Highland garb to be greeted by Sir Walter and other members of the Scottish gentry suitably adorned in elaborate family tartans and glengarry bonnets. The results were a baronetcy for Scott and a welcome boost for tartan cloths.

One can hardly overestimate the importance of Scott in popularising Scotland and her culture at this time. The wide popularity of his novels and poems, which effectively combined postwar European romanticism with a genuine love of country, exercised a major influence on fashion among both sexes. By the early nineteenth century Scotland had ceased to be to the English a synonym for barbarity and backwardness. Edinburgh's New Town, the pungent comment of the *Edinburgh Review*, the writings of Smith and Hume, and the liberal sprinkling of Scotsmen in current economic developments of importance were all indications of a virility in Scottish society that went beyond the walls of her long-respected universities. Scott's work, with its attractive characters and emotive description of Scottish events and places—

> Day set in Norham's castled steep
> And Tweed's fair river, broad and deep,
> And Cheviot's mountains lone . . .

—not only appealed to the swelling number of touring Sassenachs but also to the hearts of a large section of the European public. In this time of social flux occasioned by the French and Industrial Revolutions many sensed a loss of bearings and perceived in Scott a means of preserving a fast-fading way of life, which, though often crude and violent, was nonetheless familiar and well defined.

Such emotions were felt even more strongly by the Scottish emigrant. One practical outworking of public feeling was to purchase Scottish cloths. Thus, as a government inspector reported in 1838, the *Waverley* novels had 'conferred a very material benefit on the woollen trade of Scotland' in the temperate climates.[24]

This trade could not feed for ever, though, on sweet nostalgia. Other factors were at work which, aside from the inherent quality of tweed products themselves, encouraged fashion to stay with Scotland. The monarchy, restored to sobriety by Victoria and Albert, continued to exert a powerful influence. It encouraged a quieter taste by buying and wearing quieter tartans and tweeds. The royal visit to Scotland in 1848, trailing in its wake a large influx of tourists, stimulated demand for all types of Scottish woollens, especially, once more, the shepherd-check.[25] The Consort's adoption of the 'Balmoral' tartan led to a popular demand and encouraged Scottish landowners to adopt a distinct livery on their estates. The appearance of the Prince of Wales in 1867 wearing a complete suit of tweed confirmed the tendency towards suitings of one colour and design. Conversely death among royalty was not good for a fancy woollen trade, given the Victorian predilection for deep mourning. In 1896 Galashiels firms reported a 'smart demand for blacks and greys' on the death of Prince Henry of Battenburg,[26] while with the passing of the Queen herself in 1901 the Border fancy trade collapsed temporarily.[27]

In general, then, anything that promoted leisure helped the tweed industry. The pioneer tweed merchants were primarily concerned with exploiting the leisure habits of the British gentleman. 'Tweeds in heather and granite colours for shooting and deerstalking,' proclaimed James Locke's invoices. Golfers, too, found tweeds to their liking, while towards the end of the century cyclists began to choose the baggy knee of the tweed rather than the shiny seat of the worsted.[28]

It is difficult to say how far down the social scale Scotch tweeds eventually percolated. In 1863 a leading Scottish woollen merchant claimed that Scotch cloths were worn by all classes of society in Britain.[29] This is probably an exaggeration but a good suit of tweed was a good investment, for it was very durable, and as incomes rose it is likely that the better-off artisan would resort to a good tweed for Sunday wear at least. (Certainly employees at Scottish woollen mills bought tweed cloths, but they may have bought them on favourable terms.) What does seem beyond dispute is that Yorkshire woollen manufacturers soon began to fabricate cheap 'Scotch tweeds', using low-grade wools and patterns copied from Scottish ranges. 'A good style is no sooner out,' complained Bremner in the 1860s, 'than it is reproduced by Yorkshire makers in a lower quality.'[30] The jurors of the 1862 international exhibition reported that foreigners were up to the same trick. 'To the Scotch manufacturers belongs the credit of having found what the public like, and of having led for a considerable period the public taste. So largely have their productions been imitated on the Continent that many of the choicest fancy trouserings of France and other countries are easily traceable . . . to their Scotch origin!'[31]

Imitation was undoubtedly a major problem for the Scottish manufacturers, and 'imitation tweeds' were most likely to be bought by the British working people. The popularisation of the 'district check' suggests that this was so. Thus the more leisured classes were forced to differentiate themselves from the humbler orders by repeatedly changing the style and colouring of their informal wear and by paying much attention to the cut and styling of formal dress also. This placed a premium on quality and exclusiveness that tended to force the manufacturer to specialise in his production and in his dealings with the merchants. Manufacturers sought to exploit small differences between their goods and those of rival producers, and to concentrate on particular kinds of cloth. Thus Crombie's of Aberdeen became renowned for overcoatings, Roberts' of Selkirk for the highest grade tweeds, Wilson's of Bannockburn for military tartan cloths, Johnston's of Elgin for high quality cashmeres, vicunas and alpacas, and so on. Correspondingly merchants were jealous of their exclusive links with manufacturers. One firm of specialist yarn spinners, concerned for its reputation but forced to 'import' yarn from Leicestershire in 1879, went to the trouble of giving the suppliers special forwarding instructions so that 'the Railway Co. in Leicester will be unable to give any information as to the destination should any enquiry be made'. The buyers added : 'We trust these transactions will be kept private as if they came out it would be very awkward for us'. The yarns were, therefore, sent care of the Stationmaster in Edinburgh, forwarded in special bags and subsequently sold as if made in Scotland.[32]

Such specialisation in production and distribution tended to restrict the size of the market, and, when coupled with the need frequently to change the design, colouring and weight of goods with changes in fashion and the time of year, affected the size and organisation of the producing unit. The latter had to remain flexible enough to exploit the varied potential of the wool fibre. In the carding process there was no need to remove fibres of different length or diameter, so that nearly all the wool was employed and many differing types of wool used, often blended with one another. Thus woollen yarn was capable of infinite variety whether made from high quality wools as used in the Scottish industry or the poorer wools characteristic of the Yorkshire branch. Indeed Yorkshire woollen factories were no bigger in terms of capital per head or numbers employed than Scottish mills, despite catering for the mass market.[33] Thus is was not so much because the Scottish woollen factory catered for the quality market but because it was a woollen mill *per se* that initially gave the industry its small unit structure. But by producing slightly varying yarns and piece-goods, firms carved out a monopoly for themselves by developing sometimes marginal differences between their own goods and those of their neighbours, thus reinforcing their tendency to remain small units. The desire to control the firm, the ease of entry into the industry and the need to sell through perhaps a single merchant house also kept their size down. The tweed trade, therefore, did not readily develop the economies of large-scale production.

Under the benign influence of these changes in taste the ailing Scottish woollen producers of the late 1820s began to experience an unprecedented expansion in demand which, in turn, led to considerable investment in productive capacity, as shown in Table 1.

The number of mills grew from 90 in 1835 to 257 in 1874. Spinning capacity doubled between 1850 and 1878 to reach more than half a million spindles in that year. Weaving, too, was gradually mechanised, especially after 1860. By the mid-1870s nearly 28,000

Page 83. *Galashiels in the 1840s.* Located in a steep narrow valley, 'Gala' had to grow lengthwise in order to expand. Tall mill structures can be seen lining the banks of Gala Water, and among them the low lines of workmen's houses. The stagecoach (lower right, was soon to disappear as rail links were established to the north and south. On the left the shepherd wears his plaid, no doubt locally woven. In the right foreground cloth can be seen drying in the open on tenterhooks.

(Below). *Waulkmillhead Mill, Galashiels, 1910.* One of the earliest mill structures in the Borders, it was erected in 1802 by four local clothiers who shared it for some years. Working in this high narrow building with only a few small windows must have been depressing, and it must have been necessary to shift materials from one floor to another frequently. Its design seems to derive from contemporary domestic architecture (compare with plate on p134).

Page 84. *Innerleithen, Peeblesshire.* The woollen industry in this still peaceful valley of the Tweed was developed by the Ballantyne family from the middle of the nineteenth century (see pp 87 and 88). Scottish woollen towns never became urban sprawls, as they often did in the West Riding of Yorkshire, but, as here, became little more than industrial villages set among the heather-clad hills. The latter probably provided the inspiration of Scottish woollen designers.

TABLE 1

CHANGES IN THE PRODUCTIVE CAPACITY
OF THE SCOTTISH WOOLLEN INDUSTRY, 1835-1878[34]

Year	No of mills	No of spin'g* spindles	No of pwr looms	Amount of mov'g pwr (HP)	Total no of workers
1835	90				3,505
1838	112			1,822	5,076
1847					9,637
1850	182	224,129	247	2,533	9,464
1856	196	272,225	665	2,943	9,280
1861	184	317,185	1,303	3,906	9,812
1867	193	343,068	3,418	5,942	14,760
1871	218	421,489	10,543	9,305	23,000
1874	257	529,011	11,758		27,728
1878	246	559,031	6,284		22,667

*As opposed to 'doubling' spindles, which twisted yarns together.

TABLE 2

CHANGES IN PRODUCTIVE CAPACITY OF THE
COUNTIES OF ROXBURGH, SELKIRK AND PEEBLES, 1835-1871[35]

Year	No of mills	Per cent of total	No of spin'g spindles	Per cent of total	No of power looms	Per cent of total	No of workers	Per cent of total
1835	24	27			22	100	789	23
1838	32	30					1,046	20
1847							2,264	23
1850	40	22	77,000	34	109	44	2,573	27
1856	48	25	113,888	42	328	50	3,309	36
1861	44	24	160,257	51	559	43	4,042	41
1867	47	24	139,030	40	1,110	10†	5,180	35
1871	47	22	155,230	37	1,336	11	6,707	29

[County statistics ceased in 1871, giving way to regional computation.]
†This sharp drop was brought about by the rapid growth of power-loom
capacity in the West of Scotland carpet industry.

workers were employed in woollen factories in Scotland, plus an
unknown number of out-workers.

As had occurred earlier, most of this expansion took place in the
Borders, especially in Hawick and Galashiels, illustrated in Table 2.

About a quarter of Scottish woollen mills were sited in the Borders
between 1856 and 1867, while by 1861 the area accounted for 51
per cent of the industry's spinning, about 43 per cent of its

F

powered-weaving capacity, and 41 per cent of the factory labour force. Galashiels became the hub of the tweed industry in these years. Following the severe depression in the town in 1829, steady expansion led to great advances in the value of its trade. From an estimated level of £26,000 in 1828-9 the annual value of piece-goods and yarn produced reached about £250,000 by 1853, nearly £600,000 by 1870 and possibly about £1 million per annum, judging by productive capacity, in the early 1880s (see Table 3).

TABLE 3

GROWTH OF PRODUCTIVE CAPACITY
AND TRADE IN GALASHIELS, 1825-86[36]

Year	No of handlooms	No of power looms	No of carding sets	No of spin'g spindles	Value of the woollen trade (current prices)
1825					£58,000
1829					£26,000
1832	175				£30,000
1838	265		22		
1840			25		
1843			28		
1845/6	563		36	5,336	£200,000
1853			39		£250,000
1863	600	295	60		£490,000
1865			65		
1869			76	66,826	£570,000
1886	402	1,085	114	94,562	£1,000,000

As early as 1833 it was reported that the demand for Galashiels cloths and shawls was outstripping supply, those products having been brought to 'great perfection'.[37] In 1839, in contrast to depressed economic conditions in other parts of the country, Galashiels was described as 'the most thriving of all the woollen districts', its trade being 'rapidly on the increase'.[38] In 1842 tartan production kept Galashiels mills active for fifteen hours of the day,[39] and by 1850 so many mills had been erected or extended in the town that the available water-power was exhausted, forcing manufacturers to seek fresh locations in the upper Tweed valley and on the River Ettrick at Selkirk. Nonetheless in 1863 about one-fifth of the producing capacity of the Scottish woollen industry was located in Galashiels.

This notable rise of Galashiels as the premier centre of the new fancy woollen trade is well illustrated by the career of Henry Ballantyne who later founded the nearby industrial village of Walkerburn. Having been apprenticed to his father David at Inner-leithen, Henry returned to Galashiels about 1829 to set up business in a small way on his own account. He rented looms and jennies from another local manufacturer, and by 1834 was renting part of Wilderhaugh Mill, which contained more manufacturing appara-tus. As his operations increased, he rented space in two other local mills before building Tweeddale Mill at Walkerburn in 1855. Even then he shared with another and continued to house his weavers in loom-shops in Galashiels for some years.[40] It is clear from Ballantyne's records that the trade in fancy woollens developed very quickly in the 1830s (see Table 4).

TABLE 4

GROSS SALES OF WOOLLEN GOODS BY H. BALLANTYNE,
GALASHIELS AND WALKERBURN, 1833-1850[41]

Year	Trade with Glasgow	Trade with Edinburgh	Trade with London	Total Sales (to nearest £100)
	£	£	£	£
1833	34	158	—	200
1834	75	256	—	400
1835	148	358	230	800
1836	797	303	651	1,800
1837	874	615	520	1,700
1838	4,158	537	222	6,100
1839-40	—	No Data	—	
1841	2,040	2,112	545	4,800
1842	1,650	6,413	43	8,400
1843	2,357	5,206	66	8,100
1844	3,039	6,421	181	10,100
1845	5,746	8,490	286	14,800
1846	4,488	10,700	357	16,500
1847	3,843	2,921	1,888	9,600
1848	2,478	2,000	2,420	7,400
1849	3,036	1,876	2,471	7,600
1850	907	2,306	7,247	11,000

In 1833 Ballantyne's total turnover was only about £200 (it may have been higher previously) and consisted mainly of 'blues' and 'drabs' sold to local merchants and carriers in villages and towns in southern Scotland. By 1838 sales had reached over £6,000, with over £4,000 of business being conducted with Glasgow merchant houses, while direct accounts had been opened with others in London. Expansion continued into the 1840s and the London trade became increasingly important to Ballantyne, holding up in the recession of 1848-9 when total sales dropped alarmingly. Tartans and checks now comprised the bulk of Ballantyne's output, blues and drabs dropping from the order books by the mid-1830s to be replaced by fancy woollens with topical names such as 'railway' and 'Victoria' checks, and 'Rob Roy' and 'Meg Merrilees' tartans.

Despite renting more space and buying more machinery and handlooms, Ballantyne could not increase his productive capacity sufficiently to meet demands. Other local manufacturers were probably similarly placed, for by the early 1840s Ballantyne was forced to get yarn and semi-worsted woven goods manufactured in Holmfirth in Yorkshire, taking care to send wool samples to the firm concerned to ensure the right standards. In 1846 about 10 per cent of the value of his production was bought in in this way. He was also forced to supplement his own weavers by employing men in Alva and Paisley.[42]

Although hosiery remained very important there, Hawick also became caught up in the expanding tweed trade from the 1830s, and its firms began to specialise either in knitting or weaving. In 1837 there were no woollen manufacturers in Hawick who did not also make hosiery, whereas by 1882 only two of the ten major woollen producers did so.[43] For example, after a spell of dull sales in both hosiery and tweeds, the firm of Wm Watson & Sons abandoned hosiery manufacture in 1862 to concentrate on woven goods. The move seems to have been wise, for total sales leapt from about £35,000 per annum in the 1850s to £81,000 in 1872 and £126,000 in 1873.[44] Similarly Wm Laidlaw & Sons, prominent in the Hawick hosiery trade, began to manufacture tweeds as the trade grew, and the majority of hosiers in the burgh followed suit. By 1869 Laidlaw had left hosiery manufacture altogether.[45] No reliable estimates are available for the value of Hawick's woollen trade in the nineteenth century, but, if figures for productive capacity are any guide, it probably stood at around £500,000 per annum in the late 1860s excluding hosiery production, and nearer £1 million by 1880.

On a lesser scale the fancy woollen trade developed in other

Border centres after 1830, partly due to Galashiels and Hawick businessmen seeking room for expansion, especially in Selkirk and the upper Tweed valley. The River Ettrick at Selkirk offered a good enough 'fall' of water to permit bunched development along its banks, and, unlike Gala Water, was not so subject to drought. The Haugh provided good building land. The rising demand for industrial sites in Selkirk is evidenced by the sale there in 1838 for £210 of a corporation-owned waterfall with an upset price of £40.[46] Nevertheless local fueing restrictions continued to impede industrial progress, even in the mid-1840s.[47] In the next decade, as large new mills began to appear, one observer was led to remark that 'the old decaying burgh seems to have revived its youth . . . [the] town . . . was long thought to be in a state of hopeless decay'. In 1853 the capital invested in the burgh was estimated at £50,000.[48] By 1870 the number of power looms there had more than trebled, and the annual trade turnover was reckoned at about £220,000.[49] A large proportion of the new investment in the Border industry after 1870 was located in Selkirk.

In the Tweed valley there were smaller developments at Peebles, and at Innerleithen, where Brodie's old mill was successfully taken over by Robert Gill of Galashiels. The low rate of fall on the river made bunched development impossible and Henry Ballantyne's mill at Walkerburn never became the nucleus of a large complex. By the mid-1880s only about 35,000 spindles had been installed in the valley.

Further west the tweed trade was adopted in Dumfries and, more especially, at Langholm, where it quickly displaced cotton and thread manufacture. By 1869 about £130,000 of capital had been invested in Langholm's woollen industry. The Queen's visit to Scotland in 1848, which popularised the fine shepherd-checks made there, together with the tourist trade that followed in her wake is said to have considerably stimulated the industry at Langholm, which turned over about £200,000 annually by 1870.[50]

In the eastern borders only Jedburgh adopted the tweed trade to any extent, though not until the middle of the century. Here again hosiery tended to be displaced, the five factories there in 1869 being principally engaged on woven goods.[51]

The growth of tweed production in the Borders, therefore,

occurred mainly at the previous centres of coarse-cloth production, namely Hawick and Galashiels. In time other ancillary businesses and services became lodged in these burghs, such as rail transport, machine makers and installation engineers, merchant houses, financial agencies, specialist dyers and finishers and the large wool-stapling firm of Sanderson & Murray. By helping manufacturers to make external economies these services encouraged new investment in woollen manufacturing in these towns and round about. Thus few locational changes occurred during the nineteenth century in the Borders, despite increasingly unfavourable economic conditions as most wool came to be imported and steam power became desirable. By then other factors tended towards inertia: existing recent investments, the growing link in the public mind between high-class woollens and the Border counties and (perhaps over-rated) the manufacturing skills of the local population.

Although the years after 1830 confirmed the position of the Borders as the premier tweed district in Scotland, considerable expansion also took place in other areas, notably in the Hillfoots on the north side of the upper Forth, and in the north-east of Scot-

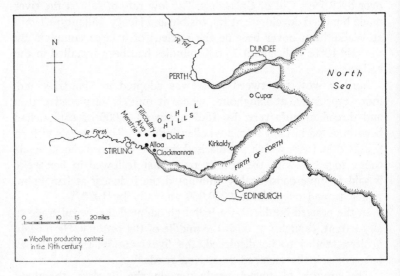

The Hillfoots Woollen District

land, especially Aberdeen. In the former region the manufacture of Tillicoultry serges, plaiding and blankets began to give way in the first decades of the nineteenth century to tartans—especially tartan shawls for ladies' wear. The shawl trade owed something both to the fashion for tartans and the popularity of the highly prized Paisley shawls that had swept into the wardrobes of wealthier ladies at the turn of the century. As the taste for patterned shawls and tartans spread, Glasgow merchants, it seems, combined the two trends and employed increasing numbers of Hillfoot workers in tartan manufacture for the ladies' trade. Thus this district became in effect the ladies' end of the tweed trade, whereas the Borders was mainly, though not exclusively, geared to men's wear. The tartan shawl was to the Hillfoots what the shepherd's plaid was to the Border counties.

By the middle of the nineteenth century there were dozens of small firms in the Alloa area manufacturing these garments, and the Hillfoot region possessed about a quarter of the country's woollen mills, about one-third of its spinning capacity, and over one-third of its factory labour force (see Table 5).

Thereafter, however, for a number of years the Hillfoots suffered severe setbacks. The number of factories, spindles and factory workers all declined both in absolute terms and relative to other

TABLE 5

CHANGES IN THE PRODUCTIVE CAPACITY
OF THE HILLFOOTS, 1835-71[52]

Year	No of mills	Per cent of total	No of spin'g spindles	Per cent of total	No of power looms	Per cent of total	No of workers	Per cent of total
1835							865	25
1838							1,410	28
1847							3,295	34
1850	45	25	72,095	32	38	16	3,669	38
1856	43	22	73,445	27	141	21	2,644	28
1861	38	21	71,261	22	278	21	2,297	23
1867	30	15	111,370	32	728	21	3,734	27
1871	33	15	143,516	34	715	7†	4,123	18

[County returns ceased in 1871; thereafter it is not possible to isolate the Hillfoot district for statistical purposes.]

†The large percentage fall in this year was the result of rapid expansion in the West of Scotland carpet industry.

Scottish areas. By 1861, for example, the region had only 23 per cent of the industry's factory labour force compared with 38 per cent in 1850.

The reasons for this decline have to do with a basic shift in the structure of the Hillfoot trade after 1850, a shift that also affected woollen manufacturers in other areas, especially in the Borders. The ladies' tweed trade was more volatile than the men's, and around the middle of the nineteenth century the demand for all-wool shawls began to wane in favour of jackets ('polkas') and cloaks, and tartans also were being gradually displaced. Although the weaving of cheaper quality shawls continued among working women, this trade came to be dominated by Bradford coarse-worsted manufacturers. The Hillfoot shawl and the Galashiels shawl both declined in favour, and, lacking the tweed trade that helped to cushion the Border manufacturers, many Hillfoot producers were left stranded.

Recovery in the Hillfoots in the 1860s began with the growth of tweed manufacture there. Several firms gave up shawl production entirely and concentrated on the more stable men's trade. Another form of diversification was the growth of specialist yarn-spinning firms, notably that at Alloa founded by John Paton. This firm grew rapidly, trebling its work force between 1861 and 1872, buying up rival firms and constructing a new factory at Clackmannan. By the 1870s Paton's net profit was averaging around 30 per cent of total capital invested.[53] Of great importance to the yarn trade was the growing desire of Border and some English manufacturers to buy in some of their carded yarns rather than produce them all themselves. The growing complexity of fancy yarns, the importance of design and variety in the industry, which compelled the retention of large stocks, together with the rapid growth of demand in the 1860s made such a policy economically desirable. After 1860, therefore, the Border and Hillfoot economies became more interdependent. The old shawl trade continued, but on a much reduced scale. The introduction of specially designed 'even-pick' power-looms capable of making a single wide (5ft), or two smaller, shawls did away with hand-weavers and raised productivity. In addition more emphasis was placed on accessories such as travelling rugs and fancy handkerchiefs.[54]

In the north of Scotland development in the woollen industry was scattered. Nowhere did a complex of mills develop. Even in Aberdeen woollen manufacture was virtually in the hands of one firm after 1850, though it was one of the largest firms in the industry. The Aberdeen woollen trade was combined till the late 1840s with cotton and linen manufacturing, as it was in the western Borders. Several firms dealing in these other fibres succumbed in the depression of 1847-8, and thereafter J. & J. Crombie became the leading woollen business in the city, concentrating on the manufacture of quality overcoatings. The firm's capital grew steadily from £2,500 in 1830 to about £17,000 by 1850, and over £35,000 in 1858. Thereafter capital growth was more rapid, reaching £135,000 in 1883, when the business was turned into a private company. Production, which had stood at only 8,000yd in 1840 reached 75,000yd in 1865 and then soared to 391,000yd in 1876, though this total was not surpassed until 1902.[55]

Outside of Aberdeen manufacturers in the rural northern areas were less favourably placed than those further south for labour, materials and markets. These difficulties were sometimes successfully overcome by intense product specialisation, which allowed some firms not only to exploit tourism and the local quality trade but penetrate the distant West End trade also, whence many goods were exported to Europe and the United States. Johnston's of Elgin, for example, developed from a small 'service' mill, in 1830, mainly engaged in carding and spinning for local people into a firm with an international reputation for high-quality cashmeres, vicunas and alpacas by the 1860s.

Since the local agricultural economy was precarious, paternally (or in some cases maternally) minded estate owners encouraged hand-tweed production and knitting in other parts of the Highlands, especially in the Hebrides, so that external markets were being served by the 1840s. By the 1870s South Uist tweeds were being ordered by London merchants via the island's lady owner, who acted as the agent for local goods. On Lewis woollen development was delayed till the 1880s, but all Highland production was encouraged by the establishment of the Scottish Home Industries Association and, to a lesser extent, by the Highland Home Industries and Arts Association, both formed in 1889.[56]

The growth of the Scottish woollen industry between the 1830s and the 1880s was generally steady. Production, as reflected in business records, increased consistently, especially after 1850. There were, however, periods of temporary difficulty when unemployment or short-time working occurred and when new investment ceased. The sharp depression of the late 1830s does not seem to have been seriously felt in the industry, probably because of the upper-class nature of its clientèle, who were largely immune to the cramping effects of short-term fluctuations. Trade was more affected by the financial crisis of 1847-8, when bad debts and falling prices were not completely offset by lower wool prices. Henry Ballantyne's sales slumped by nearly 60 per cent between 1846 and 1848 and remained below the 1846 figure for a decade.[57] Though Crombie's assets continued to grow in these years the mounting volume of debts outstanding suggests that trade was more difficult than previously.[58] In 1847 the *Kelso Mail* could remember no similar depression in the Border woollen districts for many years. Emigration from the region rose from two in 1846 to fifty-seven in 1849, dropping to three in 1850 as trade revived.[59] Some Galashiels and Hawick woollen workers found temporary work on local railway construction, which helped in some measure to stabilise local incomes.

The 1850s had their uncertain moments, too. Wool prices soared under the impact of expanding European demand (causing some adulteration of tweeds by the use of cotton), but the Crimean War, by intensifying the rise in wool prices, led to uncertainty, and compensatory military uniform contracts tended to gravitate to the West Riding. 'We are more likely to keep up each other's pluck in these dismal times', commented a Border manufacturer, 'if the French would look sharp and take Sebastopol.'[60] Postwar recovery soon ended in the financial panic of 1857, though recession in the Scottish woollen districts was not severe, unemployment tending to be confined to handloom weavers displaced by the new power looms. At Langholm and Selkirk in 1858 unemployed weavers found what solace they could working on the estates of the Duke of Buccleuch at 1s per day, with leave to return to their craft when their turn came to make a web.[61] Manufacturers at Selkirk gave their unemployed a free load of meal to be repaid

in better times, 'thus affording . . . relief without affecting independence . . . '. Welfare concerts were also arranged to soften the
pangs of hunger and humiliation. In Hawick in 1858 only twenty
four out of 160 regular hand-weavers were in full-time work.[62]

It is difficult to assess the impact of the American civil war on
the Scottish tweed districts. Theoretically a reduction in sales to
the United States, which market was particularly important to
some tweed centres, notably Galashiels, was unlikely to be covered
by an increased demand for Scottish high-quality woollens at home
as cotton prices rose. The demand was more likely to be taken up
by the lower end of the woollen market met by the West Riding
manufacturers, and even there it was more suited to the worsted
than the woollen producers. Nonetheless Border firms clearly experienced considerable growth in sales in the 1860s. Henry
Ballantyne's gross revenue grew from £51,000 in 1860 to £100,000
in 1864 and £131,000 in 1866, thereafter levelling out until the
great boom of the early 1870s.[63] William Watson of Hawick
doubled his turnover between 1861 and 1866.[64] In the absence of
precise knowledge of final markets we may surmise that such expansion had much to do with rising demand at home through
growing incomes, and with the conclusion of free-trade treaties
with France and other European countries, which were considered
by Baines to have been 'a great boon' to both English and Scottish
manufacturers.[65] Production continued to grow in the 1870s and a
good deal of new spinning plant was laid down, especially at Selkirk. The industry was only slightly ruffled by the failure of the
renegade Alexander Collie in 1875, though a few Border firms were
fatally associated with him.[66] By the end of the decade, however,
there were signs that markets were weakening and profitability
falling and the 1880s ushered in an extended period of difficulty
for the tweed trade that will be discussed in Chapter 5.

A lack of reliable statistical data makes it impossible to state
precisely the value of the Scottish tweed industry's output as it
grew in the nineteenth century; but estimates, probably based on
capacity, were made at intervals, and they give some indication.
A Galashiels manufacturer estimated local production to be about
£26,000 in 1829, so that a figure for Scotland of around £100,000
for that year may not be unreasonable.[67] Bremner, the observant

Scotsman reporter who made a study of Scottish industry in the late 1860s, suggested a figure of £900,000 for 1851, £1,830,000 for 1862 and £2,040,000 for 1869.[68] It seems clear that Bremner was not including production in areas other than the Borders, but he further estimated that production outside the Borders totalled around £900,000, so that a round figure of £3 million in 1870 appears justified. With the subsequent boom in European trade and the new investment accompanying it, together with a steady expansion of trade throughout the 1870s, the value of production by the early 1880s was probably over £4 million, representing perhaps 10 per cent of total UK production. It seems, therefore, that despite significant growth in the nineteenth century at a time when other traditional woollen producing areas declined, the Scottish tweed industry was insignificant when compared quantitatively with the West Riding. In the early years of the century some spoke of Galashiels or Hawick becoming the Leeds of Scotland. They clearly did not: they never began to approach the Yorkshire woollen centres in the scale of their industrial activities. Why not?

A possible answer could be couched in terms of geography and natural resources—the Borders were remote from large centres of population and, when steam-power became important, producers found coal too expensive for economic use. Scottish woollen mills remained long wedded to water- rather than steam-power, which placed a limit on the amount of machinery that could be driven and thus upon the size of the average enterprise. As late as 1861 about 60 per cent of total horsepower was provided by water and 68 per cent of the power used by spinning-only mills.[69] Though falling relatively, water horsepower was still on the increase in the early 1870s, and continued to be used in yarn mills well into the twentieth century. For a long time steam engines were regarded as only useful supplements to water-power or as standbys in case of emergency. As late as 1886 Ettrick Mill in Selkirk was powered by 'three magnificent water wheels . . . supplemented by a . . . steam engine'.[70] In 1910 a Galashiels mill was said to suffer from 'the defect of having no water power', and had thus 'remained closed for a longer period than it otherwise would'.[71] In the 1850s so much did the Border industry depend on an irregular water supply for power that the district factory inspector wrote that the area had 'strong claims to separate consideration' on the question of working in relays but for the administrative problems involved.[72]

The attachment to water-power, therefore, appears to have limited the growth of the industry. It forced mills to be located near water, and constrained the owners to adapt the number of looms and spindles and the size of their units to the available water supply. Yet it does appear that though coal was distant it could be obtained at an economic price when manufacturers really needed it. In the early nineteenth century quite sizeable quantities were purchased from the Lothians for heating water for dye-vats and other purposes. Steam looms were in operation in Hawick in 1830. In 1832 a large coal depot was established at Galashiels, and in the following year a gas company formed there was supplied with large and regular supplies.[73] Manufacturers had access to coal, then, long *before* the railway came but made extensive use of it for power only some time *after* rail links were established with coal-producing areas and its delivery price reduced. The availability of coal, therefore, appears not to have been the decisive factor in the retention of water-power. True, water was cheap, and this cheapness normally outweighed the capricious nature of its supply; but water-power also suited the character of the trade, at least down to the 1860s. Spinning machinery operated at a fairly leisurely pace in producing quality yarns, so that there was no premium on a speedier revolution of belts and drive wheels. Moreover the amount of plant needing to be driven in the average mill prior to the 1860s was never more than the available water power could handle, since technical problems and the fancy nature of the cloths produced gave handlooms an important place in the industry. It was the advent of powered weaving for fancy products that drove the tweed manufacturer to the use of steam-power; until then it had possessed no real attraction for him.

Power, therefore, was not an important factor in determining the shape and size of the tweed industry. More important was the structure of the market for which the industry catered. Yorkshire manufacturers specialised in the growth area of the wool-textile industry, meeting the demands of the mass market by concentrating on the lower qualities. The existence of a large working population in and around the West Riding engaged in various kinds of industrial activity provided a ready market for cheap fabrics. In Scotland these same conditions existed in Glasgow, Edinburgh and other towns in central and eastern Scotland, with large potential markets for cheap woollen cloths, and before the advent of the fancy trade in the 1830s local manufacturers were developing their business with these centres. Contemporary sources indicate, however, that Yorkshire manufacturers succeeded in undercutting Scottish clothiers, producing a better finished product into the bargain, though machinery had helped reduce any 'skill gap' in the basic manufacturing processes.

Scottish realisation of the strength of Yorkshire competition, however, did not and could not produce a major switch to quality production. It was, in fact, aristocratic demand for clothes in the style and quality of the humble Scottish shepherd's that forged the initial links between Scottish woollen producers and the quality trade. One is thus tempted to conclude that the Scottish tweed industry was a lucky development, arising from no conscious decision on the part of the producers. It happened that an increasingly mobile public found the shepherd-check plaid a useful waterproof; Sir Walter Scott, a well known and much read author, happened to live in the Borders and happened to publicise the product; Scotland was being 'discovered' as a happy hunting ground by the aristocracy; and Scottish-made cloth, therefore, became increasingly seen in important urban centres and exploited by enterprising merchants. Scottish manufacturers were willy-nilly borne along by social pressures emanating from the wealthier classes in the same way that Yorkshire manufacturers were influenced by the changing social and economic situation there. The Scottish woollen industry became associated with low intensity production and high prices, and once that identification had been made there was comparatively little room for manoeuvre. If the Scotch tweed-makers had allowed their products to be cheapened in quality, their trade would have been lost, for the West Riding dominated the lower end of the market. Yorkshire manufacturers, however, could and did aim at product improvement while maintaining an appreciable price differential between their goods and those of Scotland. Thus Scottish producers were forced to create further differentiation in the output of the two regions, so buttressing their association with quality and the upper end of the market. Though this was a growing market in the nineteenth century, it could never approach the size of the 'mass' market. The relative sizes of the Yorkshire and Scottish industries were thus a function of the clientèle to which they were orientated; this in turn was the result of social, economic and, in Scotland at least, fortuitous circumstances.

FOUR

The Means of Expansion
after 1830

'These harness looms . . . I wish them all at the ——————*!' John
Crombie, 1862*

The growth of the Scottish woollen industry charted in the previous chapter could not have occurred without corresponding
changes in the means of production—additional labour to perform
the many unmechanised tasks in the productive process, capital
for investment in new buildings and machinery, an adequate
supply of raw materials (especially wool itself), together with a
satisfactory system of communications and distribution. Of major
importance in achieving growth of output and of productivity were
the technical innovations made in the basic stages of production.
At the preparation stage the carding engines installed in the years
immediately before and after 1800 were gradually improved. As
finer wool was worked, as well as Cheviot, the carding teeth
needed to be finer, too, and the rollers closer together; and emery
sharpening rollers, introduced in 1839, made possible the effective
carding of German and, later, Australian wools.[1] Carding engines
underwent continuous improvement, often at the hands of local
mill employees or manufacturers, allowing lower costs and greater
output.[2] The greatest progress was made in spinning. The process
was gradually made more continuous, and the introduction of
large multi-spindle plant not only increased the rate of production

but improved yarn quality and allowed the manufacture of a wide variety of counts. One obstacle was the need to take the wool slivers from the carders and handfeed them on to the 'slubbing billy', a machine that performed a rough spinning task before the spinning of the final yarn. Hand-feeding was hard work for small children (until legislation intervened), and it led to uneven yarn. Sometimes the rolls from the carders varied in weight by up to 20 per cent and 'slubbers were often driven to the verge of madness'.[3] In the Borders and probably elsewhere in Scotland this problem was overcome by the use of a 'piecing machine', made in Hawick

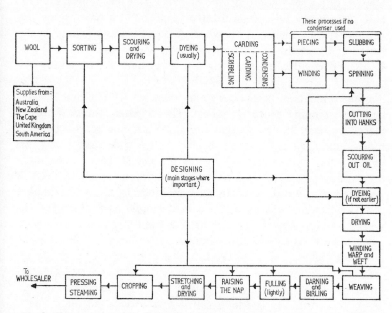

Block diagram showing the main stages in the manufacture of tweed
in the 1860s

in the early 1830s by John Melrose, a local millwright. This not only did away with child piecers but made possible the use of much wider carding engines capable of greater capacity.

The piecing machine made great strides but was eventually superseded in the 1860s by the condenser, which obviated the need for the intermediary 'slubbing' process by reducing the slivers from the carders sufficiently for them to be spun immediately into yarn. This bridging of the gap between the carding and spinning processes clearly exercised the minds of Scottish manufacturers and mechanics. Two Selkirk manufacturers, Henry Brown and Thomas Walker, patented in 1842 an arrangement for continuous stripping from the last carding roller, a process which, though subsequently more popular in Yorkshire, became established as the 'Scotch Feed'.[4] The use of the condenser in the tweed industry was also pioneered by Border manufacturers. A Galashiels emigrant in the United States sent home details of a machine he had seen there, and, after many unsuccessful attempts to build a satisfactory one at Selkirk, Galashiels and elsewhere, the condenser was finally perfected and adopted in the Borders, being widely established by the 1860s and eventually rendering the jenny-like 'slubbing billy' redundant.[5]

Improvements in preparatory and intermediary equipment made speedier spinning more necessary. The original jennies were replaced by hand 'mules'—large semi-automatic machines occupying much floor space and capable of producing a wide variety of yarns of the right texture and quality for the tweed trade.[6] Local business archives reveal tweed manufacturers of the 1840s and 1850s investing considerable sums in the new mules of up to 600 spindles per pair. From the 1860s, as a result of increasing demand and the voracity of the new power looms, the hand mule itself was gradually superseded by the fully automatic 'self-actor', adapted again from the cotton industry. Productivity gain was achieved by increasing both the speed of operation and the number of spindles under the observation of each spinner. Like its predecessor the 'self-actor' was versatile, specially suited to spinning the finer counts up to around 72 cut.

The manufacturers' success in reducing the number of stages, and therefore, the discontinuity of production, in the spinning process greatly increased production at reduced unit cost without loss of quality. The self-acting mule remained a most efficient machine, given the industry's requirements, and the ring spinning frame, which made its appearance in the 1870s, offered no real advantage to the users of non-standardised yarns.[7]

On the weaving side steam-operated looms only gradually displaced the handloom weaver, not so much because there were plenty of cheap weavers, but mainly due to technical difficulties—especially the ease with which woollen weft broke under machine conditions. Consequently, although the first woollen power looms in the Borders were installed in Hawick as early as 1830, they made slow progress. There were only 247 in the industry by 1850. Thereafter the number expanded more rapidly in tune with the demand for tweeds. Ballantyne's of Walkerburn, for example, purchased their first steam looms in 1859 and increased them, piecemeal fashion, annually until 1872.[8]

The need for innovation in the weaving process was brought about by several factors. Jacquard-type looms gave great scope to the designer, an important consideration in a fancy trade, and they also permitted a greater output per head in a given period of time. True, they did not operate much faster than a handloom —around forty-eight picks per minute—and were thus called 'slow' looms later, and in the Scottish trade a weaver normally supervised only one loom except when he was weaving plain cloths so saving in manpower was slight. Nonetheless power looms could be run regularly and continuously for long periods without a break, a feat for which Scottish hand-weavers were not renowned. Rising labour costs also appear to have played an important part in the decision to invest in powered weaving. Hand-loom weavers' earnings appear to have risen sharply in the 1850s and by the early 1860s had reached a point where it became desirable economically to replace labour with capital.[9] Again this is illustrated by Henry Ballantyne & Sons. Their male hand-weavers at Galashiels remained constant in number at a time when their average weekly earnings were rising sharply, and power looms were soon introduced—operated by female labour at half the men's wage rate. Gradually, as more plant was acquired, hand-weaving ceased, except for pattern-making, as rising wages gave manufacturers a growing incentive to employ more women.[20]

Woollen manufacturers required their machinery to be flexible and adaptable to suit various types of yarn, so, although much of the spinning and weaving plant was bought from the larger English textile manufacturers, a good deal of supporting equipment

was obtained from small local engineering firms or carpenters. Textile machines were made in Hawick, Selkirk, Galashiels and Alva,
outside of Glasgow. Melrose's of Hawick claimed to have invented
the piecing machine (accepted by Bremner); other firms specialised
in carding and drying machinery and occasionally mules were supplied from local sources.[11] Johnston's of Elgin had a foundry
attached to their mill—a fact which on one occasion led to a
Yorkshire loom firm refusing to supply them with power looms in
case they were copied and made locally.

Despite increases in capital investment in woollen production in
absolute terms and relative to the input of labour, a greatly augmented labour force was necessary. Workers seldom supervised
more than one machine, as already observed, and thus had to be
increased as machinery was installed; and, in the absence of technical change in the many other stages of production, an increasing
army of 'lookers', 'knotters', 'warpers', 'tenterers', and general
supervisory staff had to be engaged. Conversely, because of technical innovation and in the interests of quality control and general
managerial efficiency, labour was increasingly employed on factory
premises rather than in private homes or separately located loom-
shops. The factory labour force, therefore, grew from about 3,500
workers in 1835 to 31,000 by 1890.[12]

How was the labour recruited? A most important influence on
the supply of labour was the general level of population. In common with the rest of the United Kingdom the population of the
woollen districts rose until the end of the nineteenth century. In
the Borders the census returns show that the population of Roxburghshire rose from 37,230 in 1811 to 53,442 in 1881, and that
of Selkirkshire from 5,889 to 25,564, much of it in the woollen
manufacturing centres. Hawick's population grew from 3,688 in
1811 to 16,184 in 1881, and Galashiels' from 986 to 15,330. A significant proportion of these increases was due to migrants from the
surrounding districts and further afield. In 1861, for example, 45
per cent of the population of Selkirkshire and 23 per cent of Roxburghshire had been born outside those counties. By 1881 those
proportions were 52 per cent and 26 per cent respectively, although
in both cases 95 per cent of the populations had originated in Scotland.[13] In the municipal burgh of Galashiels in 1881 53 per cent of

the people had not been born in the county in which the town was sited. Most of the migrants came from surrounding Border coun- ties but about 8 per cent of the burgh's population came from western and central Scotland and the Highlands. About 3 per cent came from England and 2.5 per cent were of Irish origin. In Hawick in 1881 23.5 per cent of the town population had been born outside Roxburghshire, but 92 per cent were of Scottish origin, 6 per cent English and 2 per cent Irish.[14]

This pattern of migration suggests that most of the recruits to the woollen industry were agricultural workers. Some were no doubt former domestic woollen workers now entering factories, and others were recruited from other woollen districts in Scotland. Some migrated temporarily to the tweed districts from central Scotland, for the seasons in the Border men's trade and the Hillfoot ladies' trade did not overlap, though not of equal magnitude generally.[15] Irish immigration and movement from less prosperous branches of the textile industry or other manufacturing employ- ment do not appear to have been important in swelling the ranks of woollen workers. Other influences, such as poor housing, low wages, worker discipline, restrictive practices and lack of balancing industry for male workers, together with the general remoteness of the Borders and the north tended to restrict the supply of labour in the industry.[16]

Border manufacturers had a gentlemen's agreement not to poach each other's skilled labour, though by the middle of the nineteenth century handloom weavers were fair game. Departmental heads were specially difficult to find and retain. A number of key workers were recruited in Yorkshire, though this was made difficult by the apparent unwillingness of Scottish manufacturers to pay the going rate. Henry Ballantyne attempted to get a 'steady, honest, married man' as a mill engineer in 1857 from the West Riding, and even- tually tempted him to move north by offering him a free house and garden. At times, too, Ballantyne could not recruit enough weavers locally and was forced to send yarn to be woven in Alva, Tillicoultry and, more surprisingly, Paisley.[17] James Johnston in Elgin was constantly on the lookout for labour. He advised a col- league against setting up business in Sutherland mainly because of 'the want of competant mechanics to make and mend things' and the time it would take to 'break in and teach . . . labourers many of the processes'.[18] Difficulty was found in obtaining wool sorters, slubbers and other skilled staff in his own Elgin factory. While he endeavoured to recruit in England, he shrank from paying Yorkshire wages for fear of setting a precedent for other employees. In the 1850s Johnston employed a Galashiels bookseller to advertise for and interview potential recruits. His difficulties were increased when local workers, apart from being undisciplined, left his employment to go south. 'The two [power-loom] weavers are leaving on Friday', wrote Johnston dolefully in 1855, 'which is very unhandsome—they have no complaint but they imagine they can make better wages in the south.'[19] Later he complained of being unable to run his power looms through lack of labour, despite charging only a nominal rent for accommodation in his mill houses.

In common with other textile producers tweed manufacturers were able to make full use of local female labour. Women workers penetrated the carding room and the weaving section on the advent of power looms, and also outnumbered men in many of the later finishing processes as menders, burlers and checkers. Only wool sorting, spinning, fulling and dyeing remained firmly in male hands, due partly to tradition and partly to the degree of physical effort needed. Thus more than half the number of employees in the average woollen mill were women and girls. (The proportion was greater in solely weaving establishments but smaller in yarn mills.) The employment of both men and women in roughly equal numbers, though tending perhaps to discourage migration from other manufacturing areas, since women could often find a position easier than men, had the advantage of raising the family income and encouraged a tradition of family mill employment. Sons and daughters followed their parents almost inevitably into the local factory.

Technical change and an influx of labour would not have led to the growth of the tweed industry if wool of sufficient volume and quality had not been available at an acceptable price in relation to prevailing economic conditions within the industry. The greatest preoccupation of the Scottish woollen manufacturer was with his basic raw material. It was characteristic of the wool-textile industry that the cost and nature of the raw material assumed a greater proportional significance in production than in most other industries. The nature of the raw wool was not obscured in the process of production, so its quality was of great importance. In addition its cost constituted a large proportion of the manufacturer's gross costs, and had done so from the early days of the industry. Calculations made by a Galashiels manufacturer in the late 1820s, when wool was relatively cheap, showed that raw wool constituted between 35 per cent and 39 per cent of his prime costs, depending on the quality of wool employed. As finer, more expensive wools came to be used, and as other costs were reduced by technical innovation, the cost of wool rose proportionately.[20] In 1865 wool used by William Watson of Hawick represented more than 60 per cent of his direct costs, the precise amount varying with the weight of cloth produced. Between 1865 and 1870 the amount of wool consumed by this firm totalled almost 50 per cent of the value of the firm's turnover in the same period. In each of these years Watson's expenditure on wool and yarn greatly exceeded the total of his other direct production costs.[21] Similarly the value of wool and yarn bought by the Galashiels firm of Ballantyne & Tait in the early 1840s amounted on average to more than 50 per cent of total annual expenditure on production.[22]

An additional burden the woollen producer had to face was the volatility of wool prices. Normally the acceptance of orders for cloth preceded the sale of the final product by about one year. If the price of wool rose in the interval, therefore, as it frequently did, the margin of profit was reduced. Fluctuations in the price of raw wool are largely determined by the long gestation period before a decision to grow more wool makes its impact on the market.[23] Wool supply does not speedily respond to increases in demand. When supply does ultimately catch up, demand often slackens off, leading to more price instability. Furthermore, the woollen manufacturer's output is largely sold for wool clothing, whose price is usually considerably more than the price of the cloth, especially tweed cloth of high quality. The cut and styling of the garment is at least as important to the customer as the quality of the cloth itself. So changes in the cost of wool have little effect on the demand for clothing, and 'normal' changes in wool price have only a small effect on demand.[24] A manufacturer who bought wool when its price was high could not readily obtain an increase in the price of his finished cloth. For this reason the price of wool at any time could affect the type of production carried on in the mill. When prices were high the woollen manufacturer would find it hard to make a profit from winter qualities using more shots per inch, and would be tempted to make lighter weights or to adulterate his goods by employing inferior yarns or even shoddy or cotton. 'Wools are selling in London fearfully high . . .', complained Henry Ballantyne in 1856, 'it will add 8d to 1s 0d yard on the cost of heavy autumn goods, which we can never ask, so that we are to have a bad and profitless trade for some time . . . .' Ultimately he managed to gain increases of 3d-4d per yd for his cloths.[25]

For the Scottish tweed manufacturers to have combated high wool prices by adulterating their goods would have ruined the industry. Tweed was synonymous with quality. To have come down from this pedestal would have delivered the Scottish manufacturer into the arms of his Yorkshire rivals. Nonetheless adulteration did occur. In the mid-1850s, for example, when wool prices were unprecedentedly high, some Galashiels makers introduced cotton into thin trouserings and cheap shawls, the goods being designated 'mixed'. 'This step has been resorted to', declared the local press, 'solely from the enormous price of wool', and the dangers of the practice were roundly pointed out.[26] On the whole, therefore, though Yorkshire manufacturers could afford to juggle with the content of their cloths if wool prices or other economic phenomena made it desirable,[27] the Scottish manufacturer could do so only at his peril, for purity of material and distinctiveness of product were the foundations of his trade.

Not only was the cost of his raw wool of great significance to the manufacturer, but its grade and cleanliness were of equal importance. Wool was and is not a homogeneous product. The success of the woollen manufacturer largely turned on his ability to exploit what were often marginal variations in fibre dimension or quality. It was often this skill that made him a specialist and as such enabled him to obtain a share of the market for novelty production. The British woollen manufacturer's search for his raw wools led to the dominance of the wool market by colonial and other overseas growers in the second half of the nineteenth century.

Much of the rise of the Scottish woollen industry in the late eighteenth and early nineteenth centuries was due to contemporary changes in Scottish agriculture, in particular improvements in sheep husbandry. The 'drabs', 'greys' and 'blues' of the Borders were mainly fabricated from Cheviot wool grown locally, plus small quantities of Highland or foreign varieties. The advent of the tweed industry in the 1830s did not at first threaten the use of such wool. Indeed for a while it was intensified. Cheviot wool gave tweeds their special texture and colouring.[28] It continued to be employed, though it lost its relative importance to imported varieties as the century progressed. James Hogg, himself a local shepherd, could boast in 1832, that the manufacturers of Galashiels

> . . . consume the greater part of the wool in the country around, together with great portions of the best wool of the Borders . . . of late years, indeed, when the wool became such a drug in the market, had it not been for the spirit of the Galashiels manufacturers, the farmers of Ettrick Forest might have set their potatoes with their tarry wool, for no other person would give money for it . . . [29]

In their continued consumption of locally grown wool the woollen manufacturers represented an important factor in the economy of the Borders at a time when the large Yorkshire wool trade had diminished. Developments in the first third of the nineteenth century, however, led in time to a shift in the relative importance of the home and overseas grower. Firstly, Cheviot wool became increasingly unsuitable for quality cloth manufacture, due to farmers concentrating on rearing for mutton rather than for wool. It grew coarser and longer in the fibre, making it more suitable for worsted rather than for woollen manufacture. Secondly, fashion, as we have said, demanded lighter cloths and quieter patterns, which Cheviot could not give. Scottish wools generally did not possess 'the properties required for producing the goods now generally required, a large proportion of which are of the finest description, and as the largest profits are derived from [these] we need not wonder that capital should . . . naturally seek profitable investment . . .'.[30]

Though factors beyond the control of domestic wool producers were affecting the purchase of his clip, the Scottish farmer was his own worst enemy in marketing his product in the most casual way. Sheep continued to be smeared with tar and butter, though enlightened critics had been denouncing the practice for a century. Consequently the wool suffered greatly in quality, fetching on the market only a fraction of the price of 'white' (ie unsmeared) varieties. In addition, it was often marketed unwashed. The criticisms of Robert Boyd in the 1840s are curiously similar to those of David Loch made in the 1770s:

> Sheep washing is more imperfectly performed than any other department of sheep husbandry. In consequence of this negligence, it is well-known to manufacturers that Scotch highland wool suffers a reduction in scouring of one-half, and, when it is smeared with tar and butter . . . ⅝ths. English wool-staplers are the purchasers of Scotch wool, and, so long as it will continue to be so imperfectly managed, the amount annually paid for its transport to England will constitute a considerable proportion of its intrinsic value, independent of the expense attending the waste which wool of such description incurs in scouring, drying etc. . . . we need not wonder at having the English wool-stapler talk disparagingly of Scotch wool. Farmers complain that the small prices obtained . . . hold out no inducement to handle the fleeces better, but . . . when we view the . . . foreign wool and . . . the perfect condition in which it is sent to market . . . Scotch wool stands a higher price to the manufacturers than the foreign . . . [31]

In his last sentence Boyd hit upon the prime cause of the woollen manufacturers' growing demand for colonial wools in the 1840s. From this time up to the 1870s wool prices were steadily rising, more especially to 1863. This rise was associated with the general expansion of the British woollen and worsted industry and the great increase in demand for imported wools due to the insufficiency, and unsuitability in many cases, of the domestic clip. The supply of imported increased more rapidly than the supply of domestic wool, and, though prices of all wool rose, English wool rose more steeply than imported varieties.

When compared with native wool, therefore, colonial and foreign varieties possessed distinct advantages, which became increasingly important as time went on. The most favoured wools in Scotland were the fine 'Botany' qualities emanating from Australia and colonial cross-bred from New Zealand. Australian wool was found to be not only satisfactory in staple and quality but also soft to handle, which made it good to spin and needful of less milling than other types. 'There is no wool known to spin so well as the Australian wool from its length of staple and peculiar softness', stated a user in 1833.[32] James Johnston of Elgin wrote: 'I much prefer the Australian to the Cape wools, the latter being much harder and more difficult to mill'.[33] Moreover Australian 'Botany' wool grew whiter than Saxony Spanish or Cheviot (even in an unsmeared condition). It was not subject to the brown and yellow tinges that afflicted the other varieties. Rather it grew equal in texture and in colour throughout, with no dark strands to mar its appearance, thus making it eminently suitable to the tweed trade, where perfect colouring was required. Most of the wool used in the industry in the ninteenth century ultimately came from Australasia, though Cape and South American wool was used to some extent and German lamb's wool continued to be used for the very finest qualities. The proportion of home clip to total wool consumption declined rapidly between the later 1830s and 1850s. By the middle of the century the vast bulk of wool used in the industry originated overseas.

The precise chronology of this change is difficult to formulate. According to the writer of the *New Statistical Account* for Galashiels, about 95 per cent of the wool consumed in the town in the mid-1840s was of native origin.[34] By the early 1850s, however, Dawson reckoned that 95 per cent of the wool consumed there was imported.[35] There seems no doubt that use of the domestic clip was waning rapidly in relative terms in the 1840s, though perhaps not quite as dramatically as the figures for Galashiels suggest. In 1848 a local newspaper reported that 'Saturday last was the anniversary—for it can scarcely be called anything else—of the Galashiels wool Fair which at one time was pretty large, but has now almost dwindled down to nothing, since foreign wool has so greatly superseded the home-grown in our manufactures. The market was chiefly occupied with ginger-bread sellers . . .'.[36] Extant business records reflect the greater use of imported varieties at this time. Henry Ballantyne in Galashiels bought the bulk of his wool locally till the late 1830s, but by 1837 he was buying more imported wool than home clip. Australian varieties gradually superseded other imported wools: £2,179 worth of Ballantyne's wool in 1845-6, where the place of origin is specified, came from Australia, £464 from Germany, £237 from the Cape and £220 from Odessa.[37]

Though the tweed industry came to depend very heavily on imported wools after 1840, Cheviot wool still had a ready sale because of the expansion of the industry. Such wool remained unmatched for the coarser grades of fabric until colonial cross-bred varieties challenged it. Moreover, when prices of imported wools rose markedly, manufacturers turned to the lower qualities, thus forcing up its price. Cheviot wool prices fell steadily in the 1840s from a peak in the mid-1830s, but recovered somewhat in the 1850s and 1860s when imported wools were dearer.[38] In the boom conditions of the early 1870s Henry Ballantyne returned to the practice of buying from local farmers for the first time for about thirty years. The whiter growth of the colonial cross-bred wool gave it a comparative advantage over true Cheviot, however, whose other characteristics it also matched. This competition, coupled with the growing importance of worsted production in the medium qualities towards the end of the century, meant that Cheviot wool had permanently lost its lead, even with the coarser varieties, before 1914.

The twin facts that wool qualities varied and that it was mostly imported from distant countries led to the growth of a complex marketing system in the nineteenth century. Broadly, wool found its way to the manufacturer in two main ways: by direct buying from local growers, or through the services of the wool stapler, who might be local or not. These methods were often supplemented by the wool agent, who sold the commodity on commission either from growers or staplers.

Until the 1830s most woollen manufacturers dealt directly with local farmers, since little foreign wool was consumed. Wool was thus bought in sizeable lots at 'wool time', the manufacturer either buying it on inspection at the farm or buying it 'blind', with some financial safeguard if it was not up to standard. This method of buying may best be described as an informal ritual, an occasion on which both parties had ample scope to use their in-built shrewdness and obstinacy.

The farmer certainly knew the purpose of our call, but the subject was not broached with any indecent haste . . . the approach would as a rule be casual. By a time-honoured custom the purchaser of the clip in the previous year had the first refusal. If you happened to be in that position there was really nothing to do but settle the price; but both parties knew full well that the price would not be settled that day . . . . The conversation would drift on about the state of trade, the merits or demerits of the particular clip or the price of colonial wool; the bull points would be stressed by the vendor while the would-be purchaser adopted an unqualified pessimistic outlook. The final words were almost always 'well, we'll be seeing you at Hawick', perhaps coupled with instructions to send over your sheets. This meant that the bargain was practically concluded and the price would be amicably adjusted at Hawick fair a few weeks hence.[39]

The fairs were, of course, a method of selling in their own right if prior agreements had not been made. The fair set the price of wool not only on the day but for some months afterwards. The Borders was the scene of important wool fairs—St Boswells, Hawick and Kelso among others—visited by most of the Border sheep farmers, the wool brokers, dealers and other buyers. Their arguments were apt to be 'long and tautological, lasting often into the late afternoon, till some hardy spirit would break the ice, a bargain would be struck, the news passed round in a flash, and then there was a scramble to sell or to secure the wool'.[40] In the north much of the wool from Sutherland and Caithness, Ross and Inverness found its outlet at the great Inverness Fair, established in 1818. Northern manufacturers were sometimes engaged by their Border colleagues to buy Highland wool for them at this fair in the early part of the century, Border manufacturers sometimes reciprocating at the Border fairs. In this personal method of wool-buying, whether or not at the fairs themselves, sale was by private bargain and not by auction, as was the case with foreign wools. The farmer in trying to strike his bargain usually tried to sell at the same price as his neighbour, regardless of quality, threatening to hold it over or despatch it to England if his wishes were not met. This practice meant that there was a tendency for inferior clips to claim too high a price and superior qualities too low, as the stapler or manufacturer tried to bring down the price of the superior in order to gain the poorer clips for what they were really worth. Selling in this way gave no incentive to the farmer to improve his wool, as did the auction system. This method of purchase may, at least partly, explain why smearing died such a slow death in the industry.

Buying wool by private treaty had another major drawback— the manufacturer had to buy it for a long period ahead, thus tieing up much of his working capital. J. & H. Brown of Galashiels, for example, bought over £900 worth of wool in 1829 when their average annual turnover was in the region of only £1,300.[41] Between 1830 and 1865 the stock of wool in the annual inventory of J. Johnston of Elgin averaged over 15 per cent of his total assets, and in individual years reached well over 20 per cent.[42] Wool in stock at William Watson's mill at Hawick in 1849 represented over 12 per cent of his total assets.[43] The advent of foreign and colonial wools in large quantities in the tweed industry helped to reduce the need to carry large stocks owing to the simultaneous development of stapling facilities near or in the manufacturing districts. In 1844, for example, the wool-stapling and fell-mongering firm of Sanderson & Murray was started in Galashiels. If the Galashiels and Walkerburn firm of Henry Ballantyne & Sons was typical, the purchase of wool direct from local farmers ceased to be important in the 1840s, most supplies now coming through local brokering and stapling facilities. Table 6 shows that the number of wool brokers and dealers in the Edinburgh area increased markedly in the late 1840s, strongly suggesting a swing to imported wool, and thus to stapling services, by manufacturers at this time. Manufacturers arranged extended contracts with the staplers to be taken up as desired. The local stapler also often acted for individual manufacturers at the London wool sales once he had been given specific instructions or had come to know their particular requirements.

TABLE 6

WOOL DEALERS AND BROKERS
IN EDINBURGH & LEITH, 1836-60[44]

Year	No
1836	7
1840	7
1845	9
1850	15
1855	14
1860	16

The most eloquent testimony to the importance of local stapling facilities in the manufacturing area and to the importance of imported wools to the Scottish woollen industry from the middle of the century was the rapid expansion of the firm of Sanderson & Murray of Galashiels, who specialised in Australian skin wools.[45] In the 1830s John Murray of Jedburgh was working as a carrier between Leith and the Border towns. In 1839 he became the Galashiels agent for the carrying firm of Machell & Co, which worked between Edinburgh, Manchester and Liverpool. Murray then started buying waste wool from local manufacturers and selling it to Yorkshire. Noting the increasing amount of imported wool coming to the Borders from the Forth, Murray decided in 1844 to form a wool-merchanting business with his brother-in-law William Sanderson, a partner in a Galashiels building firm. They started to deal in local and Australian wools, the latter soon becoming the dominant part of their trade. In 1856 the firm began to buy on the London market, and at the great Hamburg wool sale, where they bought wool from Hungary, Poland and Bohemia as well as Germany for sale to Border manufacturers. A little later, William's son, John Sanderson, went out to Australia and New Zealand to buy wool directly. In this way the firm of Sanderson's of Melbourne was established. About the same time the parent firm in Galashiels appointed a Prussian wool merchant as its European buying agent. Less than twenty years after the foundation of the business extensive premises for pulling Australian, Tasmanian, Cape and Buenos Aires sheepskins had been erected in Galashiels, tanning premises had been rented in Alloa, John Sanderson had been settled in Australia and was being allowed a proportion of the considerable profits of the home firm to build up his business not only as a wool buyer but as a wool-grower, and Murray had made enough money to erect his great mansion of Glenmayne at a cost of £20,000. By the mid-1860s the firm of Sanderson & Murray was one of the largest of its kind in the world.

Such was the importance of wool to the Scottish woollen manufacturer that occasionally he endeavoured to bypass existing buying institutions and obtain supplies from their source, especially when it was felt that only the poorer grades were being sent. To this end the Hawick and London firm of Wilson & Armstrong joined with Sanderson & Murray in buying a wool farm in New Zealand in 1862, to be administered from Melbourne. The invoice ledgers of Henry Ballantyne show considerable purchases of wool from that city in the 1860s and 1870s. The same firm even went to the extent of sending George Ballantyne to New Zealand to enter the wool-buying business to supply the requirements of his firm personally, the latter giving him detailed buying instructions.[46] Such practices were probably not common, however, and the staplers continued to provide the main means of wool supply throughout the second half of the century. The London wool auctions emerged as the foremost market in the world, most imported wool being channelled though them until the later years of the century, when the great Australian wool auctions began to reduce their importance.

The growth of the tweed industry required the establishment not only of adequate supplies of raw wool and the means of its manufacture but also facilities for marketing the cloth—both the physical means and institutional arrangements for bringing producer and customer together. The first task was performed largely by the railways, the second by the woollen merchant. The greatly increased trade of the 1850s and 1860s coincided with the arrival of the railway in the Borders. Though this was clearly not a simple case of cause and effect, cheaper and more regular transport was of consequence to manufacturers. Hitherto they had been served by local carriers, who carted goods to local towns and villages, and to Berwick, Newcastle, Carlisle and Edinburgh. Goods intended for Glasgow were despatched from Edinburgh via the Forth-Clyde canal and those for London left by ship from Leith. These arrangements did not always prove satisfactory. The regularity of local services depended greatly on whether there was demand for carting grain, lime and other farm produce, while carriers in Edinburgh were often deflected into more accessible work in the Lothians. For these reasons the carrier service in Galashiels tended to be better in winter than in summer, despite bad roads. Carriers' charges also caused concern. In 1838, following an increase of 4d per cwt charged on all goods carried between Galashiels and Edinburgh, local manufacturers signed a three-year agreement with another carter operating between Preston and Edinburgh at a price of 14d per cwt, including warehousing, rent, and delivery within Edinburgh.[47]

When Galashiels was joined to the Scottish capital by rail in 1849, the price of coal there was reduced by half—from 14d to 7d per cwt.[48] In 1855 the completion of the Edinburgh-Peebles line, largely with the financial help of local investors, encouraged factory development in the Tweed valley and reduced freight charges from £1 to 9s 9d per ton between the two centres.[49] By 1862 a complete rail link had been completed through the Borders with the opening of the Hawick-Carlisle extension of the Border Union Railway. In bypassing Langholm, in order to gain access via a branch line to the Northumberland coalfield, it probably helped arrest industrial development in the burgh. Despite many quarrels between the railway companies and woollen interests over rates and delays (the latter usually being explained in terms of a lack of knowledge on the part of English suppliers as to the precise whereabouts of Border towns), the woollen industry clearly benefited from rail communications, and new mills were usually sited as near as possible to the line.

Because he produced cloth rather than clothing the Scottish woollen manufacturer had little to do with final markets. It is true that in the early years of the industry, before anything other than a local market existed, some clothiers did sell cloths to individuals who took them to a local tailor to be made up into garments. On the whole, however, middlemen linked the producer with the final purchaser. Ultimately the demand for the manufacturer's cloth not only depended on skills in manufacture and finishing but on the correct gauging of fashion trends, and on the cut, shape, and fit of the final garment. The last function was almost invariably performed by the bespoke tailor. The cloth itself was of the 'right' colouring and design because of a close association between the manufacturer and the woollen merchant, the latter becoming, in time, the lynch-pin of the Scottish woollen trade.

The services of the woollen merchant, however, were not in great demand during the industry's infancy in the latter decades of the eighteenth century, when manufacturers generally distributed their cloth themselves. At this stage goods were not always made

H

to order, and production was usually speculative, goods being made
for stock until, at various seasons of the year, the manufacturer
took his wares, or samples thereof, on his 'journeys' to all parts of
Scotland, to England and to Ireland.[50] John Crombie, founder of the
famous Aberdeen woollen firm, travelled to London carrying
samples of his cloth for his customers' inspection.[51] The Manufacturers' Corporation of Galashiels sponsored a kind of corporate system of distribution : two of their number acted as travellers for the
Corporation merchanting its wares over a wide area, but particularly in the seaboard towns of eastern Scotland.[52] Local fairs, too,
continued to be well patronised by woollen clothiers. Many carried
their pieces to them on carts from which they measured out
lengths for local individuals or for travelling merchants. William
Laidlaw, orginally a hosier, but later a tweedmaker, regularly
tramped from Hawick over the moors to Newcastle to sell his
goods, smuggling a little illicit whisky en route to help cover ex-
penses.[53] In 1829 a Galashiels manufacturer faced with high stocks
of 'blues' ferried his goods to Kirkwall and Lerwick by fishing boat,
living off oatmeal, sillocks and treacle on the way, and eventually
selling the whole of his load at twice the price it was fetching in
the south.[54] By peddling their wares in this way in the true tradition of the 'Scotch merchant' Border manufacturers built up a
reputation for their cloths.

It is not possible to state just when this type of distribution
ceased, but business records of the early nineteenth century show
that it retained its importance at least down to 1830, though formal
dealings with merchants were already frequent by then. James
Dickson of Peebles received substantial orders from 'merchants'
based in places such as Peebles, Biggar, Carluke, and Carstairs,[55]
but it is doubtful whether these men were much more than store-
men or shopkeepers engaged in both retailing and wholesaling over
a limited area. Even the occasional orders from merchants in Glasgow and Edinburgh were most likely to come from houses dealing
in a variety of goods, thus differing from the exclusive woollen
specialist houses of a later period. Galashiels manufacturers seem
to have had regular merchant connections in the early years of the
nineteenth century. An indication that Border cloth was already
attracting the attention of factoring houses in the 1780s and 1790s

was the attempt made at that time to establish Galashiels as a marketing centre. A Cloth Hall was erected in 1791 for the exposure and sale of goods, manufacturers renting shelves at 40s per annum. Though 150 pieces were disposed of in a few minutes at the Hall's inauguration in 1792, this method of marketing does not appear to have been a success. In 1798 one of its chief sponsors wrote that he hoped the Hall would 'meet the encouragement it deserves', but the venture was finally terminated in 1811.[56] The remoteness of the Borders probably discouraged merchants from visiting the centre; it was easier for them to order from individual firms, and for the manufacturers to take those orders rather than place their wares speculatively on their shelves in the Hall.

The future lay in the made-to-order trade conducted by the merchant houses operating from the larger commercial centres. Direct contact between the manufacturer and the bespoke tailor gradually diminished, and the 'journeys' were transformed from peddling expeditions into regular visits to factoring houses to show patterns. The changing emphasis towards merchanting through a middleman, which was the main marketing feature of the years down to 1830, was of great significance to the Scottish woollen trade; for at some point, possibly through a Glasgow or Edinburgh house's London connection, one of the products of Border clothiers came to the notice of London merchants dealing solely in high-class woollen fabrics. Thereafter the London factoring houses provided the main outlet for tweeds and, more important, much of the enterprise and ingenuity of the trade. The merchant rather than the manufacturer set the course for the industry. City and West End factors placed the original orders for fancy tweeds while Border manufacturers had their eyes still fixed on their local outlets for blues and drabs.[57] Merchants took the initiative in stimulating new colours and designs, which gave the goods a true Scottish flavour and made them a distinctive product; they cajoled the manufacturers into improving their commercial chances by manufacturing trials and ranges before making cloth in the piece. Visits by merchants, many of them Scots, to the manufacturing regions were frequent, and over a period of time a close relationship grew up between the producers and the middlemen in the trade. The tweed trade, and its prosecution became a joint venture: the output of the manufacturer was 'tailored' to meet the precise requirements of the merchant, who jealously guarded his claim to the exclusive use of patterns made to his specification.

In an industry made up of small production units a large proportion of the output of a mill was often channelled through a single merchant company. In 1862, for example, Henry Ballantyne of Walkerburn sold goods to the value of about £38,000, of which £35,000 worth was purchased by the single London house of Wilson & Armstrong.[58] Placing many of his eggs in one basket was a price a manufacturer in a high-class fancy trade had to pay. Exclusiveness was as much in the interest of the producer as the wholesaler. 'We are regularly in the habit of making Ranges and strictly conforming them in style to some of our wholesale customers,' declared Ballantyne; 'the interests of the merchants and manufacturer are one and cannot be separated . . . without injury to both. Therefore mutual confidence becomes necessary to success.'[59] Occasionally, though, that confidence was lost. Manufacturers, often rightly, suspected merchants of allowing their expensive patterns to be copied by cheaper manufacturers elsewhere; and merchants accused the makers of selling their own exclusive designs to other houses. But, at least while a seller's market existed (for much of the nineteenth century), both parties realised the value of close partnership in bringing success.

The services of the woollen merchant were indispensable in a novelty trade such as the tweed industry. Bespoke tailors and makers-up had no wish to buy cloth by the piece (about 50 yd), preferring suit lengths of 3yd to 3½yd from the merchants' bunches. The merchants, however, almost always ordered piece-lengths, sometimes many pieces per pattern, but more often one or two. Thus the merchant enabled even the specialist woollen manufacturer to operate on a reasonable scale by breaking down his output to meet the fragmented demand of the tailors. The merchant rather than the manufacturer was the stockholder bearing a considerable proportion of the risks of production, which were high in a fancy trade, and releasing the manufacturer's capital to finance further manufacture (though this benefit was partially offset by the habit of granting long credit to the merchant). Furthermore, by placing orders at the beginning of the two manufacturing 'seasons' (for winter and summer goods), the merchant helped to ensure steady and continuous employment in the mills when the distributive trade may have been virtually at a standstill. Above all, the merchant's virtue lay in his knowledge of the market, and, consequently, in his ability to keep the manufacturer abreast of current trends, both at home and abroad.

It follows, then, that the woollen manufacturer was, perhaps more than in other trades, dependent for his livelihood on the enterprise and integrity of the middleman. The name of the manufacturer never appeared on the cloth handled by the merchant, so that the tweed firms could not build up a market for their cloth independent of him. This was not felt to be onerous in a seller's market, but in the changed conditions during the latter years of the nineteenth century friction between merchant and manufacturer became more common. Thus Messrs Wilson & Glenny of Hawick began to stamp a brand name on to the listing of their cloth, a move resisted by the merchants and eventually discontinued.[60] The chief cause of complaint was, however, the almost complete ability of the merchant to dictate terms and prices. Pricing in the tweed trade had always been a haphazard affair. Manufacturers in their reliance on the merchant had never insisted on retaining firm control over the price for their cloth. This may have stemmed partly from the early decades of the century when the middleman acted more as a commission agent than a woollen merchant proper, taking the manufacturers' goods, which were still in the process of establishing themselves in terms of design and quality, and selling what he could for the best price available. The manufacturer had no option but to allow the merchant considerable latitude, especially in times of weak demand. Surviving letter books are full of letters between merchant and manufacturer discussing prices. After much disagreement about the colouring and quality of his cloth with a London house in 1857 Henry Ballantyne was provoked to write: 'I hope I am right that you will make as little deductions as you can on any of the goods . . . for it is very disheartening to a manufacturer to have the small profit all swept away after so much hard work in getting them made.'[61] Similarly, James Johnston of Elgin on many occasions had to request a Glasgow house to use its own discretion in altering prices of his cloths in order to get them off hand. Sometimes his instructions amounted to complete surrender. 'You will do the best you can for our interest and use your own discretion as regards reducing prices where you see cause . . .', he wrote in 1839.[62] In negotiating a military uniform contract in 1840 he stated: 'As to the price of the cloth we are quite at your mercy, and if you think 5s 6d sufficient we . . . must submit to it . . .'.[63]

Over the years, therefore, the industry was characterised by 'price-taking' rather than 'price-making'. In favourable trading conditions manufacturers received a good return, but, towards the end of the century, the tweed-makers were hard put to it to keep their mills in operation in the face of fashion change and increased competition at home and abroad. Wool prices were notoriously volatile, but merchants were reluctant to grant the manufacturers an increased price if wool prices rose, and were eager to reduce prices if the cost of wool fell between the granting of an order and its completion. In 1908 a Selkirk millowner complained that merchants had practically ' "earmarked" every manufacturer who had the temerity . . . to ask [for a price increase] and threatened to close accounts right and left . . . merchants will not take a rise in price and the manufacturers are too weak to insist upon it . . .'.[64] A few of the leading tweed-makers possessed a much greater degree of independence—Roberts' of Selkirk, for instance, makers of the highest qualities, were usually able to choose to whom they sold goods—but most firms were forced to take the merchant's terms, which led many to adulterate their cloth in an attempt to increase their margins.

The specialist woollen merchant was not always the only intermediary between the manufacturer and the tailor. Many producers, often those situated in remote areas and fully involved in the day-to-day running of their businesses, employed an agent, who was usually based in a large urban centre and sold goods on commission to the merchant, and, in some cases, to the retailers themselves. When demand for Scottish cloths rose unprecedentedly after the Great Exhibition in 1851, many factories acquired London agents, in whose offices patterns could always be consulted and orders taken. This became a general rule. Agents, too, were allowed some latitude in pricing. James Johnston wrote to a prospective agent in the 1850s as follows:

> I understand that you are willing to canvass for orders for my goods on your usual beat and afterwards settle up the accounts for a commission of 5% on the nett amount received from Retail dealers, and 2½ from wholesale purchasers ... forfeiting commission on any bad debts ... I shall keep you supplied with patterns of goods, making or on hand, charged as low as possible ... my rate is low ... but to good parties to induce an order you may always have a little latitude, say to the extent of 1d or 2d [ie per yd] in the case of Retailers and 3d to 4d for wholesale customers ... '[65]

Obviously the success of marketing in this way depended much on the calibre of the agent. Johnston was unsuccessful with his: one ran up too many bad debts, and the other invested the money he did collect, immediately went bankrupt, and paid 6s in the £.

Even when agents were employed, in the provinces or in London, most of the manufacturers dealt with their most important merchant customers personally. Some merchants refused to see an agent. Every year, often twice or thrice, manufacturers travelled to London to show their patterns, discuss prospects for the next season, obtain orders and sometimes settle debts.

Though the home trade has always been the backbone of the industry, the Scottish tweed districts have from the early nineteenth century exported a considerable proportion of their total output.[66] Owing to a total lack of firm statistical data, and to the fact that many goods found their way abroad through the home-based merchant houses, it is not possible to give an accurate figure for exports, but in the 1880s it was reckoned that 50 per cent of total production was sold abroad, and a similar proportion was suggested to the Tariff Commission in 1905.[67] The export trade, however, could have been even more important to individual firms or localities. Businesses specialising in particularly high grade cloths could expect to sell most of their output overseas—it was stated that 75 per cent of Galashiels' trade was conducted with the USA alone before 1890.[68] Predictably, Scotch tweeds found a ready sale in temperate countries with a sizeable upper and middle-class market—in the nineteenth century mainly France, Germany, Austria and the United States. After the erection of the American tariff system in the 1890s tweed-producers concentrated increasingly on their European trade, which in some areas at least was growing quickly before 1914 despite growing commercial restrictions. J. & J. Crombie, for instance, having opened a New York office in the early 1880s, closed it in 1890 and by concentrating on Europe soon were selling goods in France, Scandinavia, Holland, Belgium, Germany, Austria, Hungary, Italy and Bohemia. Even Russia, despite the high charges faced by the commercial traveller wishing to trade there, came within the company's trading pattern.[69]

Much of this trade went through the English woollen merchants, but, increasingly in the second half of the century, direct relations were established between the Scottish manufacturers and import houses on the Continent, especially in Germany. These houses regularly sent their buyers to the tweed mills in order to select patterns to make up their bunches.[70] The German houses were of particular value to the industry. German merchants, possessing unrivalled commercial know-how and usually being fluent linguists, controlled much of Eastern European and Scandinavian trade, employing armies of travellers to ferret out orders. Many opened branches in London and several German houses settled in the Borders themselves, notably Schulze & Co in Galashiels and Fuhrmann & Kramer in Hawick.

Like their English counterpart the foreign-based merchant obtained exclusive patterns from the manufacturers. Alexander & Bernhard of Berlin, for example, while not insisting that Crombies channelled all their goods through them, claimed control over the number of other German houses dealt with and had first sight of the company's ranges, first refusal of all its novelties, and cloths at 6d per yd cheaper than any of their rivals. In return the Berlin firm vigorously promoted Crombie's specialities and advised them closely on the state of the market in various parts of the continent. Adolph Bernhard was for Crombie's European trade what James Locke of Regent Street had been in earlier days to the firm's home trade.[71]

The American trade was organised in a similar way, though many firms opened agencies in New York and elsewhere as demand for tweeds grew. By the late nineteenth century imports of woollens were largely controlled by the Syndicate Trading Company, a combination of some of the most successful merchants in the States. Perhaps fortunately for the tweed trade, this group had a high proportion of Scots among its members, and was sometimes referred to as the 'Scotch Syndicate'.[72] At least a proportion of the trade between the tweed districts and North America must have been of a loosely 'sentimental' nature, owing something to the syndicate and much to the presence of a large number of Scottish emigrants. When the commercial 'chips' were down, however, sentiment played little part, and the Scottish industry suffered greatly from the US tariff system imposed at the end of the century.

Compared to the European and American trade, dealings with other countries, including colonial and dominion territories, were not large. Hot countries preferred the lighter worsteds to solid tweeds, and, more important, newly colonised territories were not particularly fashion-conscious. James Johnston of Elgin, for example, having 'no doubt there are many Scotchmen . . . who will be glad of a plaid on their way to the diggings', attempted in the mid-1850s to sell a consignment in Australia on a speculative basis through an informal agent known to him. Johnston was soon told, however, that not only had his goods arrived 'at least three months too late for the season' (because he had failed to remember that the seasons there were opposite to those at home) but that his cloths were quite unsuited to the market. 'I contrasted your goods with Silver's', wrote the agent; ' . . . in yours coatings, vestings and trowserings are respectively invoiced at 30s, 10s and 16s; in Silver's 12s 6d, 4s 6d and 7s 6d. I have no manner of doubt that yours are the superior article, but unfortunately in this country quality and workmanship are not sufficiently appreciated . . . '. Subsequently Johnston not surprisingly described his Australian venture as 'an unfortunate speculation', his goods having to be disposed of at great loss.[73] It seems that no attempt was made to capture the market by making products to suit. To have done so might have prejudiced his good connections at home.

The practice of sending speculative consignments to a colonial territory in the hope of tempting Scottish emigrants with goods from 'the auld countrie' sometimes worked well enough. Ballantyne of Walkerburn sent parcels of tweeds to the Cape and elsewhere on several occasions in the 1850s, complete with the local paper, all to be distributed by an emigrant friend on the spot. Even

Johnston, despite his failure in Australia, regularly sent consignments of cloth to Ceylon and Jamaica for sale through an emigrant
friend who was setting himself up in business.

Such examples again indicate the necessity of working through
an enterprising middleman capable of correctly judging the state
of demand. The South African situation was a further example.
In this territory, as in Australia, about 80 per cent of the clothing
around 1900 was of the cheaper 'ready-made' type. Even so, about
12 per cent of suits worn in the colony were made to measure. But
Scottish tweeds figured hardly at all among these, according to a
resident in the colony, because they were incorrectly marketed:
there were no direct selling agencies in the country for them, and,
instead, they arrived through ordinary channels 'mixed up with
tweeds charged with cotton and shoddy' so that the buyer could
not tell what was quality and what was not. Consequently most of
the trade went to the cheaper producers of Yorkshire.[74] Manufacturers showed little interest in exploiting the market properly,
though a few began to develop their trading connections in the
warmer climates before 1914 when some traditional markets
showed signs of weakening. Canada was a different story. The
replies to a questionnaire sent to firms belonging to the South of
Scotland Chamber of Commerce in 1903 indicated that the
Canadian market was showing great promise—because of the pre-
ferential tariff and to similar consumption patterns to the United
Kingdom. The Border merchanting firm of Lowe, Donald of Peebles,
previously much concerned in the North American trade, thought
Canada likely to become one of its best markets at this date.[75]

In these years the loss of traditional outlets for tweed cloths was
often followed by a new-found desire among manufacturers to
obtain Government contract work. This was not surprising, for
there were wars and rumours of wars and Britain began to rearm
seriously. But as far as can be ascertained the Scottish woollen industry for most of the nineteenth century did not compete with
Yorkshire manufacturers to secure large clothing contracts for the
army or navy. Occasionally regiments were supplied with high-
grade uniform cloth for officers' wear; some Scottish regiments
depended on home manufacturers for tartans; and local corps were
clothed usually by the local woollen producer (who equally usually

held rank within)[76]; but this sort of trade was small and cannot be compared with the large Government orders fulfilled by English woollen manufacturers. At the end of the nineteenth century, however, a considerable amount of such work was being undertaken by Scottish mills. It was generally allowed in 1901 that 'had it not been for government contracts the Border industries would have been very depressed . . . especially in the cloth department'.[77] Well known firms had no difficulty in getting on to the Government list, but the work was not profitable, and was looked for only in the absence of other business in order to cover overheads and to occupy (and thus preserve) the labour force.

In this sort of trade the maufacturers dealt directly with government departments, the specialised services of the woollen merchants not being required. Government tenders specifying the quality and price of the cloth were circulated to the interested mills, whose only requirement was to return them duly completed to an official at the ordnance department. Even in the years before World War I, however, increased government orders did not seriously disturb the existing distributive network of the woollen trade. Many firms regarded such work as undignified as well as unprofitable. Even those who indulged in it were not dependent on it, but carried on a large 'normal' trade through the merchants. Furthermore, the changed nature of distribution due to the growth of the ready-made trade was hardly felt north of the border. J. H. Clapham, writing in 1907, felt that the old type of specialised woollen merchant was faced with extinction because of the loss of his connection with the large wholesale clothing establishments,[78] which may well have been true in Yorkshire, but could hardly be said yet of the Scotch tweed trade. A few Scottish manufacturers had, with a degree of success, bypassed the merchant to deal directly with these large firms, but at this stage the ready-made trade hardly used the high-quality cloth of tweed manufacture. Even when such fabrics were required, the clothing manufacturer still preferred to deal with the merchant rather than the producer when selecting pieces; the merchant offered a greater collection than any one manufacturer and the wholesale clothier only wished to invest in stocks of cloth that were in general demand. As long as the principal outlet of the Scottish woollen industry was the bespoke tailor, the services of the woollen merchant remained indispensable, and as long as the tweed trade was identified with high-class novelty fabrics, the wholesale clothier had no real interest in buying from mills rather than merchants. In 1914, therefore, the ties between the merchant and the woollen manufacturer in Scotland were as strong and as necessary as ever.

Finally, how was the expansion of the tweed trade financed? Banks played only a small part in providing long-term capital for British industry in the nineteenth century, and the Scottish woollen industry was no exception to this rule. Permanent capital continued to be provided by close relatives and friends of the entrepreneur, and assets were increased by steady ploughing back of profits. Thus William Watson & Sons of Hawick was exclusively a family affair in the firm's formative years, all the stockholders in 1864 bearing that name.[79] Similarly nearly all Henry Ballantyne & Sons' capital in 1883, £109,323, was held by the three partners, all Ballantynes.[80] Much the same was true of Crombies of Aberdeen and Johnstons of Elgin.[81]

Internal financing of the firm forced businessmen to concentrate on capital accumulation, especially in periods of rapid technological change. By re-investing a sizeable proportion of net profits and thus living fairly frugally, net assets were increased quite rapidly. The net worth of James Crombie & Co in Aberdeen grew from £12,000 in 1847 to £35,000 in 1858, thus trebling in little more than a decade solely on the basis of retained profits. By 1883 the capital of the firm had reached £135,000, largely, again, as a result of ploughing back.[82] In the same way the assets of Henry Ballantyne & Sons doubled between 1849 and 1854-5.[83] This policy meant restricting personal consumption, and at times the partners took little more than their better paid workpeople. James Johnston took £40 a year from his Elgin business in the 1830s, and David Ballantyne, junior partner to his father Henry, took £47, £38 and £44 in 1851, 1853 and 1854 respectively, an income somewhat less than the better paid handloom weavers employed by the firm.[84] Self-discipline was also the foundation of the highly successful yarn-spinning business of John Paton & Son of Alloa. On the death of the son of the firm's founder in 1860, his two partners formed a copartnery for fourteen years. Capital of £10,000 was subscribed equally and profits could not be withdrawn, a modest salary being taken in lieu. In 1873 their sons became partners and a new agreement permitted only the two senior partners to draw on profits this privilege being allowed on the understanding that they would add to the capital of £64,000 later at a nominal rate of interest. By 1883, seventy years after the foundation of the firm, when assets totalled £162,000, the partners allowed themselves interest and profits to the value of £2,000 a year. By 1918 the firm's capital assets approached £1 million.[85]

This ability to expand capacity and trade by internal financing presupposes that the woollen trade was reasonably profitable. Few statistics have survived on this subject, since manufacturers were not prone to airing them.[86] Nonetheless the experience of two major firms suggests that a reasonable rate of return on capital was achieved during the middle decades of the century at least. Net profit, excluding withdrawals, averaged 20 per cent of capital invested in Ballantyne's at Galashiels between 1851 and 1855. The minimum annual return on capital achieved by James Crombie & Co at Aberdeen, including withdrawals, averaged 10 per cent between 1848 and 1858.[87]

From the 1860s the need to accumulate capital was not so pressing. Many firms had grown quite large by the standards of the industry, each employing several hundred workpeople. Moreover textile technology became relatively stagnant after the adoption of self-actors and before the adoption of 'fast' looms in the 1880s. Consequently, businessmen were willing to spend more on luxury. John Murray, the Galashiels carpenter and co-founder of the wool stapling concern of Sanderson & Murray, built himself a £30,000 mansion in the 1860s. In 1861 a Hawick manufacturer boasted that the palatial mansion he had erected at a cost of £30,000 had been built from the previous year's profits.[88] A whole batch of manufacturers' mansions was erected in the neighbourhood of Galashiels and Hawick at this time. Moreover proprietors of woollen businesses began to diversify their investments, especially after 1880, by buying shares in other British enterprises or in colonial ventures such as Australian mines.[89]

The woollen trade was also extended by granting generous credit to new and existing customers. Indeed, the Scotch tweed trade remained notorious for its credit terms down to World War I when, in working for the government, the manufacturers saw the benefit of prompt payments. In 1855 Henry Ballantyne advised one of his principal customers that 'we find it will be out of our power to carry on delivery of so many goods from this date [October 6th] up to April without getting supplies of cash to go on with . . . we do not consider ourselves justified . . . in not having one season's goods paid for before going on with another'.[90] Though many of the manufacturers had used the credit system to raise themselves in the past, by the middle of the nineteenth century they began to find themselves its prisoners. One declared:

> Another evil is the undue length of credit now exacted . . . I have no liking to risk two seasons' goods and mean, if I cannot limit it to one, to sheer out of that connexion a good deal—it is folly to permit such extended credits as we have to accede to—and as far as my experience goes I can hardly get a pleasant settlement now, so difficult has that evil made it . . . most of these tweed people seem to think they can treat us as they please.[91]

The local press echoed his views, which were especially pertinent in times of high discount rates. The manufacturers were considered to have too much of their capital sunk in the process of manufacture, and the advantage of introducing a prompt system of cash payments was pointed out. The members of the woollen trade took no notice, however. Despite their cooperation in the industry's early days they were now too independent to get together to agree terms. The system was not amended in the less favourable economic conditions at the end of the century. Even longer credit was often demanded by merchants, and the orders went to those manufacturers who would agree. In 1906 *The Times* declared that the tweed trade was still labouring under the long credits that were given. Then the almost universal custom in the industry was to give six months' credit, at whose expiry a four months' bill was accepted and $2\frac{1}{2}$ per cent discount allowed on payment—in practice almost a year's credit with a cash discount on top.[92] Such a system represented a most inefficient use of capital. An authority on the industry in 1914 stated that if merchants had paid cash in a month about £1,500,000 (or 50 per cent) less capital would be required.[93] Not only was capital wasted, but such favourable terms meant that it was all too easy to become a merchant, and fail in difficult years. Merchants sometimes vanished overnight without trace. The most celebrated was Alexander Collie, who contracted liabilities of over £3½ million in a few years in the early 1870s, and brought down several of the Scottish houses associated with him when he failed. Other London merchants fell with him, including one whose assets totalled only £400 but who had accepted bills for Collie amounting to £56,000, his commission for this service being his chief income.[94]

The establishment of a credit system in the woollen trade was due to lack of capital among the early entrepreneurs and lack of liquidity among the buyers of woollen goods. Its persistence for so long, however, was rather a result of the type of clientèle for whom the woollen manufacturers mainly catered. The tailor gave credit to his customer, who was the type of man whose financial standing would not normally be in question; so the merchant would have to give credit to the tailor, and repercussions would extend along the line to the manufacturer. Ultimately, of course, someone had to pay—usually the wool-stapler, since no credit was allowed at the wool sales. Some Border manufacturers relied completely on the credit given by the local wool-stapling firm of Sanderson & Murray, from whom many of them bought their wool. The normal credit given was for three months, but this was often extended to a year. Such credit enabled the manufacturers to tide themselves over difficult periods and sell their goods at an acceptable price. Sometimes the firm would grant bills to manufacturers who had run short of ready cash. Often credit given ran into many thousands of pounds, and Sanderson & Murray naturally took an active interest in the Border woollen businesses in debt to them. Occasionally partners were found who were willing to invest in the trade.[95] The value of such a well established firm, of world renown by the 1860s, was inestimable to the Border woollen industry. However, Sanderson's would perhaps have done better if they had tightened their credit more as the liquid position of the manufacturers improved. This might have forced the latter to insist on better terms from the merchants. As it was this did not happen; the giving of long credits acted as an outlet for surplus capital, gave an advantage to the larger firm in difficult times, and, insofar

as firms could be propped up almost indefinitely by credit, helped
to lower the general efficiency of the industry. It made both the
inefficient and the efficient more vulnerable, for the waywardness
of one or two badly managed firms could bring down others whose
only sin was to give them credit. In a trade where a high proportion of trade was done with perhaps a single merchant house the
risk of involvement in bad debts if long credits were given was
very great, although some firms appear to have guarded against
this eventuality by depreciating from their gross profits.

Between 1830 and 1880 Scottish woollens had achieved an international reputation for design, colour and textural quality unrivalled by the English centres of the quality trade. Having grown
from almost nothing so recently, the tweed trade by the middle of
the century was jauntily confident that it held a unique position
in the manufacture of men's wear. 'In comparing the Huddersfield
cloth with our own', boasted a Hawick tweedmaker in 1855, 'the
sun shines on the gaudy Yorkshire suit, and the colour shines no
more. A shower of rain pelts its wearer and diffuses the cheap dye
on his linen and person. The suit in a few weeks looks seedy and
miserable. Our hero in Tweeds faces sun and rain without fear.
Honesty and innate goodness triumph. The colour is permanent. A
twelve month passes; the suit looks well with a new set of buttons
and fresh pockets. The man feels proud of his economy and grateful to his tailor . . . '.[96]

The latter decades of the nineteenth century offered less reason
for such buoyant optimism and confidence. We must now turn to
this period.

Page 133. *The Burgh of Selkirk.* The woollen industry here originated as a spill-over from Galashiels six miles away whose manufacturers were attracted by the cheap power afforded by the River Ettrick and its adjacent flat 'haugh' which made an admirable industrial site. From the 1870s Selkirk became an important yarn producing centre. In contrast to Hawick (on p66) industrial and residential building in Selkirk were kept well apart.

Page 134. *Mid Mill, Gala-shiels, 1910.* Built in the 1860s to replace an earlier structure, this factory has an air of confidence and prosperity befitting the heyday of the tweed industry in the nineteenth century. The large windows and the separate stair tower gave this mill more light and room than that on p83. The bell tower is a reminder that the factory system demanded a timekeeping workforce. Notice also the link with the local rail system in the foreground.

FIVE

Tweeds in the Changing International Economy, 1880-1914

'With the goods that are produced in this district we defy the foreigner to compete, for how can . . . the miserable foreigner compete with us, an imperial race.' Galashiels Textile Workers' Union, 1905

In common with other sectors of the British economy the Scottish woollen industry showed clear signs of faltering, and, at times, decline, during the thirty years or so before 1914. All available data suggest that in this period producers lost much of the confidence and enthusiasm that had characterised the central decades of the century. The 1880s and, more especially, the 1890s were years of growing complaint and even dismay on the part of employers and workers alike.

The period between the collapse of the great foreign trade boom in 1873 and the middle of the 1890s has long borne the title of the 'Great Depression'. We shall try and discover whether the condition of the Scottish woollen industry at this time merits such a description, and why the economic climate within which the manufacturers operated changed before 1914.

It is difficult to say when the industry began to notice that all was not well. Opinion varied among the manufacturers themselves. Some felt that trade had never revived after the topping-off of the

135

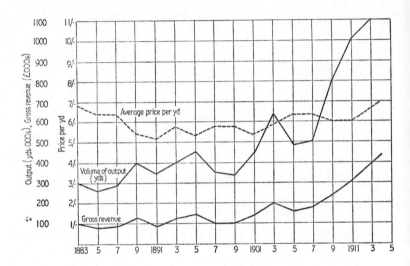

Output, Gross Revenue and Average Unit Prices, J. & J. Crombie,
Aberdeen, 1883-1914

boom in the early 1870s following the Franco-Prussian war. Others
spoke of a rare spell of prosperity in the 1880s. More traced the
downturn in their fortunes to the tariff in America in 1890.[1] Fortunately one can check these broad statements somewhat by study-
ing surviving business records, which shed some light on the movements of prices and output in the industry.

The graphs on pp 136, 137, 138 show changes in the volume of
production and in unit prices for three leading tweed-manufacturers at this time. All experienced an upward trend in production
during the 1880s and some fall-off in the following decade. Two
of the firms recovered strongly after the turn of the century,
Crombie's of Aberdeen, for instance, experiencing a period of unprecedented expansion after 1906, mainly in parson's grey cloth.
Similarly the three firms suffered price falls in the 1880s, followed
in two cases by further falls or static prices for much of the 1890s.
The general price level appears to have begun to rise after about
the middle of the decade and was more pronounced after 1900,
though, if Crombie's were typical, not surpassing levels obtained in

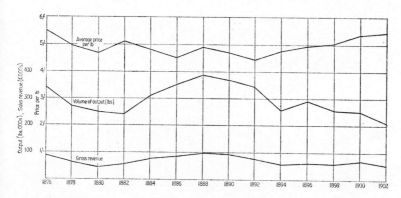

Output, Gross Revenue and Average Unit Prices, Wm Watson & Son,
Hawick, 1876-1902

the early 1880s. Prices of Ballantyne's cloths had been falling at
least from 1860, well before the onset of the 'Great Depression',
but in the 1890s falling prices were accompanied by falling production. We may conclude, therefore, that if the experience of
these firms was typical of the whole industry, the latter decades
of the nineteenth century were marked by low prices and falling
demand, at least until around 1900. Thereafter production expanded greatly, especially just before World War I, with prices rising
less steeply.

This interpretation is borne out by other evidence. Table 7 shows
that investment in new buildings, spinning plant and power looms,
and the recruitment of labour continued steadily in the 1880s, the
number of workers in the industry growing by a third. By 1904,
however, there had been a large reduction in the number of mills
(from 282 in 1890 to 239 in 1904) and more than 70,000 spindles
and 2,000 power looms had been lost. The reduction in the workforce was not so serious, however, suggesting that most of the mills
which were forced to close were small and that some of the plant
loss was due to modernisation.

That employers were having price and profit problems before
1890 despite, or perhaps because of, a high level of production is
also evident in the findings of the Royal Commission on the de-

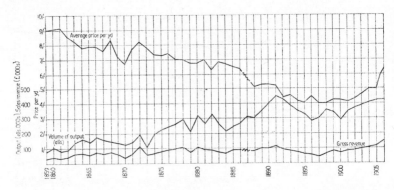

Output, Gross Revenue and Average Unit Prices, Henry Ballantyne & Sons,
Walkerburn, 1859-1906

TABLE 7

CHANGES IN THE PRODUCTIVE CAPACITY
OF THE SCOTTISH WOOLLEN INDUSTRY, 1878-1904[2]

Year	Factories	Spin/Spindles	Power looms	Workers
1878	246	559,021	6,284	22,667
1884	274	551,685	7,958	27,546
1890	282	565,146	9,386	31,077
1897				29,218
1898-9				28,223
1904	239	493,756	7,300	29,483

pression in 1886. It is here that we find the first rumblings of dis-
content in the industry. Though too much attention should not be
given to these proceedings, since they were conducted in a year
of acute depression, the 'long-term' nature of the evidence submitted by the South of Scotland Chamber of Commerce (SSCC)
gives it some significance. In accordance with the usual practice of
the tax-conscious woollen manufacturers no statistical evidence on
prices and profits was submitted. The SSCC merely stated that the
volume of trade since the early 1870s had increased, but its gross
value had declined. On the other hand capital investment was
higher, so that gross return on investment was a good deal reduced.
In the yarn-spinning section of the industry profits in the mid-
1880s were declared to be 'very much less' than in the early 1870s
—a fact which is not surprising, as the latter years were boom

years. Nonetheless the yarn-spinners had conducted little further investment after 1875, and in 1885 less capital and labour were being employed than in 1875-80. The volume of trade had already diminished. Prices and profits were falling.[3]

The severe cutback in production in the 1890s, evident in the business data, is also suggested by other sources. Between 1891 and 1901 the population of Hawick fell from 19,204 to 17,303, and that of Galashiels fell by about one quarter.[4] An observer wrote in 1899 that the Scotch tweed trade was 'withering and decaying and casting a blight over a once bright and busy part of the country'. He spoke of rows of empty houses, a dwindling population and a steady flow of emigrants to Canada and the USA, and the streets filled by 'loungers', in truth men idle due to idle plant.[5] In 1897 a mill standing at a written-down value of £18,000 was unable to find a buyer at £5,000. A year or two earlier an almost new mill valued at £12,000 was sold by a bond-holding bank for less than £6,000, payable in easy instalments at 2½ per cent interest.[6] In 1898 many Hillfoot manufacturers succeeded in obtaining reductions in their assessments because of the state of the yarn and shawl trades.[7] Prices continued to slump. Goods were sold below cost on occasion to keep mills working. The head of a Leeds clothing firm stated in 1898 in relation to a consignment of Scotch tweed: 'I bought that lot at 2s a yard . . . not long since I paid 3s 6d a yard for similar goods and I believe they could not be produced for much less than 2s 6d.'[8]

What were the causes of this depression in the industry? The falling prices shown in Ballantyne's business in the 1860s were almost certainly due to technological change in conditions of strong demand. In this decade self-acting spinning mules were installed generally in the industry to harmonise with previous investment in powered-weaving machinery. Continuing falls in the 1870s and 1880s, however, are not to be explained fully in this way. The great export boom of the early 1870s caused the industry to expand, and the collapse of the boom in 1873 left it with a good deal of excess capacity in machinery and labour. Demand still ran fairly strongly, however, above the level of the 1860s, so that production was not reduced further after 1873 but, on the contrary, continued to expand. Prices did not recover, however, and manufacturers had a real incentive to cut their costs.

The fact that production expanded while prices fell was partly due to reduced costs of production—caused by some technological innovation in weaving and a steep drop in wool prices. The bulk of the wool consumed in Britain was imported from Australasia and, because of enormous investment in wool and sheep farming there, supply was beginning to outstrip demand by the 1870s. Consequently wool prices fell dramatically. Between 1872 and 1888 the weight of wool passing through the London Wool Market more than doubled while the aggregate revenue fell by more than half.[9] This considerable reduction in the cost of raw material enabled manufacturers to withstand at least some of the fall in piece-goods prices and helps to explain continued production growth in the 1880s.

We have succeeded in explaining to some extent the falling trend of prices and profits in the years after 1873, but the real puzzle is the fall in demand. Scottish manufacturers, reporting to the committee on trade depression, blamed adverse tariffs. A high proportion of the industry's output found its way abroad—to the very countries that were imposing duties on it. As we have seen, in 1886 it was estimated that about 40 per cent of piece-goods production was exported, mainly to Europe and North America. Some firms and even entire communities were even more heavily committed to exports: Galashiels, for example, was almost totally committed to the North American market. Thus the erection of tariff barriers was a severe threat to the industry.

The return to protective commercial policies in Europe, begun in the 1870s, initially did not seriously embarrass the industry. Woollen industries abroad needed immediate protection from cheap imports, not quality goods. Nevertheless, over time, the Scottish manufacturers, especially those most concerned with medium and plain goods, felt the adverse effects of protective duties.

The real blow to the industry, however, was the erection of a stiff American tariff against woollen goods in 1890, since the incidence of both specific and *ad valorem* charges fell more heavily upon better quality goods.[10] The McKinley tariff of 1890 imposed on woollen goods valued at more than 40c per lb a specific duty of 44c per lb, plus 50 per cent *ad valorem*. Conditions were relaxed under the short-lived Wilson revision in the mid-1890s (which coincided with a temporary upturn in the fortunes of several Scottish firms) but under the Dingley tariff of 1897 a new category brought the *ad valorem* duty on cloth (and dress goods) valued at 70c per lb or more up to 55 per cent. In round terms the duties imposed on most woollen goods under the 1890 tariff structure were equal to more than their foreign value, while the severe Dingley legislation was specifically designed to 'preserve the home market as far as possible to our own producers'.[11] Though a further revision of the tariff was embodied in the Payne-Aldrich Act of 1909, woollen duties remained virtually unchanged down to 1914 apart from a slight reduction on the cheaper yarn and dress goods.[12]

The imposition of Continental tariff protection was also undoubtedly prejudicial to the trade of the Scottish woollen manufacturers and spinners, being sufficient to turn some of the staunchest free traders into retaliationists, and a few into downright protectionists.[13] Yarn spinners were severely affected. A Border spinner testified before the Tariff Commissioners in 1905 that an increase in the price of yarn of 1d per lb caused by import duties was 'more than enough to decide an order in a trade where quotations are made by the farthing'.[14] As early as 1886 there was talk of retaliation to stem the 'inch by inch decay' of the yarn trade caused by Continental tariffs.[15] By 1901 European yarn orders were reported only one-third of those in the 1870s and 1880s, and what *was* required had to be much more intricately fabricated and designed. A Selkirk yarn spinner stated that it was 'impossible to send plain carded yarns to the continent'. The value of yarn exports through Scottish ports fell from £129,000 in 1896 to only £56,000 in 1902.[16]

The tweed-manufacturers were also adversely affected, progressively so as tariff adjustments were made. In 1903 a questionnaire was distributed by the SSCC to all its members engaged in woollen manufacture regarding the effect of Continental tariffs upon the level of business, and replies unanimously stated that Continental trade was indeed hampered by protective barriers. A Galashiels manufacturing firm put the general opinion of Border businessmen succinctly : 'France, dwindling down; Germany ditto; Russia after a last struggle now dead; Austria, very difficult and risky; Italy, sometimes a bit of business in a novelty if we give them it for nothing.'[17] W. B. Sime of Hawick advised that the last increase in the French tariff had so seriously diminished his business that he had been compelled to dismiss his French agent because the amount of trade he could do would no longer pay the cost of his patterns.[18] By 1906 *The Times* reported that Scottish dealings with France had 'degenerated into a petty trade in short lengths . . .' Not unnaturally the effect of protective commercial policies was most fully felt in the cheaper ranges.[19] 'When it comes to plain goods in the medium and cheaper qualities', wrote a leading tweed merchant, 'the Tariffs kill business . . . trade is practically limited to the extent in which we are successful in producing novelties. The constant cry is for "novelty" and catering for that alone enables us to sell at a profit.'[20]

Not all the Continental tariffs, however, were equal in their effect on the Scottish tweed- and yarn-makers. It was felt that the French tariff was more of an impediment than the German (though the latter was felt to be prohibitive by some) and many manufacturers paid more attention to the German market after the McKinley tariff of 1890 because it was also the base for trade in Eastern Europe and Russia. A. J. Sanderson of Galashiels stated in 1903 that, though his French trade had been gradually diminishing for the past two decades, that with Germany had been growing considerably.[21] The effect of tariffs depended directly upon the nature of the goods produced by the exporting firm: specialists in high-grade fabrics, with the accent on design, were more successful in combating it than manufacturers of plain goods in the medium qualities because of the sophisticated skills embodied in their products and the comparative irrelevance of the price factor. There were still many German merchants in this period, for instance, who dealt exclusively in British goods because they thereby obtained superior cloths and patterns.[22]

If, however, Continental commercial policies after 1880 hit the Scottish woollen producer pretty hard, the policy of the USA in the 1890s was little short of disastrous. The North American market, with its large number of British emigrants, especially Scots, with similar consumption patterns to their native countrymen, was, be-

fore the erection of the McKinley tariff, probably the best overseas
outlet for Scottish woollen products. The McKinley tariff of 1890,
however, effectively placed a 90 per cent duty on woollens sent
from Scotland. Woollen yarn that sold in Selkirk at 1s 3d to 1s 8d
per lb was, on entering the USA, subject to a duty of 1s 4½d per
lb, besides 35 per cent of its value. So on yarn invoiced at 1s 3d per
lb a duty of 1s 9½d or 143 per cent had to be paid. Taking 4s per
lb as the average value of Border cloth suitable for the American
trade, this was liable to a total duty of about 3s 10d per lb.[23] After
the Dingley legislation of 1897 the average duty on such cloths rose
to over 100 per cent, and under the later Payne-Aldrich schedules
the tariff on Scottish products still ranged from 95-145 per cent. Not
surprisingly American tariff policy was regarded as 'unquestionably
the worst slap in the face that the tweed industry ever got', which
'practically severed the commercial intercourse between the Scottish Border towns and the United States'.[24] Before 1890 the trade of
Border manufacturers with the USA was over £500,000 annually,
but by 1905 this had dropped to about £50,000. Galashiels was particularly adversely affected: before McKinley's tariff about 75
per cent of the town's trade was directed to the American market,
but by the early 1900s this had slumped to only 5 per cent.[25] The
following table shows the experience of three Border firms engaged
in the American trade.

TABLE 8

ANNUAL AVERAGE SALES TO USA[26]

	FIRM		
	a	*b*	*c*
Before McKinley	£25,000	£10,000	£30,000
After McKinley	£12,000		
After Dingley	£2,000	£500	£3,000-4,000

Another firm reported trade as having been 'cut to pieces, and in
many cases rendered worthless to any manufacturer who has to
look to these markets to do more than help pay his working ex-
penses'.[27] Members of the SSCC in 1903 were unanimous in their
condemnation of the American tariff, employing freely phrases
like 'practically ceased', 'almost stopped', 'market practically
closed' and 'ruinous conditions'. Where merchants had been used to
ordering 1,000yd to a colouring, they were now content with 50yd

or less. The Hillfoot manufacturers suffered no less than those in the Borders: by 1905 the Hillfoot trade in ladies' dress goods had been cut by half, the American trade having been 'killed by the McKinley tariff'. One firm, whose average annual turnover with the USA before 1890 had been around £20,000, sold only £2,000 worth in 1891 and nothing at all by 1894.[28] Again, the manufacturers and spinners of the cheaper qualities suffered most. Only the purest aristocrats of the trade were little worried, though most firms combined work of various levels of quality, for the market was not large enough for all to produce solely for the highest class trade. Nevertheless high-class American tailors were always anxious to get the best goods, and were willing to pay any price for a fetching novelty. The well-to-do American thought it 'the right thing' to wear the latest novelties in imported goods, in this way proving his financial standing. The volume of such trade was small, however, amounting to perhaps only about 5-10 per cent of total trade before 1890, the loss of which would not have been materially felt by the industry.[29] Such cloths had prestige value and acted as 'kite flyers' for the more modest products that made up the bulk of the trade.

Undoubtedly the protectionist policies of foreign governments, especially after 1890, had an extremely depressing effect on the Scottish tweed and yarn industry, but tariffs cannot be held wholly responsible for its misfortunes. They were still in effective operation when the tweed trade revived in the early twentieth century, though admittedly the bulk of the export trade had shifted from America to Europe, where the tariff was less severe. However, Continental tariffs also had been the subject of much bitter criticism by manufacturers in the questionnaire returns of 1903. While allowing for the importance of the tariff issue, therefore, a full insight into the problems of Scottish woollen manufacturers demands that we look at other companion factors.

Contemporary opinion saw the increase in competition, both from foreign and English manufacturing, as another major threat to the Scotch tweed trade. To some extent intensified competition in third markets or at home was a function of protective policies. One of the principal objects of erecting tariff barriers was to protect the home market and thus subsidise exports by obtaining good

returns on home sales. Over time, also, the skills and capital equipment of foreign manufacturers improved greatly, thus adding to
the range of goods in which they could successfully compete.
There were many in the Scottish woollen industry who felt in the
1880s and even after 1890 that their goods were so distinctive in
quality, colouring and design that they had no need to fear tariffs
and foreign competition. Such complacency was unjustified, as we
have seen. By the early twentieth century Scottish manufacturers
were beginning to feel the cold draught of competition in overseas
markets. By 1905 Scotch flannel suitings, for example, were being
successfully matched by Dutch manufacturers in the German market. The decline in the vesting trade between Galashiels and Italy
was thought to be due more to Italian progress than to the tariff.[30]
More alarming was the fact that French and German competition
was being increasingly felt on the domestic market, especially in
ladies' costume cloths. Robert Noble & Co of Hawick complained
in 1905 that they were 'practically cut out' of their own home
trade due to cheap German and French piece-dyed products. Similar
competition was felt from low-priced German shawls, and some
spoke alarmingly of a 'systemised German invasion' of such
fabrics.[31] On the whole, however, tweed manufacturers were not
seriously affected by imported woollens. The experience of the
cheap dress goods branch was the exception, not the rule. At home
competition stemmed mainly from Yorkshire.

In common with many other British manufacturers Scottish employers reacted irrationally to foreign manufacturers, accusing
them of all manner of underhand tricks. A Dumfries firm, for example, was in no doubt that competition on the home front was
the result of 'spurious imitations' as well as all the other 'vile practices which the foreigner introduces into every trade he touches'.[32]
Others claimed that the still existing US trade was only tolerated
by that country so that the American merchants could buy high-
grade goods in small quantities to 'coach' their own manufacturers.
'Buyers look at our styles' grumbled Keddie, Gordon & Co of Galashiels, 'buy a few bits to save their shame, and then make up their
bulk in cheaper goods on this side, or know better what to buy on
the other. We lose patience when speaking of this country [USA]
which takes 95 per cent of a start . . . and then struts about as

Lord of creation.'[33] Fume as they might, however, the fact remained that by a combination of skill and knavish behaviour Scottish manufacturers were being successfully imitated by foreign manufacturers. Even the Clan tartan trade was being successfully imitated in low qualities and 'bastard substitutes'.

Foreign competition in the woollen trade was mainly felt by the yarn spinners, who were faced with ever-increasing consumption of cheap Belgian yarn by home and overseas manufacturers. Belgium, herself largely excluded from the American market by the tariffs of 1890 and 1897, turned increasingly to Britain as a trading outlet. Yorkshire makers, too, who hitherto had obtained a good deal of their carded yarn from Scotland, turned more and more to inferior imported varieties. Even some Scottish manufacturers, seeking refuge in cutting costs, turned to Belgian yarn (which contained about 10 per cent cotton). In 1905 a Hillfoot manufacturer estimated that three-quarters of the yarns used there were of Continental origin, while the remaining 25 per cent were only home-produced because they were sold at cost price or less. In that year a Galashiels firm reckoned that Belgian yarn was 3d to 4d per lb cheaper than local yarn.[34]

It was an added burden to the Scottish woollen industry that increasing competition from overseas manufacturers and the loss of foreign markets should also be the occasion of intensified competition from England. West Riding manufacturers, also faced with the disruption of their trade in cheap goods by hostile tariffs, particularly in America, began vigorously to exploit the home market in fancy goods. At first Yorkshire attempts at emulating Scottish cloths in inferior qualities were viewed with some contempt, but the Colne Valley manufacturers showed great skill and enterprise in making—from a combination of low-grade wool, torn-up stockings, pulled waste and cotton—good imitations of even the most characteristic Scotch tweed patterns. As a result Yorkshire tweeds began to make great inroads on the sale of the genuine article. It was claimed in 1898 that Yorkshire was making 'as good cloths as the regular Scotch makers, at less price, and in as good designs and colours'.[35] The Yorkshiremen were helped in their efforts partly by the time-worn custom of copying Scotch patterns, partly by the luring of Scottish designers to Yorkshire by better wages, and also by many Scottish firms seeking salvation from the crisis by reducing their standards and fighting the battle on Yorkshire's terms. This resulted in even Scottish warehousemen increasingly turning to cheaper Yorkshire tweeds. Thus by 1906 it was estimated that about three-quarters of the 'Scotch Tweeds' produced in Britain were made in England, a fact that is also suggested by the increasing concern of some Scots to obtain an adequate trademark.[36]

The striking success with which Yorkshire manufacturers reacted to the dwindling American trade by exploiting the home market was aided by the current movements in fashion. Woollen cloths were giving way to worsteds as consumers came to prefer lighter and less formal garments, and the demand for quality cloths began to wane as public taste moved towards cheaper, less durable dress. Fine men's broadcloths went down before fine worsteds, while 'rough'-textured woollens gave way, to some extent, to worsted serges. The growing ladies' trade aided the movement towards lighter, more fancy fabrics, as did the requirements of what remained of the American market. Thus Scottish manufacturers, already beseiged by tariff barriers in their important export sector and by increasing foreign competition at home and overseas, were further embarrassed by arbitrary fashion changes. Thus in 1898 an observer could write that 'a few years ago Scotch tweeds were all the rage, while at the present time no man with any pretensions to being considered well-dressed is to be seen arrayed in the productions of the looms of Caledonia'.[37] The changes in demand were particularly harmful to the sale of average tweeds. 'People do not now go in for the clothing which may descend from grandfather to grandson, nor do they pay the old-fashioned prices for them . . . the present generation preferring repeated changes to the plain goods which suited our forefathers . . . taste, comfort and variety, not to mention prices, being the chief consideration.'[38]

The demand for Scottish woollens had spread through the social classes since the middle years of the nineteenth century. Though careful to maintain the purity of raw wool content, manufacturers produced a wide variety of qualities. One way of keeping costs down to the more humble buyer, whose tweed suit in any case was usually reserved for Sundays and other formal occasions, was to restrict the amount of designing that went into its production.

Consequently these cloths were fairly plain and patterns were more or less repeated year after year. By the last quarter of the century it was this part of the trade, which had never been quite as novelty-conscious as the aristocratic branch, which was under heavy fire from Yorkshire woollen and worsted producers.

A further consequence of the change in fashion and the battle for the home market was the gradual evolution of the multiple clothier and the ready-made trade. From its origins in the mid-1850s in London, Norwich and Glasgow the ready-made clothing industry had mainly used inferior cloths.[39] By the 1890s, however, buying 'off the peg' was beginning to affect the purchasers of medium qualities also, and the Scottish tweed manufacturers were no longer exempt from its economic implications. Moreover this movement in tailoring was even more seriously affecting overseas markets, especially the USA. A 'ready-made' suit there carried none of the social stigma that it did in Britain, and by 1914 it was reported that the bulk of American business and professional classes bought ready-made clothes. By the late 1880s in Britain, too, large wholesale tailoring houses were swamping drapers throughout the country with bunches of cloth patterns representing stock at headquarters. Would-be purchasers chose the pattern, were measured by the local agent, and the manufacturing tailor made a garment which, though mass-produced, combined attractiveness of style with cheapness of cost. This type of tailoring naturally required large quantities of standardised cloth identical in weight and pattern—a demand more easily supplied by the Yorkshire woollen factories, employing considerable quantities of 'recovered' wool and other fibres, than by the Scottish manufacturers, for whom quality rather than cheapness had always been the governing factor. The ability of the Yorkshire manufacturers to imitate accurately the genuine Scottish article ensured their victory in the market for medium qualities on the home front.

This quiet revolution in distributing woollen articles to the consumer, which heralded the decline of the bespoke tailor, the principal outlet of the merchant dealing in Scotch goods, was noted by the Scottish manufacturers. True, those dealing principally in top-quality products were again not alarmed, and others questioned whether the ready-made principle would ever extend to the genuine

Scotch tweed, but many were more realistic. As one remarked, the top quality trade was 'only a small outlet, no trade centre can exist on the plums without getting a share of the good solid bread'.

As the stigma attached to mass-produced clothing began to ease, manufacturing tailors began to employ medium and even high-class cloths for ready-made clothing, thus bringing quality cloths to the consumer at considerably reduced prices. As a result of these developments and a general concern to diversify Border industry, calls were made upon local manufacturers to employ surplus capital in establishing clothing factories to make up the local cloth. A number of local commercial interests strove to get Glasgow firms to open up in the Borders, pointing out that they would be better placed to command a range of goods and plan their work on the spot than they would by merely seeing pattern ranges. It was generally realised, however, by the proponents of these ventures that a wider range of qualities than those made in the Borders would have to be stocked, because of the type of market and competition from the West Riding. Though one factory was eventually opened at Galashiels (which still operates), the idea did not in general appeal to local capitalists. They feared the introduction of low-class labour (as did existing workers—owing to the threat of a lower wage-level); they were sceptical of the demand for high-class ready-mades; and, more important, feared, not without some cause, that they would lose a good deal of their merchant trade. They thus preferred to leave well alone, and trust to orders for multiple tailors being placed through the merchant as were those of the bespoke tailor, and the making-up trade continued to be conducted elsewhere.[40]

Important as the external influences of tariffs and competition were, however, it would be wrong to conclude that the Scottish woollen trade was the innocent victim of inevitability. Ineffective adjustment to market conditions was to some extent a result of internal weaknesses. Before the 1880s little competition had been felt from other branches of the woollen industry in Britain; Scottish manufacturers had successfully captured the quality market and had no trouble in selling their output. For the most part capacity was fully occupied. The long existence of a seller's market bred a spirit of inertia and complacency in the industry. Little attention was given to sounding out new markets, and manufacturers came to rely increasingly in the medium qualities on repeat orders for well tried patterns. Profits were good, as the increasing number of fine mansions dotted around the manufacturing centres indicated. Management became less involved in the activities of the mill floor, and gradually owners delegated more control to subordinates, though not abandoning their predilection for family businesses. In common with other industries the local businessman bore much of the criticism for the palpable weakness of the tweed trade at this time. 'We cannot compete if we content ourselves with wringing our hands and speaking of the prosperity of the Borders as having passed away', complained the local press.[41] The energy and perspicacity of the founders of the industry was felt to be lacking, and it was argued that too much unproductive capital was lying in the owners' hands.

Manufacturers were accused of dallying at the smoking concert, the billiard table and the Riviera. ('I'm afraid we have both got the gadabout fever and won't be satisfied unless we see a new country every year', wrote one in 1892.)[42] Some became victims of conspicuous consumption. J. T. Laing, examined for bankruptcy in 1909, admitted to keeping four servants, a coachman and drawing a high income from the business for personal expenditure.[43] 'We [have] had many men' observed a Hawick minister in public, 'chiefly in the founders of our businesses—men not afraid of very hard work, keeping pleasure in its place, sticking fast to their posts. In the second generation, however, we have often seen a different spirit; sometimes contempt for trades, an aping of the fine gentleman, an aspiring to be what they were not . . . love of ease, self-indulgence and lack of grit and back-bone. They must work in the spirit of their fathers . . . study the technique of their business, bend their energies and talents in one direction . . .'.[44] A Hawick burgh councillor considered the local manufacturers in general to be an 'effete body' who ought to retire and give place to men with more energy and less money. They were likened to Mr Micawber: rather than face the crisis in the industry squarely they merely waited for something to turn up.[45] More than ever before dynamic leadership was required, but many tweed-makers were unable to supply it. In the past they had been able to apply the dictum 'let those

Page 151. *Workers in a Galashiels mill in the 1920s.*

Page 152. *The weaving shop of Robert Noble & Co Ltd, Hawick, about 1920.* In contrast to the cotton handloom weaver the woollen weaver's position was only slowly undermined by machinery, largely because of the intricacy of tweed designs. By the end of the nineteenth century, however, little hand-woven cloth was sold compared with that made by power looms. These men are doubtless pattern weavers, that is, skilled men who executed the ideas of the firm's designer and from which the season's patterns were chosen. The men in the photograph probably started with the firm as boy apprentices (no girls or women were so trained) and were retained as pattern weavers when commercial hand-weaving died out.

who will sell their goods by the pound, we sell our brains' with some justification. But, largely unnoticed, the industry had been outpaced in the good years by its competitors, leaving it to face the lean years with outdated and expensive production methods.

The *Hawick Advertiser* sounded the Clarion call: 'Technical education, application, energy and thrift must be the war cry, combined with capital . . . whether in worsted, high-class tweeds or low goods to suit the million, there should be no reason why Border goods should be second to any in price, quality or general excellence.'[46] But traditional attitudes were firmly ingrained. Even on the enactment of the harsh McKinley tariff, many tweed-makers were unmoved. They 'shrugged their shoulders', and said, 'America must have our goods and if she chooses to pay double price for them that is her lookout'.[47] For all the criticism levelled at them at public gatherings, from the pulpit and the press, manufacturers largely refrained from comment. Their contributions to local newspapers mainly confined themselves to fond remembrances of yesteryear or harangues against the foreigner, with his guileful ways and low labour costs. What energy they did display was often channelled into local politics. It is perhaps not insignificant that the head of one of the most successful Hawick tweed firms, until he retired through ill health, was Mr Blenkhorn, a Yorkshireman who was stated to be 'not prominently identified with the public life of the town'.[48] The canker of traditionalism and self-adulation was equally prevalent in Galashiels at annual mill 'soirées', and in the welter of verbiage spilled at annual dinners of the Manufacturers' Corporation, an event which eventually prompted a Selkirk yarn spinner to remark that 'the time is past for comforting ourselves at corporation banquets with the assurance that "the enterprise which distinguished us in the past will etc . . . " and for all such flattering platitudes'.[49]

Having said all this, it would be wrong to conclude that the leaders of local industry in the Borders were completely devoid of energy and enterprise. Further investigation of the response made by the industry to changing market conditions is necessary before a disinterested evaluation of managerial efficiency can be made.

Scottish woollen manufacturers possessed three possible lines of action, short of doing nothing, in order to meet the problems dis-

K

cussed above. In the first place new markets could be sought out where tariff restriction or competition was not so great. Secondly, they could endeavour to latch on to prevailing trends and try to cater for the mass market in cheap products. Thirdly, the industry could raise the quality of its products to even higher levels and concentrate on catering for the discriminating buyer to whom price was of only secondary importance. This might require the evolving of entirely new products while retaining quality and distinctiveness. All these policies might involve the re-equipping of mills with the latest machinery.

A fair test of entrepreneurial response to the challenge of competition is the degree to which it embraces technical progress. Though textile technology, especially in woollens, advanced only slowly in the nineteenth century, important technological changes were being made at this time in the major processes of spinning and weaving. On the spinning side the chief invention was the ring-spinning frame, which operated on a different principle to the established mule, occupied less space and produced yarn more quickly.[50] Several of these machines do appear to have been installed in Galashiels from the mid-1870s, but they seem not to have been regarded highly, probably for technical reasons. Scottish manufacturers were not alone in their conclusions. Vickerman in his book *Woollen Spinning* (1894) scoffed at the idea of employing the continuous spinning frame for woollen yarns, saying that the inventor had done nothing more noteworthy than the perpetration of a piece of mechanical mischief. It is true that the self-acting mule was more versatile than the frame in its ability to spin a wide variety of yarns, especially the finer counts. The early ring frames were quite capable of spinning the heavier or thicker yarns but not the finer counts. The woollen manufacturer needed to vary the structure of his yarn, and to this extent the frame was less relevant than the older mule; and, though continuous in operation, the early frames had to be stopped before making a 'piecing' if a slubbing broke at the condenser bobbin. The early frame did not, therefore, produce much more than the new 'self-acting' mules. Both machines operated around 2,000 rpm. The self-acting condensers were recent, having themselves displaced the piecing-machines and the slubbing 'billy'. Combined with larger carding machinery, the

self-actor had greatly accelerated the process of yarn-making without loss of quality. There were good technical reasons, therefore,
why the ring-spinning frame should be so little employed in the
Borders, and lack of innovation here should not blind us to the investment in self-actors that had proceeded apace in the 1860s and
1870s.

More scope for investment offered itself on the weaving side,
especially as weaving machinery wore out more quickly than the
leisurely 'mules'. The new 'fast' loom operated at an average of
100 'picks' per minute—about twice the speed of the old looms—
and, therefore, offered scope for considerable productivity gains
and cost reductions. There were no serious technical drawbacks to
their introduction, and it seems clear that many manufacturers
did take advantage of the new weaving machinery: 'fast' looms
were rapidly replacing the 240 'slow' looms on Crombie's books
in the 1880s, and the last was replaced by 1895.[51] Ballantyne's of
Walkerburn possessed 450 'fast' looms in 1896 out of a total of
around 1,100.[52] Indeed, to obtain trade, it became increasingly
necessary to introduce fast high-capacity weaving and spinning
plant since, in times of uncertainty, merchants refrained from placing orders till the last moment and then demanded delivery almost
immediately.

Despite some modernisation in the industry, however, the local
head of the Galashiels Woollen Technical College could claim in
1914 that many firms had been slow to scrap redundant machinery
and had clung to old practices for far too long. This was especially
true in the finishing processes.[53] Though specialist dyers and
finishers did appear in the Borders during the later part of the century most firms retained control over these processes. Scotch
tweeds had never been renowned for their finish: tweeds by
definition did not permit of lengthy finishing; rather they were
known for design and durability; and the Scots had never needed
to develop the finer arts of this part of the manufacturing process.
Now, however, the vigorous competition in design and finish
shown by Yorkshire manufacturers increased the significance of
this stage of production.

We may conclude, therefore, that most of the leading Scottish
woollen manufacturers at least displayed enough awareness of

current needs to take advantage of improved weaving plant while they shunned the spinning frame for avowedly technical reasons. Increases in productivity by weavers, therefore, were obtained, and, due to the general slackness of demand, we may explain part of the unemployment problem in the 1890s by investment in this better plant. Part of the problem of the industry at this period, therefore, resulted from over-capacity, caused by modernisation, at a time of reduced or stationary demand. The manufacturers' detractors could not have it both ways: retention of old plant or investment in new were both likely to produce unemployment.

How far did manufacturers seek out new markets? The organisation of the trade was such that a good deal of the initiative here lay with the merchant, not the manufacturer, but there is some evidence that producers did seek out fresh outlets for their products or exploited older ones more vigorously. The German market was given more attention after the McKinley tariff in 1890; and a big boost was given to manufacturers by increased dealings with Canada. The Canadian tariff was felt to be 3s 4d in the £ cheaper than the German and it was estimated that trade to Canada quadrupled between 1896 and 1908.[54] In addition Australia and New Zealand were rising in importance, as was South Africa. Some manufacturers even pioneered the Indian and Chinese markets.[55] Unfortunately no quantitative assessment of the exploitation of new markets is possible, but there is no case for concluding that merchants and makers made no adaptation at all to changed market conditions.

Faced with the seeming eclipse of their products, it was natural that some manufacturers should have forsaken their former high standards of materials and adulterated their goods by the use of poor and mixed yarns. In this they sought to extend their range downwards to cater for the growing mass market in inferior qualities. Such a policy of apostacy entailed meeting the West Riding on its own ground. Yorkshire woollen manufacturers were renowned for their ability to 'spin anything with two ends'.

These ventures, by compromising the reputation of Scotch tweed, brought little success, and embarrassment to all. A well disposed Yorkshireman declared in 1898 that 'some Scotch makers have ruined their trade and name by making low-cloths and the word

Scotch is getting of less value as a character every season'.[56] 'In the old days', echoed the *Yorkshire Post*, 'Scotch tweed, the genuine article, like Scotch whisky, enjoyed as much immunity as Caesar's wife. [Now] Scotchmen cheapen their goods in imitation of the Yorkshiremen. The old Scotch trade has been dished by . . . not sticking to the pure old Scottish tweed that made them their fame and money.'[57] Yarn spinners, too, were involved in this regressive policy, in order to compete with each other and with Belgian yarn in a shrinking market for carded yarns.

This 'putting on the gloves with Dewsbury' usually brought failure to those concerned. As one retired yarn spinner scripturally observed: 'Those who bowed the knee to Baal had grievous reason to regret their apostacy'. Their own individual reputation as producers of genuine tweeds suffered. The market preferred Yorkshire cloth, which, though lacking the superior reputation of Scotch tweed, at least was all it claimed to be.

It seems clear, however, that most of the more important firms in the industry, those who were the largest employers of labour and capital, responded differently to the situation. They modernised their plant, and they refused to lower the standards that had given their products their superlative reputation. Instead they devised new products that followed the general movement in fashion but retained good materials and designing. In practice this meant a shift towards worsted production rather than woollen tweeds in men's goods. The 'Scotch Worsted', which became so popular in these and later years, was born of the problems of the late nineteenth century. By 1897 it was estimated there were many large Scottish firms whose output ranged from 20 per cent to over 90 per cent worsted cloth, and ten years later the same writer concluded that nothing had been so remarkable in the history of the trade than the 'extraordinary increase in worsted fabrics'.[58] Other firms took advantage of the growing 'athletic' trade, by the manufacture of flannel suiting, which required only loosely made light yarns and no milling, coping or tentering. Others began to exploit the growing taste for light tweeds for ladies' wear. In the Hillfoots the most novel development came in infant shawl production—a logical extension of the staple trade of the district. This change was made possible by the introduction of Raschel warp-knitting machines, imported from Germany, which produced fabric made from warp only, without the insertion of any weft.

Such diversification kept the principal Scottish woollen piece-goods manufacturers afloat in a difficult era. By producing genuine products, some businesses maintained a good enough record in this period. Blenkhorn, Richardson of Hawick in the latter years of the century were an example of how energy and enterprise could yield dividends. With mills closing their doors around them, the firm made consistently good profits in the 1890s, and, when it became a limited liability company in 1898, the available shares were subscribed many times over.[59] Crombie's of Aberdeen also responded vigorously to depressed conditions. After the McKinley tariff they switched to the Continental trade, especially to Germany. Though profitability was lower than formerly, Crombie's suffered less than the Border firms, partly perhaps because of their preoccupation with overcoatings, which suffered less than suiting from the worsted invasion, but in part also, to bold management.[60]

There were few crumbs of comfort, however, for the yarn spinners. They were only geared on the whole for the manufacture of carded yarns and their mills were fairly replete with recently acquired capital equipment. Their prosperity largely depended on manufacturing demand, but, as shown above, the manufacturers were increasingly buying in worsted yarn for their mills. On the carded side Belgian and inferior grades were making a profound impact on the Glasgow light woollen and wincey market. Perhaps many spinners were too conservative in outlook, for no attempt was made to introduce worsted spinning into Scotland on any scale. One firm that did install combing plant, however, Paton's of Alloa, achieved a real measure of expansion during this period both in manufacturing and hand-knitting yarns.

One cannot generalise, therefore, about the level of entrepreneurial ability in the Scottish woollen industry. Manufacturers reacted in different ways with varying degrees of success or failure. Like most other sectors of the economy the Scottish woollen industry had its fair share of talent and inadequacy. Certain areas of general difficulty and weakness in the industry, however, militated against successful adaptation to new highly competitive conditions, and its production costs were probably higher than

Yorkshire's and the Continent's. Its concentration on quality had ensured that prices were thought of as being added to cost, rather than costs being assessed in relation to a preconceived final price. On the whole Scottish firms had acted as price leaders to the whole British industry and had usually obtained their figure when trade was buoyant. The nature of production ensured that costs were high. Normally only virgin wool was employed, not waste or mungo, and individual tastes were catered for. The Scotch tweed trade was largely a 'one-off' trade, with few lengthy runs. The shorter the warp the greater the cost per unit of production. Such a trade put a premium on designers and pattern-weavers, who were expensive to maintain; large numbers of trial patterns had to be produced from which merchants could choose. A firm with an annual turnover of about 12,000 pieces made about 1,500 ranges of eighty to 100 patterns each in a year, or 150,000 different patterns. For every pattern chosen, manufacturers had to make large patterns varying from ¼yd to 2¼yd each, which cost about double price but were charged the same price as the goods. Commonly buyers only ordered piece-lengths from about half the large patterns supplied; and half those orders would be for two pieces per pattern (manufacturers endeavoured to make this a minimum) and the lengths for the rest would vary from three to thirty pieces per pattern, though runs as high as this were not common in novelty lines.[61] Thus warping was a constant and expensive task, as the procedure was complicated and led to an excessive amount of machine down-time. In addition the amount of warp yarn wasted was the same for patterns as for any cloth length—about 1yd—so in pattern weaving about half the warp was lost. Designing was, therefore, an exceptionally costly part of the productive process, since most of it fell on the manufacturer himself. The hostility expressed by manufacturers towards merchants and others who poached their designs (and there were too many to register them all) was consequently motivated by strong economic as well as ethical considerations. In the highly competitive conditions of the late nineteenth century the procedure by which a Scottish cloth got into the customer's hands was too protracted and costly to enable manufacturers to compete on price with other areas.

Then the industry paid less attention than it should have done to technical education. It was little different from the rest of British industry in that, but such education was perhaps more important to the tweed trade than to some other branches of the economy. The sale of Scottish woollens depended very largely on artistry and superlative skills in the blending of wools and the dyeing of wool yarn and piece lengths, and powerful competition in Europe, clearly portrayed in the Paris International Exhibition of 1867, resulted in the SSCC sending a manufacturer to the Continent to investigate the state of technical education there. In the following year, subsequent to a visit from the Organising Inspector of the Science and Art department, a committee of manufacturers and interested parties was formed with a view to starting classes in Galashiels. Little was achieved, however, and when the Inspector returned in 1871 he was impelled to 'preach a scathing sermon' on the lack of Scottish enterprise, adding that as many examination papers were sent to one small town in Ireland as were sent to the whole of Scotland.[62] As a result a designers' association was formed in Galashiels but soon faded away, though private classes in weaving and designing continued for a few years under the direction of the association's secretary. Buoyant trade for much of the 1870s pushed the need for such training into the background, but interest revived a little as trade faltered in the 1880s. Again classes operated perfunctorily in Galashiels under the auspices of the Mechanics Institute and paid for by a manufacturers' levy. Though the Galashiels local school board adopted the Technical Schools Act of 1887, little was done, and not until 1901 was a movement set in motion to establish a Technical College geared to the woollen industry, a venture that achieved final success only in 1909.[63]

Though certain manufacturers displayed some interest in technical education for their workpeople, most of them failed to see the importance of the issue. They looked askance at formal education, preferring men firmly rooted in traditional mill practices. 'As everyone who works in a factory knows,' stated a student in the local press, 'a good church membership, with a capacity for whistling the proper tune into the ear of the proper person is far more likely to advance your interests than all the technical education that could ever be imparted.'[64] Technical training, insomuch as there was any, was regarded more as a convenient way of extending mill education than important for its own sake. Hence fresh ideas did not reach the mills, so that when the resources of the industry were stretched, much was found wanting. The Yorkshire manufacturers and Continental spinners appeared to some at least to manipulate the various grades of wool to better advantage. Technical training was regarded either as unnecessary or irrelevant by short-sighted manufacturers. C. J. Wilson of Hawick in 1905 thought it 'a good thing' but no good for breaking down tariff barriers.[65] A Galashiels colleague spoke similarly: 'I have not much belief in a two or three years' course at a technical centre turning out the best workmen. Practical training is required adapted to the stage the workman is at . . .'.[66] Perhaps it was significant that when Crombie's of Aberdeen wanted to train their manager in designing they sent him to Germany.[67]

Another handicap in the late nineteenth century was the industry's highly competitive and fragmented structure. This was equally applicable to the English branch of the trade, but the way out for the manufacturer there was comparatively simple—a reduction of costs and prices by the increased use of recovered wool. Scottish manufacturers and workpeople alike showed an excessive degree of independence. 'They seldom agree about anything', was the verdict of a prominent Borderer. Competition and individuality had contributed to the virility displayed by the industry in its formative years, but what had hitherto been on balance an asset was now in the changed circumstances of the late nineteenth century a distinct liability. The most important manifestation of this spirit was the lack of a common policy on the terms on which the woollen trade was conducted. Consequently the industry played straight into the hands of the merchant, who could in bad times impose more or less whatever terms he cared to choose. He could always find someone to accept a lower price than his neighbour, and this further encouraged cloth adulteration and a general lowering of standards. The result was suspicion and disagreement at a time when a common front was most desirable. 'The manufacturers have themselves to thank in no small measure for the present unsatisfactory condition of the industry', reproved *The Times*. 'Internecine competition is very keen and combination seems impossible . . . the idea of [any] "gentleman's agreement" is scouted as not worthy of consideration.'[68] The same theme was echoed by the *Glasgow Herald*, which warned that some regulation of pattern lengths, terms and even prices would have to be considered.[69] No cooperation was achieved, or indeed sought, on these matters, however. The industry continued to be notorious for the length of its credit terms and its liberal policy on patterns, and made little headway before 1913 in obtaining a trademark for its products owing to difficulties in arriving at a satisfactory definition of 'Scotch tweed'.[70]

In the first part of this chapter it was noted that the surviving business records suggest that some improvement in prices and profits, and considerable increases in output, took place in the industry from the early years of the present century down to World War I. Those firms strong enough to survive the 1890s took full advantage of the reduced capacity of the industry during these years. Ballantyne's, for example, increased production from 300,000 ells in 1900 to 433,000 ells in 1907. Sales turnover rose 50 per cent between 1903 and 1911 as prices and production moved upwards.[71] Crombie's likewise expanded output greatly, from fewer than 9,000 pieces in 1901 to 22,000 pieces in 1910. These firms shared in a general recovery, for the value of piece goods exported through Scottish ports rose from £202,000 in 1900 to £257,000 in 1912.[72] One cause of this recovery was the great rise in Australian wool prices, which tended to switch demand from Botany worsteds back to the Scotch woollen tweeds made from Cheviot or similar qualities. The latter rose in price also, but not so steeply as imported long wools. Cheviot white wool, whose price had fallen from 30s per stone (24lb) in 1880 to only 13s in 1902 rose to 27s in 1906. Though dropping temporarily, in the ensuing depression, the price of Cheviot remained inflated down to the war.[73] Australian wools were even dearer, however, advancing from 6d to 10d per lb between 1901 and 1906 because of stock depletion from severe drought and to the great demand stemming from America and other countries. Manufacturers, though busier than previously, were not able at first to improve their profitability. Demand recovered only slowly in the early years of the century and there were setbacks in 1904-5 and again in 1907. Thus cloth prices, though rising, did not keep pace with wool prices. When the latter fell in 1907-8, merchants immediately demanded a reduction in cloth prices, though some manufacturers had not yet paid for their wool stocks. Profitability was improved when better supply coincided with good demand after 1909. Wool prices then fell as supply more than met demand. Even so, many firms still found it hard to keep busy, some falling back on government orders and commission work. The revival in trade that undoubtedly occurred, therefore, should not deceive us into thinking that the industry's troubles of previous decades had been permanently overcome.

To summarise, the decades before 1914 were an unprecedented test for the Scottish woollen industry, as they were for the economy in general. Throughout the nineteenth century the Scots had taken full advantage of a product of distinctiveness and craftsmanship that led the way in men's, and sometimes ladies', fashion. A large, perhaps over-large, export trade had been built up with primary producers and young industrialising nations in the temperate zone. Many of these were peopled either by British expatriates or other Europeans with similar consumption patterns to those in the United Kingdom. By the 1880s, however, the industry's honeymoon period was ending. Other countries were experiencing their own industrial revolutions, and, as Britain had done, though to a greater extent, made use of a widely diffused indigenous craft to foster their textile industries. Immigration policy and borrowed technology ensured that knowledge and output was quickly built up. The tariffs erected, therefore, soon affected a wider range than the cheapest products. This was particularly true of the United States, with the result that the Scottish-American trade was all but wrecked. Partial compensation was obtained by exploiting Continental and colonial markets, Canada's especially, but here, too, tariffs made progress difficult. The logical step was to turn to the home market, but here again the industry suffered frustration as fashion turned from the tweedmakers towards the manufacturers of light smooth-faced cheaper fabrics. Simultaneously progress in ready-made clothes was causing a radical change in distribution methods, which, by favouring long runs of standard-type cloths in the medium qualities, worked against the Scottish woollen trade.

Severe competition was felt from Yorkshire—from the Colne Valley mills in cheap woollens and from Huddersfield fancy worsted makers in the novelty trade. Whereas the Yorkshire woollen trade overcame international restrictions by reducing material costs, this course was fraught with dangers in an industry with a reputation for quality. Scottish firms that sought the same solution as the West Riding generally brought calamity to themselves and suspicion to all. Mill closures, idle plant and unemployment resulted. On the whole the successful mills were those who invested in new plant and, more important, in new products.

The long-term prospect for the industry was not bright. The size of the market for individual and durable fancy clothing was no longer sufficient to maintain all firms in full employment for long periods. The drift towards more standardised, more expendable clothing was permanent. Meanwhile, however, the inevitable reckoning with these problems was delayed. The clouds were thickening on the political horizon of Europe, and the tweedmakers had fortunes to make in a very different market—service uniforms. The industry turned from multiple fancies to the production of long runs of standardised khaki cloths, where designing was at a discount.

SIX

Labour Earnings
and Industrial Relations

'Orr—*invariably late of a morning and meals which don't like . . .*
Morgan—gross carelessness, annoys the women and saucy when spoken
to . . . ' Jas Johnston, 1863

In his study of the industries of Scotland first published in 1869
David Bremner stated that the Scottish woollen workers enjoyed
'a [family] income equal to that of many persons who have to
maintain a far higher social position' and that 'trade unionism, if
not a thing unknown, has seldom or never exercised its power for
evil in the trade'.[1] If this was so, one must needs ask how it came
about and whether this observation is applicable to later decades
in the nineteenth century.

Any person attempting to measure accurately the return of
labour in the woollen industry is immediately confronted with
special complicating factors. Firstly, for most of the nineteenth
century there was no standard pricing system for labour in the industry—each mill paid its own rates. It is probable, however,
that wage rates between various mills in Hawick or Galashiels did
not vary too much. When asked by the Royal Commission on
Labour in 1891 whether wage rates differed much between mills,
C. J. Wilson of Hawick replied: 'I should say not very much'.
Variations were due to differences in the kind or quality of work
performed in the mills, which highlights a further general problem

that some workers with a common designation were not necessarily engaged upon identical work and did not receive comparable rates of pay. For example, a weaver of plain goods was paid differently to one weaving fancies; the latter may have possessed more skill and the intricacy of his work would be taken into consideration, for he probably had to work more slowly to avoid breakages or take more time over careful darning when faults did occur. Again, towards the end of the century, the rates of remuneration for weavers depended on whether they were engaged on 'fast' or 'slow' looms. Furthermore, some workers were employed on a piece work basis, others were paid by the hour, and a few annually. Thirdly, actual net earnings varied much according to local conditions: before 1849, for example, the weavers of Galashiels had to pay for their own light and weft winding, a burden assumed by the employers after a three-week strike. Spinners' seemingly high earnings were considerably reduced by their having to pay a substantial part of the wages of their piecers. Tartan weavers in the Hillfoots had to pay for their own weft winding. Cottage weavers there in the 1830s were subject to incidental costs amounting to about 1s 8d weekly, made up of 1s for winding, 4d for loom stance or rent, 2d for lighting, and 2d for wear and tear of looms, mounting, etc.[2] Thus it is difficult to compile figures for earnings that are comparable over periods of time or between different districts. Further, money earnings were sometimes supplemented by real benefits such as cheap accommodation or gardens. Finally there is the general problem of inadequate data, especially in the early years of the century. For other decades extant business records are useful but by no means numerous enough for one to generalise on the level of earnings.

In the absence of perfect tools, however, the enquirer must use imperfect ones. The data discussed below are largely based on official estimates given by the Hand-Loom Commissioners in 1838, on estimates given by various other commentators, and on the small sample of business archives—probably enough to show the trend of earnings in the nineteenth century. Much of this evidence relates to handloom weavers, important workers in the industry till the mid-1860s. Other workers' incomes, except those of departmental foremen and perhaps some male spinners, were lower.

Since the weaving process is basic to the industry, it is likely that fluctuations in weavers' earnings were accompanied by variations in those of other workers.

Table 9, compiled from fragmentary data from the southern counties of Scotland, suggests that a handloom weaver (invariably a man in this region) could earn between 15s and 18s weekly in the early 1830s, a level about double that which obtained at the outset of the Napoleonic Wars. Unfortunately the evidence is too slim to indicate what happened to wages during the remainder of the war or whether any real gains were made when prices fell afterwards. Trade revived strongly in the 1820s, however, and, given that he was not threatened as yet by technical change, the handloom weaver probably made real gains in income during these years.

TABLE 9

AVERAGE WEEKLY GROSS EARNINGS OF HANDLOOM
WEAVERS IN THE BORDERS, 1793-1850[3]

	s	d		s	d
1793	8	0	-	9	6
1794	7	6	-	10	0
1829	12	0			
1830-32	15	0	-	18	0
1833-35	13	0	-	17	0
1836-8	12	0	-	17	0
1846-8	14	6			
1849-50	12	0			

Table 9 also suggests that earnings from weaving tended to fall through the 1830s, though the industry expanded considerably during the decade. This fall was, however, mainly experienced by weavers of plain goods, reflecting the decline of the old trade in traditional blues and drabs. One interpretation of the data is that many coarse-goods weavers who switched to making fancy tweeds had a mildly deflating influence on the earnings of the first-class weavers, but the evidence is too weak for certainty. By 1846 weavers at Ballantyne's loom-shops in Galashiels were averaging 18s weekly if employed full time. The depression of the late 1840s struck hard for a brief period, however, and average earnings fell to only 10s 4d in 1849.[4]

For skilled male machine-spinners during this period there is even less evidence. A jenny-spinner in the Hillfoots was reckoned to net about 9s per week in the 1790s and probably 13s in Galashiels in 1829 (a bad year for local industry).[5] By the mid-1830s Galashiels spinners were said to earn about 17s weekly, but piecers' earnings (maybe the spinner's own children) of about 3s would have to be deducted from this sum.[6] If one bears in mind that charges for light, weft-winding and sometimes loom space were deducted from handloom weavers' earnings till 1849, there was probably little difference in the earnings of male operatives engaged in spinning in the main centres of the industry.

Individual earnings, however, were often markedly different from the occupational mean: one Robert Bryden, for example, a Hawick weaver, earned a weekly average of £1 3s 5d over six weeks of full work in 1838, but a colleague was able to muster only 10s 8½d.[7] Earnings among handloom weavers depended not only on the regularity with which they were supplied with webs but on their energy and skill and on the type of goods upon which they were engaged. The finer and more intricate the work, the higher was the weaving 'price', which usually meant that piece-work earnings tended to be higher also. The price allowed for particular grades of goods was not often altered, but in times of technological change or dull trade employers had an interest in revising it downwards.

Table 10 suggests that earnings of handloom weavers improved considerably once more in the 1850s, in Galashiels at least, faltered in the depressed conditions at the end of the decade, to recover once more in the 1860s despite the presence of an increasing number of power looms operated by cheap female labour. Indeed the peak earnings for hand-weavers at Ballantyne's occurred as late as 1864, five years *after* the first introduction of steam looms, under the impetus of rapidly expanding output and (possibly) the reservation to hand-weavers of a considerable proportion of the more intricate work.

However, the steam loom spelt the eventual doom of commercial hand-weavers and with them went the considerable differential between their earnings and other workers'. From Table 10 it can be seen that from the outset power-loom weavers (mainly women) earned much less than the average for all the firm's workers, and

TABLE 10

AVERAGE WEEKLY NET EARNINGS OF WOOLLEN
WORKERS (FULL-TIME) AT HENRY BALLANTYNE & SONS,
GALASHIELS AND WALKERBURN, 1850-79[8]

Date	Handloom weavers (m) (Galashiels)		Power-loom weavers (f) (Walkerburn)		All workers	
	s	d	s	d	s	d
1850-2	13	7	—		9	3
1852-4	15	4	—		10	0
1854-6	20	3	—		12	6
1856-8	10	10	—		12	10
1858-60	19	7	11	8	14	0
1860-2	19	10	11	1	13	10
1862-4	21	8	12	9	15	3
1864-6	22	7	13	2	15	9
1866-8	20	10	12	10	15	0
1868-70	—		13	6	13	9
1870-3	—		11	7	14	1
1873-6	—		12	10	17	8
1876-9	—		13	11	17	4

this remained so after the inflationary effect of hand-weavers' earnings had ceased to operate in the firm. The records of the business, nonetheless, suggest that woollen workers made substantial gains in the third quarter of the century. Taking 1850 as 100, this firm's wage index rose to 179 in 1864 and 197 by 1876.

In the later years of the century national prices dropped distinctly while wages remained stagnant. In consequence, the standard of living rose, especially as food prices fell steeply. As we have seen, in the 1880s the Scottish woollen industry itself en-

TABLE 11

AVERAGE WEEKLY EARNINGS OF ALL WOOLLEN
WORKERS AT H. BALLANTYNE & SONS, WALKERBURN, 1876-1906 (NET PAY)[9]

	s	d
1876-9	17	4
1880-2	18	0
1883-5	17	6
1886-8	18	3
1889-91	19	7
1892-4	17	4
1895-7	17	10
1896-1900	15	7
1901-3	21	5
1904-6	22	7

L

tered upon a long period of dull trade, falling prices and sagging margins, and the long period of growth in employees' incomes was halted for a generation or so. Table 11 shows that wages at Ballantyne's remained virtually static from the late 1870s to the late 1890s, reviving again only when the national price level began to rise at the end of the century.

A rather similar picture in a northern specialist firm is revealed in Table 12, though here revival seems to have occurred a little earlier, in the mid-1890s.

TABLE 12

AVERAGE WEEKLY NET EARNINGS OF ALL EMPLOYEES
AT JAMES JOHNSTON & CO, NEWMILL, ELGIN, 1877-1911[10]

	s	d
1877-9	9	3
1880-4	11	4
1885-9	11	2
1890-3	11	7
1894-9	13	5
1900-5	15	10
1906-11	18	11

Other evidence suggests that the experience of these firms was typical of the industry. In 1905 it was stated that labour prices at Innerleithen had remained unchanged for twenty years, suggesting stagnant earnings also. In the same year the general level of weavers' earnings in Hawick was held to be a good deal lower than 'formerly', a clear allusion, in the context, to the years before 1890.[11] Again, the average earnings of power-loom weavers in Hawick in 1901, at about 18s weekly, were no higher than in the mid-1880s.[12]

Given the absence of strong unionism in the industry, we should be more surprised that earnings did not fall appreciably rather than fail to rise in these years of difficulty. Doubtless some firms cut their workforce, thus permitting more regular work for the remainder, and manufacturers who installed the 'fast' power looms passed on some of the benefit from increased productivity to their weavers. We should also bear in mind that in this period of generally falling prices static money earnings, or even mildly falling ones, nonetheless represented some gain in real terms.

Trade revived markedly, however, in the years down to 1914,

except between 1907 and 1909. Average earnings of Galashiels power-weavers began to rise slightly from about 1905 to around £1 for all classes compared with about 18s formerly.[13] At Ballantyne's mills average earnings of the whole labour force rose sharply from 15s 7d in 1900 to 22s 7d by 1906. At Johnston's mill in Elgin average earnings reacted similarly.[14] Thus on the eve of World War I earnings in the industry were probably 50 per cent higher than in the 1880s and 1890s in many firms, but no higher than had been achieved by some workers in the 1860s.

Wage movements, therefore, fall into three distinct periods from 1830 to 1914: from the 1830s to the mid-1880s the trend was upward, gently at first but more strongly in the years after 1850; then earnings remained the same for much of the period between the mid-1880s and about 1900-05; thereafter a steep increase occurred down to 1912-14. Despite these quite sharply defined spans of time, earnings could fluctuate considerably over short periods. Table 13 shows earnings of a group of handloom weavers employed full-time by Henry Ballantyne between 1846 and 1856.

TABLE 13

ANNUAL NET EARNINGS OF FOUR FULL-TIME HANDLOOM
WEAVERS, H. BALLANTYNE OF GALASHIELS AND WALKERBURN, 1846-56[15]

Year	*D. Tait* £ s d	*Will Rankin* £ s d	*Will Cockburn* £ s d	*Rob Turner* £ s d
1846	38 11 0	43 1 6	42 0 0	not employed
1847	28 14 8	39 4 4	34 14 0	,, ,,
1848	25 11 4	30 11 7	not employed	,, ,,
1849	28 6 10	33 6 0	,, ,,	,, ,,
1850	39 0 6	not employed	34 0 0	37 16 3
1851	36 8 10	43 10 4	38 18 0	38 7 4
1852	30 9 8	37 2 4	30 11 0	not employed
1853	40 3 0	42 1 6	not employed	44 2 0
1854	44 3 3	37 10 9	,, ,,	50 0 3
1855	not employed	36 12 7	,, ,,	55 17 6
1856	48 3 2	not employed	,, ,,	69 6 6

As most of the work in the industry was done to order, any oscillation in the state of trade made itself immediately felt in employment and activity, so that earnings provide a good barometer of the state of trade in general.

Any attempt to compare earnings between different regions

associated with woollen manufacturing is difficult. One of the chief problems is the selection of an area comparable to the tweed industry in type of work and conditions. The nearest approach was the Huddersfield fancy worsted industry, where goods of superior quality were made, a similar high percentage of female labour, especially weavers, was employed in the second half of the century, and a weaver usually operated no more than a single loom, as in the Borders.

The earnings of handloom weavers in the Huddersfield district in the 1830s appear to have been comparable to those in the Borders, averaging between 12s and 14s weekly. For the 1840s the evidence is limited, but probably little change took place in the relative levels of the two areas: Huddersfield hand-weavers earned about 14s per week in 1843 and, in the depressed years at the end of the decade, 10s to 12s,[16] which may be compared with the earnings of Ballantyne's weavers in Galashiels in 1847-9 of 11s 9d. The wages of handloom weavers in the Borders in the 1850s may have increased more rapidly than those of Huddersfield, since between 1859 and 1861 the latter averaged about 16s weekly and Ballantyne's workers over £1.[17] Female power-loom weavers in the 1860s and 1870s in both areas appear to have been roughly similar, from 12s to 15s weekly; the level in Huddersfield in 1871 of 11s to 16s compares with an average figure for all weavers at W. Watson's Hawick mills of 12s 6d in 1872 and about the same figure at Ballantyne's at Walkerburn. A more detailed comparison is afforded by the Returns of Wages in 1877 (see Table 14). According to these, men's wages in many occupations in the tweed industry were consistently lower than their counterparts in Yorkshire, especially for departmental heads. A scribbling foreman in the Galashiels district, for example, could expect to earn 25s to 50s per week, compared with 50s to 60s in Huddersfield. However, certain categories of design and finishing work were better paid in the Borders—clearly apparent on the women's side—skilled knotters, menders, and burlers, for example, earning between 15s and £1 weekly in the Galashiels area as opposed to 9s to 12s in Huddersfield.

Wage returns for various districts of the United Kingdom also were taken in 1885, and are reproduced in Table 15, though the fact that 1885 was a depressed year invalidates this evidence some-

TABLE 14

COMPARISON OF WEEKLY EARNINGS IN GALASHIELS
& DISTRICT AND HUDDERSFIELD, 1877[18]

| | Men | | Women | |
Occupation	*Galashiels*	*Huddersfield*	*Galashiels*	*Huddersfield*
Wool sorters	27s	27s	-	-
Foremen sorters	30s	-	-	-
Securers & Driers	20s-24s	21s-23s	-	-
Dyers	18s-20s	22s-24s	-	-
Foremen dyers	30s-44s	50s-60s	-	-
Teazers & Willyers	18s-21s	-	-	-
Scribblers	17s-18s	-	-	-
Foremen scribblers	25s-50s	50s-60s	-	-
Feeder scribblers	17s	-	11s	11s (1880)
Condenser minders	17s-18s	-	-	10s-12s
Spinners & Twist	25s-13s 6d	30s-40s	-	-
Foremen spinners	28s	35s-45s	-	-
Warpers/beamers	25s-28s	25s-28s	-	-
Healders	25s	-	15s	-
Foremen healders	25s	-	-	-
Winders	-	-	12s-14s	9s-12s
Fettlers	19s	20s-22s	-	-
Pattern designers	32s-70s	50s-60s	-	-
Pattern weavers	25s-30s	25s-30s	-	-
Weavers	22s	20s-35s	15s	-
Foremen weavers	28s-30s	-	-	-
Burlers	15s	-	15s-16s	9s-12s
Knotters/menders	-	-	15s-19s 9d	10s-12s
Fullers	18s-19s 6d	22s-25s	-	-
Foremen fullers	23s-34s	40s-50s	-	-
in Yarn store	20s-24s	-	-	-
Foremen in yarn store	30s	-	-	-
Dressers/Giggers	26s	24s-25s	-	-
Tenterers	18s 6d-20s	24s-25s	-	-
Cutters or Croppers	20s-28s	24s-26s	-	-
Press setters	18s-22s	26s-28s	-	-
Steamers	16s-19s 6d	24s-26s	-	-
Finish/Foremen	26s	-	-	-
Drawers	24s	-	12s	-
Engine tenters	24s-28s	25s-30s	-	-
Stokers	23s-25s	24s-28s	-	-
Mechanics	26s-31s	30s-40s	-	-
Warehousemen	31s 6d-50s	20s-25s	-	-
Labourers	18s-19s	20s-22s	-	-
Floor brushers	-	-	11s	-

what. The actual level of earnings in the returns may not be typical, but the relative earnings' level of the various districts were presumably not affected by a recession that was general rather than local in its incidence. Table 15 shows that the Scotch tweed industry in 1885, at £35 per head per annum, fell well below several Yorkshire districts in its average rate of earnings per head, including Huddersfield. But the Border workers were paid about the average rate for the whole industry. Other branches of the Scottish woollen industry, including the Hillfoot shawl trade, with a high percentage of female workers, received less than average earnings. The yarn trade, with average income per head at only £26 per annum, was the worst paid section of the whole industry outside of Ireland. These low averages for branches other than the tweed trade in Scotland brought the Scottish annual average income per head down to £31 compared with £35 in England. As in England earnings in Scotland tended to be higher in the towns, there being considerable differences between earnings in the Borders and elsewhere, where the market for labour was less favourable, seasonal fluctuation more severe, or plainer goods made.

TABLE 15

COMPARISON OF AVERAGE ANNUAL RATES OF PAY
PER HEAD IN DIFFERENT BRANCHES OF THE
WOOLLEN INDUSTRY OF GREAT BRITAIN IN 1885[19]

	£
Dewsbury (coatings)	39
Huddersfield	39
Halifax	38
Dewsbury (blankets)	36
Scotland (tweeds)	35
Leeds and district	35
Scotland (shawls)	34
West of England	31
Scotland (shirtings and blankets)	31
Wales	30
Scotland (yarn)	26
Ireland	21

Detailed comparisons of earnings throughout the industry were also taken in one pay week in 1906, and these are set out in Table 16. Here the high earning power of female weavers is very marked, and the high proportion of these workers in the main Border

TABLE 16

EARNINGS IN THE WOOLLEN INDUSTY (WKLY, FULL-TIME), 1906[20]

Average Earnings of Operatives working Full Time in the last pay week, September 1906

District	Men		Boys Full Timers		Boys Half Timers		Women		Girls Full Timers		Girls Half Timers		All Workpeople	
	s	d	s	d	s	d	s	d	s	d	s	d	s	d
Huddersfield	27	4	11	2	3	2	17	1	9	8	3	3	20	1
Leeds	29	2	10	5	3	7	13	9	9	10	3	8	15	11
Dewsbury & Batley	27	2	11	1	3	4	15	0	9	11	3	0	17	11
Halifax	26	0	9	7	3	2	12	4	9	0	3	3	13	0
Bradford	27	2	9	9	3	9	12	7	9	5	3	8	12	11
Keighley	26	2	10	3	3	10	13	6	10	2	4	1	14	0
Rest of WR	27	0	9	8	3	5	12	11	7	9	3	6	15	9
All Yorkshire	27	3	10	3	3	8	13	10	9	6	3	8	15	9
West of England	21	9	9	4	3	6	11	3	8	6	—		13	11
Rox, Selk, Peebles	27	7	10	6	—		18	6	8	6	—		19	8
Rest of Scotland	23	11	8	11	3	0	11	8	7	4	3	2	14	0
Rest of UK	24	10	9	8	3	2	12	11	7	9	3	2	14	11
All UK	26	10	10	2	—		13	10	9	3	3	8	15	9

counties helped to give all women workers there higher average earnings than in any other district in the industry in Britain. Men, too, appeared to have improved their position since the 1880s, though only marginally, perhaps as a result of considerable emigration from the Borders in the 1890s. Their average weekly earnings per head were slightly above those in Huddersfield but still well below rates in Leeds. The average weekly income of all workers in the main Border manufacturing counties in 1906 was about the same as in the Huddersfield district, but appreciably more, even when the shortcomings of the evidence are allowed for, than in other districts.

As in 1885 other parts of Scotland compared less favourably with English districts in 1906. According to Table 16 men's earnings in the Rest of Scotland were below the UK average, though higher than in the West of England trade; Women, too, earned less, averaging only 11s 8d per week compared with 18s 6d in the Borders. The large difference between wages in the Borders and in other Scottish districts is again borne out by other evidence: female power-weavers at Aberdeen's Grandholm Mills in 1891 averaged only 13s 9d per week compared with between 16s and £1 in the Borders; workers' earnings in 1905 were more than 25 per cent lower at Newmill, Elgin, than at Ballantyne's of Walkerburn in 1906.[21]

It may be concluded then that workers in the tweed district of the woollen industry in Scotland were paid at roughly the rates prevailing in the main manufacturing centres in England, while some, especially women weavers, earned rates that were second to none, to some extent justifying certain manufacturers' claims that workers there were the highest paid in the country. Other Scottish districts, however, were some of the worst paid woollen areas in the industry.

There is some suggestion in the evidence that male earnings in the Borders suffered from the lack of balancing industry in the area, but the main conclusion to be drawn is that the charge sometimes put forward that the industry grew up on high profits and untypically low wages cannot be substantiated. By the standards operating in the whole of the woollen industry at the time most Border woollen workers were reasonably well paid, though unskilled workers must perhaps be excluded from such a generalisation. Some manufacturers kept up wages in order to preserve good standards of workmanship and prevent migration to other industrial areas, and actually entered into agreements to keep up wages of woollen weavers in order to maintain the quality of the fabric.[22] Employers sometimes appear to have been motivated by other than purely economic reasons in this respect. Border workers became identified with intelligence and responsibility in their conduct as citizens and employees, so that employers had no desire to see the workforce diluted by other lower elements. If wages remained satisfactory, good workers would not leave, and any would-be incomers could be handpicked if a 'high-wage policy' was operated. This attitude, which is underlined by the fact that many of the manufacturers were leaders of local society, some becoming magistrates and provosts, is well illustrated by their refusal to use their capital to diversify the local economy in the 1890s. Suggestions for the erection of ready-made clothing factories foundered mainly on the grounds that they would encourage the import of cheap labour into the area, with all the social strain that might ensue.[23]

Observers of Border life in the nineteenth century were unanimous in describing the condition of the working classes as good, and notably better than many workers elsewhere. In the late 1830s the Assistant Handloom Commissioners felt that woollen weavers were 'wholly removed from distress', in marked contrast in weavers in the cotton industry. The weavers' homes exhibited 'every sympton of comfort'; and the class was removed from 'the demoralising influences and the physical disadvantages of large towns', uniting the 'cleanliness and salubrity of the country with the comfort of easy circumstances'. They were also 'more moral' and generally educated their children.[24] Weavers were then the aristocrats of labour in the woollen industry, and we must not suppose that all workers shared their standard; the towns became more unhealthy as they grew, but there was no doubt in the Commissioners' minds that woollen workers had a materially better standard of life than had the western cotton weavers. In the 'Report on Arrestment of Wages' presented in 1854 very few cases of small debt were said to occur in the district, and when they did the culprit was often an incomer. The Report was careful to stress the thriftiness of the local population, pointing to the prosperity of the cooperative stores by way of example (as did the Royal Commission on Labour in 1891). It concluded that 'in the Border manufacturing districts . . . the habits of the people are conspicuous for a self adjusted regularity . . . '.[25] Bremner added in the late 1860s that squalid poverty was unknown in Galashiels, the workers being able to afford high rents. Building societies, banks and benefit institutions all throve in the district.[26] This picture of general prosperity among the working classes did not change much in the difficult years towards the end of the century. In the 1890s the manufacturers, at any rate, considered that workers had never been so well off despite increasing irregularity of work, while Hawick in 1912 was described as one of the best paid industrial towns in the country, the population being well housed, well dressed and 'able to maintain themselves in comfort'.[27]

Table 17 attempts statistically to assess this evidence, none of which was given by workmen themselves. The index of real income for handloom weavers at Ballantyne's in the 1850s shows that solid gains were made in the period. Real income in the period 1858-60 averaged about 30 per cent more than at the beginning of the decade, which was, admittedly, a time when the industry was emerging from depression. This level was maintained into the early 1860s and, after a brief fall, rose to new heights around the middle of the decade. All workers shared in this rise in the standard of living. After an initial fall in real earnings in the early 1850s rapid increases followed down to the mid-1860s, whereafter the index shows a considerable fall in real income per head down to the early 1870s. Rapid gains in the so-called 'Great Depression' years, however, continued unchecked into the early 1890s. Thereafter came a further loss in real income during this depressed decade, but, as a high level of activity was resumed after the turn of the century, real earnings also moved upward and stood in 1906 about 130 per cent above the level of 1850. The workers in this firm, therefore, experienced no marked turning point in the mid-1890s, as occurred in some other sections of British industry. This may have been partly due to the fact that many workers had left the district, creating a labour shortage in the area when trade revived.

The trend of real earnings after 1906 is hard to determine, because of lack of data, but there is some evidence that prices rose more rapidly than wages. The wages paid at Galashiels between 1905 and 1912 were said to have remained unchanged, whereas provision and fuel prices were purported to be extremely high.[28] The 'Report on the Cost of Living of the Working Classes' in 1908 claimed that Galashiels prices were the highest in Scotland, and a similar survey taken in 1912 revealed that food and coal prices were higher in only one other town of eighty-eight investigated in Britain. Between 1905 and 1912 rents in Galashiels rose by 7 per

TABLE 17

INDEX OF REAL AND MONEY INCOME OF HAND-WEAVERS
AND ALL WORKERS AT
H. BALLANTYNE & SONS, GALASHIELS & WALKERBURN, 1850-1906[29]
(1850 = 100)

Period	Handloom Weavers (Piece-work)		Total Workers (Piece & Time)	
	Average money earnings	*Real Income*	*Average money earnings*	*Real Income*
1850-52	99	101	98	99
1852-4	115	106	105	96
1854-6	148	119	130	104
1856-8	146	123	135	115
1858-60	143	131	147	134
1860-62	145	129	156	140
1862-4	158	117	161	149
1864-6	165	152	171	156
1866-8	152	134	158	139
1868-70	—	—	145	128
1870-73	—	—	148	126
1873-6	—	—	177	154
1876-9	—	—	184	173
1879-82	—	—	181	173
1882-5	—	—	187	186
1885-8	—	—	189	205
1888-91	—	—	200	221
1891-4	—	—	195	217
1894-7	—	—	185	214
1897-1900	—	—	176	201
1900-03	—	—	195	215
1903-6	—	—	232	233

cent, the highest increase except one among ten Scottish towns surveyed.[30] Thus it would appear that the steady increases in real income over the second half of the nineteenth century were halted and even reversed in the decade before 1914.

Nonetheless the development of the factory system of woollen manufacture in the Borders not only brought rich rewards to its promoters but real improvement in the lives of its labour force. In the 1870s and 1880s many of the main Border towns were rebuilt; and factories on the whole were clean, well lit and airy. In the early 1890s many woollen workers were buying their own houses through local building societies.[31] The coming of industrialisation in the Borders was gradual enough to avoid some of the more violent social stresses associated with the factory system in other areas. The craft element in the industry was never completely eliminated by mechanisation, and skilled intelligent workmen predominated. Despite some fondness for the bottle they took a keen interest in politics, religion and, ironically, the temperance movement. Hawick took to Chartism with much enthusiasm, and was the site of one of the earliest and most successful Chartist stores in Scotland. Galashiels soon followed suit, under the leadership of William Sanderson, a prominent advocate of co-operative trading.[32]

An outstanding feature of the Scottish woollen districts was the almost total lack of formal union organisation among the workpeople for much of the century. One Hawick employer in his evidence before the 1891 Labour Commission said that he had few dealings with union officials because unions hardly existed.[33] Later, in 1905, the same manufacturer suggested with pride that the industry paid the highest wages in the country 'in the absence of unions'.[34] In 1907 J. H. Clapham observed only one union in the Borders among the woollen workers, and that had only 114 members.[35]

It is tempting to link the weakness of trade unionism with the high proportion of female workers, for in the Border mills about 60 per cent of the workforce were women. Female earnings were often part of family income, 'extra' to earnings of the breadwinner. With several children employed at the local mill family income could be quite high. No doubt the demand for female as well as male labour helped to reduce tension through poverty in the workforce, but it can hardly be claimed that women were inherently less militant than their menfolk. In 1907 there were twice as many women in unions than there were men, and women figured prominently in the Hawick weavers' strike in 1887.

The weakness of trade unionism might have been due to the number of trades in the workforce, workers possessing different skills not always having identical interests. This was particularly clear among the weavers. When combined action did occur it tended to be along craft lines within the mill workforce, without embracing the whole of it. Furthermore the units of production were small, men and management were not far removed and, in the formative period of the industry, usually possessed common roots. Industrial relations, therefore, in the first generation of ownership at least, were intimate and informal, employers taking their places on the mill floor to further production in one department or another. Some mills did not even possess a proper office, ledgers being piled on a windowsill or similar shelf.[36] Management and men recognised no social barrier; for the mills and the mill towns were closely knit, and no serious class differences could readily evolve. Millowners on the whole identified themselves with their town, living there or nearby rather than in exclusive residential suburbs, and actively participating in local politics and social life.

In the second half of the nineteenth century such relationships were forced to change. As business expanded, the mill proprietor had to spend more time off the floor and to delegate responsibility. With the greater use of expensive plant, informal working attitudes could no longer be accepted and fines for lateness and poor performance were widely introduced.[37] Inevitably a wider gulf began to separate workers and management, accompanied by some increased tension between the two groups. Towards the end of the century a combination of unstable trading conditions and technical change led to sporadic outburts of union activity, in contrast to normal times, when the main objects of trade unionism—security of employment, 'adequate' pay and conditions—could be attained without recourse to formal organisation. Though the unions that emerged towards the end of the century were usually ephemeral, they often lasted long enough to secure their immediate objectives. Dyers, for example, who formed a union in Hawick in 1889 secured a pay increase and then dissolved themselves;[38] in 1887 women 'fast' loom weavers in Hawick organised themselves to secure the pay differential between themselves and the 'slow' loom weavers before the union disbanded; and dull trade and the threat of piece rate reductions led the Galashiels power-loom weavers to form a branch of the Amalgamated Weavers Association in the town in 1895.[39]

This kind of formal grouping was even then the exception rather than the rule. The prevailing attitude was of discreet paternalism, which in practice meant a fairly typical Victorian diet of help for self-help. Labour disputes were expected to be settled individually by private interview with the owners, not by official, organised delegations. Workpeople were encouraged to save through mill savings schemes, interest being granted by the employer on funds lodged with the firm. Some businesses operated profit-sharing schemes in which selected workers and salaried staff participated.[40] Though occasionally pensions were granted to faithful servants, or handouts made to celebrate anniversaries or the retirement of a partner, the emphasis was placed on individual thrift and sobriety. A Hawick tweed manufacturer, C. J. Wilson, was happy to state before the Royal Commission on Labour in 1891 that many local workpeople saved with the local building societies, had shares in the local co-ops and were never so happy as when they were cultivating their allotments at the fringes of the burgh.[41] J. & J. Crombie of Aberdeen actually awarded a pay increase to some of their men in the 1880s on condition that it was 'invested in Societies, Insurance or Endowments so as to provide for old-age, ill-health or absence from business'.[42]

In this atmosphere of intimate family-type relationships it is little wonder that unionism failed to germinate. It was viewed as unnecessary by a workforce which, till late in the century, experienced few serious threats to its livelihood and which was not fined or fired arbitrarily by a management that shared the life of the people and knew its workers by their Christian names. But the formal absence of trade-union organisation did not necessarily mean that workers could place no pressure on their employers. The

Galashiels Weavers' Corporation existed into the 1840s, and, by holding a common stock of reeds for the looms, was still strong enough then to place severe obstacles in the way of a newcomer who sought to ignore it; and although it could no longer dictate terms on apprenticeship, it could regulate the supply of labour to some extent. When in 1838 a government inquirer asked if ex-cotton weavers had been engaged by Galashiels clothiers, he was told that the woollen weavers there would not permit it. He himself noted darkly that 'the weavers possess, and equitably exercise the power of preserving a just remuneration for their labour; there is no excess of hands'.[43] In this respect the woollen weavers were able to avoid the weaknesses of their counterparts in the West of Scotland cotton industry; and their bargaining position was enhanced by their not being scattered about in individual country cottages but grouped together in loom-shops, often actually located on mill premises, under the watchful eye of their employer. Though the latter might gain in quality control and have less of his yarn and wool embezzled, the weavers gained the physical proximity that was a prerequisite of successful combination. That such combination could be effective was shown in the depression of 1848-9, when the Galashiels and district weavers struck for three weeks against the employers' attempts (they appear to have combined themselves on this occasion through the Galashiels Manufacturers Association) to reduce weaving prices. After the employers had rejected a schedule of prices submitted by the weavers, the latter sent a delegation to Hawick and the Hillfoots to see what employers were paying there. Eventually they settled for some alteration in prices, but succeeded in ending their own payments for light and weft winding.[44] Such stoppages were rare in the industry, though, because of the complicated job and piece-rate structure, minor disagreements were not. 'The question of pay was a constant source of wrangling and annoyance', wrote an elderly worker concerning the 1840s. 'Few weeks wages were paid without some degree of feeling being shown.'[45]

There is little evidence of combined hostility to the introduction of power looms later. Bremner suggested that weavers refused to work them, so women operatives took them over; but a more likely explanation is that power looms were eased in piece-meal and many hand-weavers employed on highly intricate work were not threatened at first, especially as trade was expanding,[46] and their position was only slowly undermined.

Other highly skilled operatives, especially male supervisory staff, also knew their position to be a strong one. A Galashiels manufacturer admitted to a colleague in the 1850s that his carding manager was most reluctant to train others in his trade, and, because he knew himself to be almost irreplaceable, worked very differently.[47] In 1900 P. & R. Sanderson of Galashiels experienced their 'unorganised' workers' power to protect their position. In an effort to improve productivity the firm endeavoured to break the long tradition of one loom per weaver (itself evidence of strong bargaining power) by putting one worker in charge of two looms operating on plain goods. Presumably a policy of non-cooperation among their employees led Sanderson's to obtain workers from Bradford to operate the looms, but the Yorkshiremen were soon 'influenced to go back' and the experiment was brought to a premature end.[48] Unskilled labour found its own methods of intimidation, for example, by refusing to urinate in the receptacles provided by the management, thus depriving the scouring department of its main source of ammonia!

If the working classes in the woollen industry showed little inclination to form long-term union organisations, the manufacturers showed a similar disregard for employers' associations, cherishing their individuality and often regarding each other with the utmost suspicion. This is important in understanding basic worker attitudes in the industry. It was not a simple 'we' and 'they' situation, although this element is a little more apparent in the 1890s. Each mill was a unit on its own, making its own products in its own avowedly inimitable way. Employees did not sense any major differences of interest between themselves and their particular employer. They acted more as a team with the proprietor of a factory often playing his part as a craftsman on the factory floor, or in the design department. Contact with workers was never lost, for expansion in the industry did not produce large units of production. If one may speak of a 'we' and 'they' attitude, it must be with reference to different mills or manufacturing districts, not different classes. This close identification of the worker with his firm or his type of product and not his class or status is important in explaining the relative lack of concerted action in the industry. For the same reason employers did not band together either. Even when all the dyers' labourers struck in Hawick in 1889 the employers settled the matter at their own mills without referring to one another. Thus workers were not encouraged to combine or agitate on a broad front, for they saw no combination among the potential opposition. One must add this strong psychological factor to the other important economic considerations to explain the relatively uneventful history of labour relations in the industry in the nineteenth century.

M

Epilogue

In 1907, according to the Census of Production, the Scottish woollen industry was responsible for a little over 7 per cent of the total value of the British industry, including worsted manufacturers (see Table 18). If worsted goods are excluded, Scotland accounted for about 11½ per cent of the yardage of woollen goods produced and about 17 per cent of their value. Moreover she produced about 16 per cent of the volume and nearly one-third of the value of carded yarns manufactured in Britain. Although the position of the West Riding, therefore, in the woollen industry was clearly unassailable, the Scottish industry was not insignificant. If one could isolate high quality products from the rest of production, the share

TABLE 18

THE OUTPUT OF THE SCOTTISH AND UNITED
KINGDOM WOOLLEN INDUSTRIES, 1907[1]

Type of goods produced	Quantity produced (Scotland)	Quantity produced (UK)	Value of production (Scotland) £	Value of production (UK) £
Woollen yarns	10.2m lb	62.2m lb	779,000	2.4m
Woollen tissues (broad & narrow)	21.2m yd	183.6m yd	2.8m	16.5m
Total value of all products (exc carpets)	—	—	5.1m	66.9m

186

TABLE 19

VALUE OF OUTPUT OF THE PRINCIPAL INDUSTRIES
OF SCOTLAND, 1907[2]

Industry	Value (£ million)	
Mines	21.2	
Iron & Steel	19.6	
Jute, Linen	16.2	
Engineering	16.0	
Shipbuilding & Marine Engineering	15.2	
Building	10.7	
Bread and Biscuits	8.5	
Woollen & Worsted	5.1	(excluding carpets)
Total (all main industries)	145.8	

going to the Scottish manufacturers would be considerably higher.

The relative importance of the main Scottish industries in 1907 is set out in Table 19. In value of output the woollen industry was clearly very inferior to the heavy industries of the Clyde Valley, and only about half as important as building and contracting. In sum we find that the woollen sector accounted for only about 3½ per cent of the value of production of the country's major industries, and did not, therefore, occupy a central position in the Scottish economy before 1914.

But if regional considerations are substituted for national ones then clearly the woollen industry in Scotland was of much greater significance. Its existence was crucial to the local economy of several areas of Scotland, especially the Borders. In Selkirkshire, for example, 33 per cent of the total male population of the county was directly concerned in wool manufacture in 1911, and 57.4 per cent of the female population.[3] The Border towns of Hawick, Langholm, Galashiels, Innerleithen, and Selkirk owed their growth, and Walkerburn its very existence, to the woollen industry. They were still almost totally committed to it in 1914. The same was only a little less true of Peebles and Jedburgh. Clearly a very large proportion of the population of the Border region was either directly or indirectly connected with the manufacture of wool. The woollen factories controlled the income-earning abilities of most of the trades in the area. This lack of balance was not serious while the woollen industry was sound, but today it lies at the root of the economic difficulties of the area.

Subsequent history has shown that the century before 1914 was the heyday of the Scottish tweed industry. It had a virtual monopoly of quality woollen fabrics and fashion ran strongly in its favour, especially during the middle decades of the century and the years just before World War I. The century between 1780 and 1880 witnessed a remarkable metamorphosis of the industry. From the low-grade traditional fabrics of a peasant craft characterised by intermittent production, inferior techniques and localised markets—the limited horizons of a backward agricultural community —grew an industry of wide international repute unsurpassed in the standard and variety of its products. 'Scotch Tweed' became the aristocratic cloth of the British textile industry, a byword for genuineness and quality. This change was achieved and accompanied by a fairly speedy transition from subsistence production in the peasant home, through a brief 'putting out' phase which made use of certain centralised processes, to a factory-based production system characterised by technical aids and a centrally located, specialised workforce. The tweed industry evolved, then, by the gradual commercialisation of a peasant occupation linked to agriculture. Indeed, as we have seen, it was a shepherd's plaid that formed the foundation of the trade.

The tweed trade thus witnessed the reverse of what happened in some other branches of textiles. The cotton industry owed much to the desire of the humbler orders to emulate their 'betters', first in dressing in the latter's cast-off clothes;[4] but with tweeds the 'betters' copied the dress of their 'inferiors'. For these socio-cultural reasons, together with important advances in textural quality and dyeing techniques, the Scottish woollen producer became linked with the 'new' wealth of the Industrial Revolution and the 'old' wealth that adjusted to that revolution—wealth that could well express its status and leisure-purchasing power by the clothes it wore. Thus industrial expansion in Scottish woollens took the form of a multiplicity of small units of production specialising in quality cloths of many different varieties seeking to satisfy a novelty-conscious clientèle. Underlying this was the production of more standardised quality cloths such as parson's grey and navy blue for more formal wear, and this sort of wear percolated through the social strata to the upper working class eventually. To further their interests the Scottish tweedmakers made early use of practices commonplace today—the adoption of the brand name 'tweed' and repeated product changes to stimulate demand.

The economic and social conditions of the present century have not been so conducive to the growth and prosperity of the industry. In common with other sectors of the British economy its nineteenth-century framework has proved a liability. Fashion since the late nineteenth century has favoured lighter, more expendable mass-produced fabrics rather than heavy tweeds. This has taken the form of a general shift towards worsted products and artificial fibres. The wool-textile industry as a whole has ceased to be a major growth sector in the economy and the Scotch tweed manufacturer, strongly conscious of his high reputation in world woollen markets and wedded to purity of raw materials and 'expensive' production and distribution practices (for example, large design departments and multiple patterning), has found it difficult to adjust to demand changes. Many small family firms have survived because their machinery has ceased to depreciate and because of consumer resistance to standardised clothing, but economic pressures are forcing many to group together, sometimes with English concerns. Though improved marketing and more streamlined management and production procedures have resulted to a degree, grouping has also, in some cases, tended to weaken the association of Scottish people with their local industrial enterprises and to reduce these to the status of vulnerable satellite concerns.

Fashion has also decreed that knitted rather than woven goods should hold the centre of the woollen stage. Indeed, many firms formerly associated with the tweed industry, especially carded yarn spinners, have only survived by switching to the manufacture of hosiery yarns. The decline of the Hawick trade in plainer tweeds has been more than balanced by the rapid growth of the knitwear industry which is equally dedicated to quality and exports. In 1970 the Scottish hosiery industry employed 20,000 workers in the Border counties specialising in the manufacture of cashmere, Shetland and lamb's wool garments.[5]

Despite organisational change in recent years and fashion shifts which have favoured the products of their competitors, Scottish woollen producers have retained their world reputation for superior quality cloths earned by their nineteenth-century forbears. Continuity and change co-exist: tweed made in Scotland remains as David Bremner of the *Scotsman* reported it over a century ago, 'an honest stuff honestly manufactured'.[6]

Glossary of Technical Terms

Bays (or Baize). A cheap lightweight woollen cloth. Probably one of the 'new draperies' of the seventeenth century.

Carding. The process of passing wool through a series of rollers covered with wire teeth and revolving at different speeds in order to disentangle it or to mix together various classes of fibre throughout the mass.

Card 'clothing'. The wire teeth referred to under *Carding*. These were usually wire nails driven through lengths of leather that were then wrapped round the rollers of the carding engine.

Cheviot. Originally this term was applied exclusively to cloths made from the wool of the Cheviot sheep but, for the sake of convenience, it came to denote any cloth in a particular quality range whatever wool was employed in its manufacture. Broadly any cloth below 60s quality may be classed as 'Cheviot', ie a cloth in which 1lb of wool can be spun into 60 x 560yd—about 19 miles. The latter is termed the 'Gala cut', ie the measurement used in the Galashiels district.

Condenser. A machine that produces a fine enough sliver of wool from the cardings produced by the carding process for it to be spun immediately into yarn. The condenser did away with the intermediate slubbing process performed by the 'slubbing billy'.

Cropping. After the 'nap' of the cloth had been 'raised', it was cut (cropped) by highly-skilled men using very large hand shears. In Scotland these were quite early replaced by cropping machines, which acted a little like a lawnmower. Many tweeds were either not cropped at all or only lightly.

Doubling. The twisting together of two yarns, used in the tweed trade to obtain subtle designs.

Drab. A thick yellow/brown woollen cloth.

Drugget. A coarse stuff, often undyed and unmilled, used by the peasantry for everyday clothing till the last century.

Duffle. A coarse milled cloth similar to that used in duffle coats today.

Fells. The skins of sheep with the wool still attached. Fell-mongering was the practice of removing and selling this wool.

Fetler. A person who cleaned a carding set (see *Carding*).

Fingram. A coarse serge made in Aberdeenshire in the seventeenth century and earlier.

Fulling. The thickening and shrinking of woollen cloth, often performed in Scotland by stamping on the fabric in water; in some Highland areas this activity (known as 'waulking') persisted into the present century. Usually performed by machinery (fulling stocks).

Kersey. A coarse but smooth-faced woollen cloth.

Milling. See *Fulling.*

Nap. The surface of woollen cloth. It was often brushed with teasles (raised) and then cut (cropped or sheared).

Noils. Short fibres of wool that are combed out in the worsted process. Being short, these were very suitable for carding in the woollen process.

Pick. The action of carrying the shuttle across the face of the warp in the weaving process. Power-loom efficiency tended to be measured in 'picks per minute'.

Piecing. Before the invention of the *Condenser* (qv) the ends of wool coming from the *Carding* machines had to be joined (pieced together) and then passed on to the *slubber* (see *Condenser*). This was an irksome and often dangerous task, usually performed by children before factory legislation forbade it.

Plaiding. A long piece of coarse woollen cloth usually worn over the shoulder (see p65). In Highland areas it was normally a tartan and in the Lowlands a check. Worn by both sexes, a plaid could be used as an overcoat, a blanket or a bed-pallet. Sometimes it was drawn up between the legs to form a kind of skirt.

Raising. See *Cropping* and *Nap.*

Range. A series of patterns woven on to one warp from which a firm's cloth designs for a particular year would be chosen.

Reed. A comb-like instrument on a weaving loom to keep the warp threads steady and to separate them as they were passed through it. Often more than one warp thread was passed between each tooth ('split') in the reed.

Saxony. Originally a term denoting cloth made out of fine wool from Saxony, it came to refer to any cloth made from merino quality wool, ie anything above, say, 60s quality (see *Cheviot*).

Scribbling. The first stage of the carding process or the process of unravelling the wool before carding it (see *Carding*).

Self-actor. A fully automatic spinning mule, in which the carriage holding the spindles did not require to be pushed in and out by hand.

Serge. A twilled cloth, sometimes with a worsted warp and a woollen weft, but usually all worsted.

Shalloons. A twilled worsted cloth of a coarse variety, often used for undergarments.

Slubbing. See *Condenser.*

Sorting. The fleece of a sheep is made up of several qualities of wool which, in order to obtain an even fabric, have to be sorted out into their respective categories.

Tenters. Before cloths were dried by machinery they were hung in the open to dry on a series of hooks placed on a rectangular wooden frame. Hence to be 'on tenterhooks' (see p83).

Warping. Warp threads run lengthwise in the cloth. Before weaving, these have to be fastened to a warp bar at one end and then wound around a warp beam. This was a slow process, and, since it had often to be done in the fancy tweed trade where short runs prevailed, it raised costs.

Waulkmill. The old name for a fulling mill.

Web. A piece of cloth that has just been woven in the loom but has received no further treatment.

Weft. The crosswise threads in a piece of cloth.

Wincey. In Scotland this was a cloth that had a linen or cotton warp and woollen weft. Originally termed a 'linsey-woolsey', it was mainly made in the Glasgow area, and also for a while in Aberdeen.

Winding. Yarn for warp threads was wound on to bobbins ready for use, and weft yarn was wound on to pirns.

Woollens. Strictly, cloth made of yarn that has been carded not combed, ie cloth made from short wool and from noils.

Worsteds. Fabrics made from longer wool that has been combed— ie the fibres have been straightened and laid parallel to each other.

Abbreviations

Used mainly in References and bibliography

APS	Acts of the Parliament of Scotland
EJ	*Economic Journal*
EcHR	*Economic History Review*
GRL	Galashiels Reference Library
HRL	Hawick Reference Library
JBTS	*Journal of the Bradford Textile Society*
J of EcH	*Journal of Economic History*
JRSS	*Journal of the Royal Statistical Society*
NLS	National Library of Scotland
PP	*Parliamentary Papers*
PRO	Public Record Office
RPCS	Register of the Privy Council of Scotland
SHS	*Scottish History Society*
SJPE	*Scottish Journal of Political Economy*
SPP	*Supplementary Parliamentary Papers (Scottish)*
SRO	Scottish Record Office
Scot Stud	Scottish Studies
SSCC	South of Scotland Chamber of Commerce
THAgS	*Transactions of the Highland and Agricultural Society*
THAS	*Transactions of the Hawick Archaeological Society*
TNAPSS	*Transactions of the National Association for the Promotion of Social Science*
YBESR	*Yorkshire Bulletin of Economic and Social Research*

References

REFERENCES TO CHAPTER 1

1. Heaton, H. *The Yorkshire Woollen and Worsted Industries*, 2nd Ed (Oxford 1965)
   Minchinton, W. E. (ed). *The Growth of English Overseas Trade* (1969), 18
2. Lythe, S. G. *Economy of Scotland 1550-1625* (Edinburgh 1960), 38
3. Smout, T. C. *Scottish Trade on the Eve of Union* (Edinburgh 1963), 191
4. Cf Black, D. *Essay upon Industry and Trade* (1706)
5. Lythe. *Economy*, 83-4; Smout. *Trade*, 216
6. Cf Anon. *A Letter to a Member of Parliament concerning Manufacture and Trade* (1704), 8. For an opposing point of view see Anon. *A Speech in Parliament concerning the Exportation of Wool* (1704), 8
7. Smout. *Trade*, 215-16; Keith, T. *Commercial Relations of England and Scotland 1603-1707* (Cambridge 1910), 2
8. It is possible that this legislation was more effective than previous attempts to ban wool exports; see Keith. *Relations*, 83
9. Black. *Essay*, 8; SRO. *SPP*, XVII, 88 (1)
10. Smout. *Trade*, 217
11. SRO. *Tarred Wool Census* (Berwickshire 1708). MSS uncatalogued

196

12. SRO. Clerk of Penicuik MSS, GD 18/5897
13. Black. *Essay*, 8; 'Reasons against continuing the Act allowing the Exportation of Wool', SRO. *SPP*, XVII, 88 (1)
14. Black. *Essay*, 8
15. Keith. *Relations*, 18, 24, 38-9
16. Ibid, 103-4
17. Ibid, 104-8
18. Black. *Essay*, 8
19. 'The Petitions of the Manufactories of this Kingdom', SRO. *SPP*, XIX. 52 (1704)
20. 'Reasons against etc.' It was declared in Aberdeen that wool exports were causing the making of cloth 'so slight as renders it unvendable abroad'; Keith. *Relations*, 82
21. Anon. 'Memorial Concerning the State of Manufactures Before and Since the Year 1700', SRO. *SPP*, XIX, 63 (c 1703)
22. Ibid
23. Scott, W. R. *Constitution and Finance of English, Scottish and Irish Joint Stock Companies* (New York 1951), iii, 152
24. 'Proposal of Lord Anstruther', SRO. *SPP*, XIX, 52 (7); 'A Short Proposal Anent the Export of Wool', Ibid, XVII, 88 (2); Black. *Essay*, 7; Anon. *A Letter to a Member of Parliament etc.* (1704), 4
25. Keith. *Relations*, 23-4; Lythe. *Economy*, 221
26. Smout. *Trade*, 216
27. APS, x, 275
28. SRO. *SPP*, 94 (c 1702?), 3
29. Anon. 'A Short Proposal etc.'
30. Smout, T. C. 'The Development and Enterprise of Glasgow', *SJPE*, vii (1960), 204
31. Keith. *Relations*, 78
32. Lythe. *Economy*, 238-9
33. 'Memorial Concerning etc.'
34. Keith. *Relations*, 2, 22-3; Smout. *Trade*, 234n
35. 'Memorial Concerning etc.'; Black. *Essay*, 9; Smout. *Trade*, 235
36. 'Memorial Concerning etc.'; Black. *Essay*, 7; 'Reasons against etc.'
37. Smout. *Trade*, 112, 235
38. Anon. *A Scheme of Scotland's Product and Manufactories*

(nd), 20

39. 'Memorial Concerning etc.'; cf Keith. *Relations*, 81-2
40. Anon. *A Speech Without Doors*, 7
41. Quoted in Keith. *Relations*, 21
42. Cf Lythe. *Economy*, 38-9
43. Smout. *Trade*, 233, 236
44. Quoted in Bremner, D. *The Industries of Scotland* (Edinburgh 1869, reprinted Newton Abbot, 1969), 146
45. Keith. *Relations*, 21; Grant, I.F. *Social and Economic Development of Scotland before 1603* (Edinburgh 1930), 464 ff
46. Ibid
47. Ibid
48. This and subsequent paragraphs draw heavily on Scott. *Joint-Stock Cos*, iii, 138-62
49. APS, viii, 348
50. Ibid, xi, 190
51. See Scott, W. R. (ed). 'New Mills Cloth Manufactory 1681-1703', *SHS*, XLV (1905), upon which this account is based
51a. *Acts of the Privy Council* (1685 ff), 137, 138; cf the discussion in Scott 'New Mills', lxviii
52. RPCS, sev 3, x. 355, et alia
53. 'Memorial Concerning etc'
54. SRO. *SPP*, VIII, 27 (2)
55. Cf Scott. 'New Mills', 255, 262, 269, 274; 'Supplication by the Incorporation of Taylors in Edinburgh 1684', RPCS, x, 384
56. 'Memorial concerning etc.'
57. 'Petition of the Managers of Newmills' (Oct 1696), SRO. *SPP*, XV, 104; Lindsay P. *The Interest of Scotland Considered* (Edinburgh 1733), 112-13
58. Lythe. *Economy*, 36-7; APS, xi, 81-2
59. Scott. *Joint-Stock Cos*, iii, 148
60. 'Petition of James Lyell of Gardin' (1704), SRO. *SPP*, XIX, 25
61. APS, vii, 261-2; Scott. 'New Mills', *passim*. The New Mills enterprise seems to have had to abandon frame-knitted hosiery largely because of internecine labour disputes
62. Smout, T. C. (ed). 'Sir John Clerk's Observations on the Present Circumstances of Scotland, 1730', *SHS*, X (1965), 189

63. PRO. *Treasury Papers* (1704), xcii, 84

64. For example, Kilmarnock flannel weavers complained in 1729 that they were unable to obtain Galloway wool as most of it was sent to Sweden (SRO. *Minutes of the Board of Trustees*, NG 1/1/2/12)

65. Heaton, H. *The Yorkshire Woollen & Worsted Industries* (Oxford 1965), 205

66. Ibid, 253

67. SRO. Mins Bd of Trust, NG 1/1/1/46, 72

68. Anderson, J. *Observations on the Means of Exciting a Spirit of National Industry etc.* (Edinburgh 1777), i, 323; Naismith, J. *Thoughts on Various Objects of Industry in Scotland* (Edinburgh 1790), 475

69. PRO. *Treasury Papers* (1719), ccxxiii, 15

70. Loch. D. *Essays on the Trade & Manufactures of Scotland* (Edinburgh 1778), i, 128

71. Stockholm, Royal Library, MS 'Journal of Travels in Scotland 1719-20', by H. Kalmeter (not paginated)

72. Lindsay, P. *The Interest of Scotland Considered* (Edinburgh 1773), 105-6

73. Postlethwaite, M. *Universal Dictionary of Trade and Commerce* (1774), ii, section on Scotland (not paginated)

74. SRO Mins Bd of Trust, NG 1/1/2/123-4; Lindsay. *Interest of Scotland*, 106; SRO. Clerk of Penicuik MSS, GD 18/5897 (1733); Postlethwaite. *Universal Dictionary*, section on Scotland. Further evidence of the expansion of woollens at this time is the establishment of a Glasgow tartan manufactory in the 1740s by local tobacco merchants. Glasgow City Archives B 10/15 *Glasgow Burgh Court Register of Deeds*. I owe this to Dr John Butt of the University of Strathclyde

75. Coleman, D. C. 'An Innovation and its diffusion: the "New Draperies" ', *EcHR*, ser 2, xxii, no 3 (1969), 425n

76. MS Journal by Kalmeter; Lindsay. *Interest of Scotland*, 105-6; Postlethwaite, *Universal Dictionary*, section on Scotland

77. Quoted in Craig-Brown, T. *Presentation of Relics of Galashiels Weavers' Corporation* (1908, no pagination)

78. SRO. Clerk of Penicuik MSS. GD 18/5897 (1733)

79. SRO. *SPP*, XVII, 94; MS Journal by Kalmeter

80. Smith, Adam. *Wealth of Nations* (Everyman edition), i, 98, 106, 173; Scott, W. R. *Joint-Stock Cos*, iii, 148

81. It is noteworthy here that English manufacturers were unable to undersell peasant production in Norway in the eighteenth century, while considerable quantities of cloth were imported there from Russia and Germany. See Tveite, S. 'The Norwegian textile market in the 18th century', *Scandinavian Economic History Review*, xvii, 2 (1969), 161-78

82. Somerville, T. 'My Own Life and Times, 1751-1815', quoted in Fyfe, J. G. *Scottish Diaries and Memoirs 1746-1843* (Stirling, 1942); Sinclair, Sir J. *Analysis of the Statistical Account of Scotland* (Edinburgh 1831), appendix i, 18

83. *Wealth of Nations*, i, 216

84. SRO. Clerk of Penicuik MSS, GD 18/5901 (1738), 5904 (1739)

85. Ibid, GD 18/5926 (1759)

86. SRO. Mins Bd of Trust, NG 1/1/2/93; NG 1/1/3/181

87. Loch, D. *Tour Through the Manufacturing Districts of Scotland* (Edinburgh 1778), 45

REFERENCES TO CHAPTER 2

1. Mitchell, B. R. with Deane, P. *Abstract of British Historical Statistics* (Cambridge 1962), 191-2

2. Ibid, 189

3. SRO. Annual Reports of the Board of Trustees (1784), 9

4. Ibid (1791), 185

5. Ibid (1814), 291

6. Quoted in Kennedy, W. *Annals of Aberdeen* (1818), i, 203n

7. Quoted in Hall. R. *History of Galashiels* (Galashiels 1898), 299

8. Shairp, J. C. (ed). *Recollections of a Tour made in Scotland, A.D. 1803* (Edinburgh, 1874)

9. Hall. *Galashiels*, 90

10. Douglas, R. *Agricultural Report of Roxburghshire* (Edinburgh 1798), 212

11. SRO. Ann Repts Trustees

12. Loch, D. *A Tour through most of the Trading Towns and Villages of Scotland* (Edinburgh 1778), 44-5; Douglas R. *Agricultural Report of Selkirkshire* (Edinburgh 1798), 329-31;

SRO. Minutes of the Board of Trustees, XXXV, 84

13. Loch. *Tour through etc*, 46-7; Douglas. *Roxburghshire*, 212-13; Wilson, R. *History of Hawick* (Hawick 1825), 252

14. Sinclair. Sir J. (ed). *The Statistical Account of Scotland* (Edinburgh 1791-9), viii, 523, 529n; SRO. Scroll Minutes of the Board of Trustees, 12 Feb 1794; Wilson. *Hawick*, 255

15. SRO. Soap Drawback Certificates (MSS uncatalogued)

16. *Pigot's New Commercial Dictionary of Scotland* (1826), 645

17. Loch. *Tour through etc*, 46-7; *Stat Acct of Scotland*, viii, 529; Douglas. *Roxburghshire*, 213; Wilson. *Hawick*, 253; SRO. Mins Bd of Trust, XXXV, 84

18. SRO. Ann Repts Trustees (1791-1814); Douglas. *Roxburghshire*, 213-14; Pigot. *Dictionary*, 649; Report of the Assistant Handloom Weavers Commissioners, *PP*, (1839), XLII, 159

19. *Stat Acct of Scotland*, x, 576ff; Weavers Commission, *PP* (1839), XLII, 159

20. Hogg, Jas. 'Statistics of Selkirkshire', *THAgS*, (1832), ix, 299

21. Findlater, Rev C. *Agricultural Survey of Peeblesshire* (Edinburgh 1802), 27, 218

22. Rept of Handloom Comm, *PP* (1839), XLII, 159

23. A. Dickson & Co, (Galasheils), MS ledger of Jas Dickson

24. *Stat Acct of Scotland*, xiii, 587 ff; xxi, 245-6

25. Wilson. *Hawick*, 287-8

26. Ibid

27. *Stat Acct of Scotland*, vi, 538-9

28. *New Statistical Account of Scotland* (1845), ii, Pt 2, 13

29. *Stat Acct of Scotland*, xvi, 13-14

30. Ibid, ii, 87-8

31. *New Stat Acct*, i, section on Edinburgh

32. *Stat Acct of Scotland*, viii, 283-4

33. Scottish College of Textiles (Galashiels). J. & H. Brown, MS Account Book 1828-9

34. Wilson. *Hawick*, 150

35. *Stat Acct of Scotland*, i, 16; ii, 315-16

36. Brown. Account Book, 14 May 1829

37. Anon. *Border Tour* (Edinburgh 1826), 146; Wilson. *Hawick*, 11

38. Peacock, W. T. 'The Early Stockingmakers etc', *THAS*, (1960), 25

39. Hall. *Galashiels*, 61, 100

40. Cf Handley, J. E. *The Agricultural Revolution in Scotland* (Glasgow 1963)

41. Ryder, M. L. 'The Evolution of Sheep Breeds in Scotland' *Scot Stud*, xii (1968), 147

42. Sinclair, Sir J. *Plan for Improvement of British Wool* (Edinburgh 1791), 4

43. Report of the Committee on the British Wool Trade, *PP* (1828), VIII, 515; Hartwell, R. M. *The Yorkshire Woollen and Worsted Industry 1800-1860* (Oxford DPhil unpub thesis, 1955), 24

44. Edinburgh University Library MSS Gen 921 Order Book, 1828; Brown. Account Book, *passim*

45. Ure, D. *General View of the Agriculture of Roxburghshire* (1794), 70

46. See pp35 and 36 above

47. Brown. Account Book, 13 August 1828

48. Rept on Wool Trade, *PP* (1828), VIII, 515

49. Jas Johnston to G. Gunn, 10 February, 1849, Letter Book ii, Jas Johnston & Co, Newmill Elgin (hereafter referred to as *Johnston Archives*)

50. Hamilton, H. *An Economic History of Scotland in the Eighteenth Century* (Oxford 1963), 93

51. Sinclair, Sir J. *Analysis of the Statistical Account of Scotland* (Edinburgh 1823), appendix i, 19

52. Kyd, J. G. 'Scottish Population Statistics', *SHS*, 3rd ser, XLIV, 1952

53. For example, 'under the present system of husbandry in Roxburghshire [women and children were] needed in the field from the beginning of spring until the harvest is over' thus permitting less yarn to be spun (Ure. *Roxburghshire*, 70)

54. Loch. *Tour through etc*, 44-52

55. SRO. Ann Repts Trustees (1780-1830)

56. Low, Alex. 'Report on the Estate of Gala', quoted in Craig-Brown, T. *History of Selkirkshire* (Edinburgh 1886) ii, app vii, 393

57. The Laird of Gala appears to have granted 99 year tacks before feus became general. Sir Walter Scott occasionally lent

his weight to petitions from local clothiers to the Board of Trustees. Cf Craig-Brown, *Selkirkshire*, i, 570-71

58. Hall. *Galashiels*, 286
59. Sinclair, Sir J. *General View of Agriculture in Scotland* (1814), iii, 294
60. Allan, J. R. (ed). *Crombies of Grandholm and Cothal 1805-1960* (Aberdeen, nd), 19
61. SRO. Ann Repts Trustees
62. Ibid (1785, 1791); Craig-Brown. *Selkirkshire*, i, 575-6
63. Pollard, S. *The Genesis of Modern Management* (1965), 37
64. Brown. Account Book, 25 May 1829. See also the *Stat Acc of Scotland, passim*
65. Douglas. *Selkirkshire*, 330
66. Thompson, F. *Harris Tweed* (Newton Abbot 1969), 79-80
67. Smout, T. C. 'Scottish Landowners and Industrial Development', *SJPE*, XI, (1964), 3
68. Allan. *Crombies*, 22-5
69. Letter Book i, *passim, Johnston Archives*
70. According to Brown, Account Book indigo-dyeing started in Galashiels about 1770
71. See Hall. *Galashiels* for a list of members of the Dyers' and Manufacturers' Corporations in the Galashiels area at this time
72. Douglas. *Selkirkshire*, 329-31
73. Caledonian Insurance Co, Edinburgh, MS Fire Book (1805), Policy no 364. The difficulties of interpreting insurance records are fully realised
74. SRO. Scroll Mins of Bd of Trustees, 21 January 1795
75. This is suggested by the Fire Book mentioned in 73 above
76. Allan. *Crombies*, 16-17
77. Records of the Sun Insurance Co, MS 11937, CD Series, *Guildhall Library*, London. I am grateful to Dr John Butt of the University of Strathclyde for this information
78. Letter Book i, 7, 15, 20, *Johnston Archives*
79. *Stat Acct of Scotland*, ii, 315
80. Brown. Account Book, *passim*
81. Hall. *Galashiels*, 303
82. SRO. Ann Repts Trustees

83. Douglas. *Roxburghshire*, 329-30
84. PRO. Customs 14
85. Weavers Commission, *PP* (1839), XLII, 159
86. SRO. *Report of the Special Committee of the Board of Trustees on Premiums* (1830), 28
87. Brown. Account Book, 24 July 1828
88. Ibid, 14 February 1829
89. House of Lords Record Office. *Journals of the House of Lords,* 9 Geo IV, LX, 487
90. Brown. Account Book, 25 May 1829

REFERENCES TO CHAPTER 3

1. For this and the following section see Craig, Alexander. 'Reminiscences of the Tweed Trade', *Border Advertiser* 9 Dec 1874; 'The Early Stages of the Tweed Trade', Ibid (20 Oct 1875)
2. Locke, Jas. 'The Origins of the Tweed Trade', Ibid (18 Sept 1863)
3. Cochrane, Adam. 'The Scotch Tweed Trade', *TNAPSS* (1863), 793
4. Craig, 'Reminiscences'. Locke had close associations with several Scottish firms, including Crombies of Aberdeen. As a tailor he was patronised by Queen Victoria and her Consort. Cf Allan. *Crombies*, 52-3
5. See records of Henry Ballantyne & Sons, Edin Univ Lib MSS Gen 921 Day Books (1844-50)
6. This is the usual story and there seems no reason to disbelieve it (see Wilson, B. 'The Industrial Development of Hawick', *THAS*, 1953). Naturally, however, others wished to take the credit, one such being Ebenezer Harvey & Co, merchants in London, who figure prominently in order books of the 1830s (see *Hawick Advertiser*, 27 Oct 1855). Jedburgh manufacturers also claimed responsibility, arguing that it was the weather-resisting quality of their cloth worn by the Marquis of Lothian and Lord Polworth that gave rise to the trade which took its name from their parties of gentlemen fishing the Tweed river (see Craig-Brown. *Selkirkshire*, i, 563). For

what it is worth the word 'Tweed' does not figure in any business data seen by the author before the early 1840s, though the word was said to have been coined in 1826

7. Locke. 'Tweed Trade'
8. Dodd, G. *The Textile Manufactures of Great Britain* (1844), 44
9. Edin Univ Lib MSS Gen 921 Day Book (1850)
10. Robt Gill to Jas Johnston, 17 Jan 1852. 'In-Letters' (1852-4), *Johnston Archives*
11. Ibid, 23 March 1852
12. This section relies entirely on the work of E. S. Harrison. See his recent *Our District Checks* (Edinburgh 1969) and *Scottish Woollens* (Edinburgh 1956), Chaps 6 and 7. It is difficult to know just how much the Scottish estate owners really encouraged the manufacture of a variety of district checks, or how much the trade was just a successful sales gimmick prosecuted by northern manufacturers. Certainly it is difficult to believe that the translation of the traditional border plaid of black and white check into the 'Glenfeshie' by the addition of a red overcheck added much to its protective qualities
13. Lovat was important to the growth of this trade. 'You say that you must give over making the Lovats as they do not pay you. Lord Lovat and his family have been the means of putting many a good £20 note of profit in your pocket and in mine, he it is that introduced a taste for shooting tweed made in the North.' D. McDougall to Jas Johnston, 12 Sept 1855. 'In-Letters' (1854-6), *Johnston Archives*
14. The importance of the 'districts' and the evolution of design in one Galashiels firm after 1850 can be seen in Johnston, W. N. 'A Study of the Galashiels Fancy Woollen Trade 1850-1900', a dissertation in the Scottish College of Textiles, Galashiels
15. Ibid
16. For example, the pattern books of J. & A. Ogilvie preserved by Geo Harrison & Co (Edinburgh) Ltd, woollen merchants, Edinburgh
17. See Glossary for general meaning of 'Cheviot' and 'Saxony' in the trade
18. Galashiels Manufacturers' Corporation, MS Minute Book, 68

19. Ibid (page unnumbered)
20. *Hawick Advertiser* (27 Oct 1855)
21. Henry Ballantyne to Messrs Wilson & Armstrong, 17 July 1856. Edin Univ Lib MSS Gen 921. Letter Book ii
22. E. S. Harrison (ed). *Scottish Woollens*, 147-54
23. Cochrane. 'Tweed Trade', 794-5
24. Rept of Asst Handloom Comm, PP (1839), XLII, 159, 186n
25. Craig. 'Reminiscences'
26. *Hawick Advertiser* (14 Feb 1896)
27. *Hawick News* (8 Feb 1901)
28. Ibid, supplement (12 Feb 1897)
29. Locke. 'Tweed Trade'
30. Bremner, D. *The Industries of Scotland* (1869, reprinted Newton Abbot 1969), 157
31. Ibid
32. A. P. Forrester Paton to Mr Ewan, 14 Oct 1879. Letter Book in care of the firm
33. This is made clear on a careful examination of the returns of woollen factories made at intervals during the century (see 32)
34. PP (1836), XLV, 138; PP (1839), XLII, 310; PP (1847), XLVI, 294; PP (1850), XLII, 745; PP (1857), XIV, 7; PP (1862), LV, 23; PP (1867-8), LXIV, 453; PP (1871), LXII, 440; PP (1875), XVI; PP (1878-9), LXV, 324. The 1871 returns are not regarded as very reliable
35. As for reference 34.
36. Bremner. *Industries*, chap on woollen manufactures; Brown. Account Book, 25 May 1829; Craig-Brown. *Selkirkshire*, i, 575; Chambers, R. & W. *Gazetteer of Scotland* (1883), section on Galashiels; Dawson, J. H. *A Statistical History of Scotland* (Edinburgh 1853), 988-90; *New Stat Acct of Scotland*, iii, Selkirk, 11 ff; Rept of a Handloom Comm, PP (1839), XLII, 159, Rept of Dr Harding
37. Quoted in Hall. *Galashiels*, 317
38. Rept of Handloom Comm, PP (1839), XLII, 159, Rept of Dr Harding
39. Repts of Factory Inspectors, PP (1843), XXVIII, Rept of Jas Stuart, 44

40. Edin Univ Lib MSS Gen 921 Account Book (1829-31), Balance Book (1828-38), Wage Books (1855-68)
41. Ibid, Day Books (1844-50)
42. Ibid, Henry Ballantyne to Messrs T. & D. Wood, 30 Dec 1845, Letter Book i, Invoice Book (1840-46), Wage Books (1855-68)
43. Pigot. *Dictionary*, 749; Groome, F. H. (ed). *Ordnance Gazetteer of Scotland* (1883), iv, 251
44. Edin Univ Lib MSS Gen 921 Sales Book (Wm Watson)
45. Bremner. *Industries*, 196
46. Rept of Handloom Comm, *PP* (1839), XLII, 159, Rept of Dr Harding
47. '[There is] little encouragement given to trade or enterprise from the severe burgh restrictions in force . . . ' *New Stat Acct*, iii, Selkirk, 7
48. Dawson. *Statistical History*, 994
49. Bremner. *Industries*, 198
50. Ibid, 200-203
51. Ibid, 200
52. Sources as for 34
53. Based on private MS shown to the author
54. Cf Christie, D. R. *Scottish Tweeds: Four Hundred Years in Fashion* (Wool Education Society 1958)
55. Allan. *Crombies*, 44, 67, 73, and data from surviving records supplied privately to the author
56. For a descriptive account of the Hebridean industry see Thompson F. *Harris Tweed* (Newton Abbot 1969)
57. Edin Univ Lib MSS Gen 921 Day Books (1846-56)
58. Allan. *Crombies*, 73
59. *Kelso Mail* (14 June 1847); *PP* (1851), XL, 680
60. Robert Gill to Jas Johnston. 22 Feb 1855. 'In Letters' (1854-6), *Johnston Archives*
61. *Hawick Advertiser* (6 Feb 1858)
62. Ibid, 30 Jan 1858
63. Edin Univ Lib MSS Gen 921 Day Books (1860-72)
64. Ibid, Ledger B (1841-93)
65. Ponting, K. G. (ed). *Baines's Account of the Woollen Manufacture of England* (Newton Abbot 1970), 112
66. Scott, R. *A Century of Commercial History and Progress:*

The SSCC 1860-1960 (Hawick 1960), 12

67. Brown. Account Book, 25 May 1829 (mentioned in Bremner. *Industries*, 156)

68. Bremner. Industries, 156-8

69. Return of Woollen Factories, *PP* (1862), LV, 23

70. Craig-Brown. *Selkirkshire*, i, 180-81

71. *Textile Mercury* (Oct 1910), 351

72. Rept of the Inspector of Factories, *PP* (1851), XXIII, Rept of Jas Stuart, 31 Oct 1850, 39-40

73. Hall. *Galashiels*, 113-14

REFERENCES TO CHAPTER 4

1. Locke. 'Origins of the Tweed Trade', *Border Advertiser* (18 Sept 1863)

2. According to a Selkirk yarn spinner in 1871 his 'old carders' dealt with 15lb per hour at 2s 2d. His 'new carders' dealt with 11lb per hour at 2s—a difference of 3d per lb carded. T. Craig-Brown to Jas Lees, 16 May 1871, MS Private Letter Book (shown to the author)

3. Locke. 'Tweed Trade'

4. Mitchell, J. A. B. 'Brown's Patent Self-Acting Feeder', *Scottish Woollen Technical College Bulletin* (3 March 1967), 8-10. (Brown & Walker's patent is dated 20 Oct 1842, no 9493)

5. Bremner. *Industries*, 192

6. Cf Catling, H. *The Spinning Mule* (Newton Abbot 1970)

7. See below, Chap 5

8. Edin Univ Lib MSS Gen 921 Invoice Books (1845-1919); Valuation Book, Tweedvale Mills (1876)

9. See below, Chap 6

10. Edin Univ Lib MSS Gen 921 Wage Books (1858-68). See below in Chap 6

11. Ibid, Invoice Books (1845-1919); Purchase Day Books (1800-1904), *Johnston Archives*. Special power looms for weaving tartans were supplied to the Hillfoots by a Glasgow firm. Normally woollen power looms were bought from Yorkshire firms and mules from Platts of Oldham

12. Returns of Woollen Factories, *PP* (1836), XLV, 138; *PP* (1890),

LXVII, 328

13. *Census Returns*, Scotland

14. Ibid

15. Bremner. *Industries*, 211

16. Galashiels Manufacturers' Corporation Minute Book (page unnumbered) refers to poor lodgings and the need for new workers to try to build their own houses. A Selkirk firm in 1910 converted an old mill there into workers' flats to overcome the local 'house famine' (*Textile Mercury*, Dec 1910, 466)

17. Edin Univ Lib MSS Gen 921 Letter Book (19 Feb and 16 Mar 1857)

18. Jas Johnston to Geo Gunn, 10 Feb 1849, Letter Book ii, *Johnston Archives*

19. Jas Johnston to J. Crombie, 18 Sept 1855. 'Officials 1852', *Johnston Archives*

20. H. Brown. Account Book 1828-9 (26 Mar 1828)

21. Calculations from private diary kindly shown to the author by Lindsay Watson

22. Edin Univ Lib MSS Gen 921 Ledger B (1841-93)

23. See Philpott, B. P. 'Wool Prices 1870-1950', (Leeds Univ PhD unpub thesis 1955)

24. Rainnie, G. F. (ed). *The Woollen and Worsted Industry* (Oxford 1965), 1-15

25. Edin Univ Lib MSS Gen 921 Letter Book (19 May 1856)

26. *Hawick Advertiser* (7 June 1856). Cf *Border Advertiser* (23 Mar 1881)

27. See Sigsworth, E. M. & Blackman, J. 'The Woollen and Worsted Industries' in Aldcroft, D. H. (ed). *The Development of British Industry and Foreign Competition 1875-1914* (1968), 153

28. See Chap 3 above

29. Hogg, Jas. 'Statistics of Selkirkshire', THAgS, (1832), 300

30. Boyd, Robert. 'On the Woollen Manufactures obtained from the Wool of our Mountain Sheep', Ibid (1843-5), 134-5

31. Ibid

32. *PP* (1833) VI, 690, 77-8

33. Jas Johnston to E. C. Goodhart, 22 Nov 1847. Letter Book ii.

Johnston Archives
34. *New Stat Acct of Scotland*, iii, Selkirk, 21
35. Dawson, J. H. *Abridged Statistical Survey of Scotland* (1853), 988
36. *Border Advertiser* (14 July 1848)
37. Edin Univ Lib MSS Gen 921 Invoice Books (1823-9, 1845-6)
38. For Cheviot wool prices see annual *THAgS*
39. Harrison, E. S. *Scottish Woollens*, 97-8
40. Ibid
41. Brown. Account Book (1829), *passim*
42. Inventory Ledgers (1830-65), *Johnston Archives*
43. Edin Univ Lib MSS Gen 921 Balance Book (1849)
44. *Post Office Directories of Edinburgh and Leith*
45. McLaren, M. *Sanderson & Murray 1844-1954* (Galashiels, nd), upon which the subsequent account is based
46. Edin Univ Lib MSS Gen 921 Letter Book II (20 Apr 1857)
47. Galashiels Manufacturers' Corporation, Minute Book (page unnumbered)
48. Buchan, J. W. (ed). *History of Peeblesshire*, i, 117
49. Ibid
50. Brown. Account Book, *passim*. Letter Book i, *passim, Johnston Archives*
51. Allan, J. R. (ed). *Crombies of Grandholm*, 31
52. Gala Manuf Corp Minute Book (page unnumbered)
53. *Border Magazine*, ii (1897), 81
54. Hall. *Galashiels*, 339-40
55. Account Book (in care of Arthur Dickson & Co, Galashiels)
56. Douglas. *Selkirkshire*, 329-30; *Third Statistical Account of Scotland*, Selkirkshire, 308
57. See Chap 3 above
58. Edin Univ Lib MSS Gen 921 Day Books (1862)
59. Ibid, Letter Book, H. Ballantyne to Craigs Bros (16 June 1858)
60. I am grateful to Alfred Harrison of Edinburgh for this point and for discussing the role of the woollen merchants with me
61. Edin Univ Lib MSS Gen 921 Letter Book, H. Ballantyne to W. Armstrong (24 Oct 1857)
62. Alex Johnston to Urquhart Blackwood & Co. 9 May 1839. Letter Book ii, *Johnston Archives*

63. Ibid, Alex Johnston to Col Brown, 10 June 1840
64. *Glasgow Herald* (13 June 1908)
65. Jas Johnston to Alex Johnston (no relation), 24 & 29 Nov 1855. Letter Book iii, *Johnston Archives*
66. Royal Commission on the Depression of Trade and Industry, 2nd Rept, Evidence of the South of Scotland Chamber of Commerce, *PP* (1886), XXI c. 4715
67. Rept of the Tariff Commission (1905) ii, pt ii, paras 1305-6
68. *Glasgow Herald* (6 Oct 1913)
69. Allan. *Crombies*, 105
70. Tariff Comm, ii, pt ii, evidence of P. & R. Sanderson
71. Allan. *Crombies*, 105-6
72. *Textile Mercury* (Apr 1891), 325
73. Jas Johnston to A. B. Spark, 11 Mar 1853 (and subsequent correspondence). Letter Book iii, *Johnston Archives*
74. See letter in *Hawick News* (8 Apr 1898)
75. *The Scottish Woollen Trade & Foreign Tariffs* (Hawick 1903), 10-12
76. Craig, Alex. 'The Early Stages of the Tweed Trade', *Border Advertiser* (20 Oct 1875); Wilson's of Bannockburn specialised in army tartan cloths
77. *Hawick News* (14 June 1901)
78. *The Woollen and Worsted Industries* (1907), 165
79. Edin Univ Lib MSS Gen 921 Balance Book (1864)
80. Ibid, Ledgers A (1883-1903)
81. Allan. *Crombies*, 44, 73; 'Journal' (1829-38), *Johnston Archives*
82. Allan. *Crombies*, 44, 73, 102
83. Edin Univ Lib MSS Gen 921 Ledger B (1841-93)
84. Ibid; 'Journal' (1829-38), *Johnston Archives*
85. Based on private MS kindly supplied by the firm
86. Cf 'The manufacturers are exceedingly averse to affording information concerning the extent of their operations.' E. H. Groome (ed). *Ordnance Gazetteer of Scotland* (1883), iii, 68
87. Edin Univ Lib MSS Gen 921 Ledger B; Allan. *Crombies*, 77
88. *Scotch Tweed* (Scottish Woollen Technical College), xii, 99
89. Edin Univ Lib MSS Gen 921 Investment Journal (1902-5) and Private Investment Ledgers (retained by the firm); 'Letters

1880s', *Johnston Archives*

90. Edin Univ Lib MSS Gen 921 Letter Book. H. Ballantyne to Messrs Wilson & Armstrong. 6 Oct 1855. Cf 'from a large number of our customers we do not get a single penny between January and August' (John Paton to James Lord Sept 1873. MS Letter Book at Paton & Baldwins, Alloa)
91. Robt Gill to Jas Johnston. 'In-letters' (1854-6), *Johnston Archives*
92. *The Times Financial & Commercial Supplement* (21 May 1906)
93. Oliver, Dr T. 'Some Lines of Development', *Glasgow Herald* (30 Dec 1914)
94. Scott, R. 'The Collie Disaster', *THAS* (1962), 31 ff
95. Edin Univ Lib MSS Gen 921 Invoice Books, *passim*; McLaren. *Sanderson & Murray*, 70-71
96. *Hawick Advertiser* (27 Oct 1855)

REFERENCES TO CHAPTER 5

1. Wilson, C. *Address to the Border Counties Commercial Travellers' Association* (Galashiels 1903); Oliver, Dr T. 'Some Lines of Development', *Glasgow Herald* (30 Dec 1914); Tariff Commission, ii, pt ii, para 1,314, inter alia
2. Factory Inspectors Returns of Woollen Factories, *PP* (1904), XII, 841
3. R. C. on the Depression of Trade and Industry (1886), 1st Rept, *PP* (1886), XXI, 110
4. *Census Returns (Scotland)*, i, pt ii, para 2059 (1911)
5. McBain, W. C. in *The Liberty Review*, (15 Apr 1899). Cf *Glasgow Herald* (14 Sept 1897)
6. Ibid
7. Edin Univ Lib MSS Gen 921 Private Letter Book, 273
8. Letter to *Hawick News* (11 Mar 1898)
9. Ponting, K. G. *The Wool Trade: Past & Present* (1961), 176; Thompson, R. J. 'Wool Prices in Great Britain', *JRSS*, 65, (1912) 503-13
10. For full details of the American tariff structure see Taussig, F. W. *Tariff History of the United States* (New York 1931), esp 260, 263 and 333-4

11. Ashley, W. *Modern Tariff History* (1904), 219-20
12. Tausigg. *Tariff History*, 393 and note
13. The best source for Scottish opinion on this matter is *Scottish Woollen Trade & Foreign Tariffs* (South of Scotland Chamber of Commerce, 1903). For the opinion of one influential yarn spinner see Craig-Brown, T. 'Tariff Reform', a paper read before the Hawick Constitutional Club, 16 Oct 1903
14. Tariff Comm, ii, pt ii, para 1,968
15. Craig-Brown, T. *Foreign Tariffs* (Hawick 1886), 14. Cf R.C. on Depression (1886), 1st Rept, evidence of W. Shulze, paras 5,369, 5,383, 5,481
16. *Scots Woollen Trade & For Tariffs*, 6; I am indebted to Prof Michael Flinn for information on the value of yarn exports
17. Ibid, 7
18. Ibid, 8
19. *The Times Financial & Commercial Supplement*, (21 May 1906)
20. *Scots Woollen Trade & For Tariffs*, 8
21. Ibid
22. Tariff Comm, ii, pt ii, evidence of P. & R. Sanderson, para 1,824
23. *Textile Mercury* (July 1891), 62
24. 'Problems and practices of the Tweed Trade', *Glasgow Herald* (13 June 1908)
25. Tariff Comm, ii, pt ii, para 1,314
26. *Glasgow Herald* (4 Oct 1913)
27. Tariff Comm, ii, pt ii, para 2,016
28. Ibid. paras 1,348-9
29. *Scots Woollen Trade & For Tariffs*, 4; Craig-Brown. *Tariff Reform*, 6
30. Tariff Comm, ii,pt ii, paras 1,343, 1,346
31. Ibid, 1,939, 1,953
32. Ibid, 2,016
33. *Scots Woollen Trade & For Tariffs*, 3-4
34. Tariff Comm, ii, pt ii, para 1.351
35. Letter from 'A Leeds Gentleman', *Hawick News* (25 Feb 1898)
36. Oliver. 'Lines of Development', *Glasgow Herald* (30 Dec 1914); Rept of the American Consulate in Edinburgh, *Textile*

Recorder (Dec 1906), 226

37.   Letter to *Hawick News* (11 Mar 1898)

38.   Ibid (21 Jan 1898)

39.   For a good account of the growth of the multiple clothier see Thomas, J. 'A History of the Leeds Clothing Industry', *Yorkshire Bulletin Occasional Papers*, i (Jan 1955), upon which the subsequent discussion is based

40.   One has to rely on the local press for the industry's attitude to the ready-made trade. See especially *Hawick News* (7 and 14 Jan 1898). Dr T. Oliver, first principal of the Woollen Technical College at Galashiels was a keen proponent of the establishment of clothing factories in the Borders

41.   *Hawick News* (28 Jan 1898)

42.   T. Craig-Brown to G. Hyman, 12 Aug 1892 (private Letter Book shown to author)

43.   *Hawick Advertiser* (19 Feb 1909)

44.   Ibid (8 Jan 1909)

45.   *Hawick News* (31 Dec 1897)

46.   24 Mar 1899

47.   Craig-Brown. 'Problems of Tweed Trade', *Glasgow Herald* (13 June 1908)

48.   *Hawick Advertiser* (14 May 1909)

49.   I cannot find the reference for this quote!

50.   This discussion relies heavily on the author's discussions with the late J. A. B. Mitchell of the College of Textiles, Galashiels

51.   Allan. *Crombies*, 108

52.   Ibid, 78

53.   Oliver. 'Lines of Development'

54.   *Scots Woollen Trade & For Tariffs*, 10-12

55.   Ibid; cf *Hawick Express* (27 Dec 1912)

56.   *Hawick News* (25 Feb 1898)

57.   Quoted in *Hawick News* (21 Apr 1899)

58.   Craig-Brown. 'Problems of Tweed Trade'

59.   *Hawick News* (12 Oct 1898). The firm's records show, however, that no dividend was paid for some years after the company was formed

60.   Allan. *Crombies*, 107

61. Craig-Brown, T. *The French Tariff on Woollen Goods* (Hawick 1881)
62. Oliver, T. *The Rise of Scotch Tweed Technique* (Galashiels, nd), 3
63. Ibid, 4-13
64. *Hawick News* (4 Oct 1901)
65. Tariff Comm. ii, pt ii, para 1,837. To be fair, C. J. Wilson was largely responsible for founding the technical college at Galashiels in 1909
66. Ibid, 1,822
67. Allan. *Crombies*, 116
68. *The Times Financial and Commercial Supplement* (21 May 1906)
69. 30 Dec 1914, 40
70. Cf Scott, R. E. *A Century of Commercial History and Progress*, 14-15
71. Edin Univ Lib MSS Gen 921 Wage Books (1900-07); Day Books (1903-11)
72. Figures kindly supplied by the firms concerned and export values by Prof. Michael Flinn
73. See prices quoted in *THAgS*, XXVII (1914)

REFERENCES TO CHAPTER 6

1. Bremner. *Industries of Scotland*, 172
2. Rept of Asst Handloom Comm, *PP* (1839), XLII, 159, 185 ff
3. Ure, D. *General View of Agriculture of Selkirk* (Edinburgh, 1794), 35; *Stat Acct of Scotland*, viii, 622; Brown. Account Book, *passim;* Hall. *Galashiels*, 306; *PP* (1839), XLII, 159, 13, 15. 39-42, 185-7; Edin Univ Lib MSS Gen 921 Handlooms Book (1826-31); Wage Book (1846-50)
4. Edin Univ Lib MSS Gen 921 Wage Book (1846-50)
5. *Stat Acct of Scotland*, viii, 622n; Brown. Account Book (25 May 1829)
6. *New Stat Acct of Scotland*, iii, Selkirkshire, 22 ff; Edin Univ Lib MSS Gen 921 Account Book (1829-38)
7. *PP* (1839) XLII, 159, 15
8. Edin Univ Lib MSS Gen 921 Wage Books (1850-79)

9. Ibid, Wage Books (1876-1906)
10. Pay Books (1877-1912), *Johnston Archives*
11. Tariff Comm, ii, pt ii, paras 2,134, 1,834
12. *Hawick Express* (18 May 1887); *Hawick News* (28 June 1901)
13. Tariff Comm, ii, pt ii, para 1,825
14. See Tables 11 and 12 above
15. Edin Univ Lib MSS Gen 921 Wage Books (1846-56)
16. Bowley, A. L. 'Wages in the West Riding of Yorkshire' *JRSS*, LXV (1902), 102-26
17. Ibid
18. Ibid, 118-19; *Miscellaneous Statistics*, X (1879), 397-8
19. Returns of Wages in the Textile industries, *PP* (1889), LXX, 843, C-5807, xiv
20. *PP* (1909), LXXX, xli
21. Allan. *Crombies*, 91; Tables 11 and 12 above
22. Rept of Asst Handloom Comm, *PP* (1839), XLII, 159, 56
23. See Chap 5 above
24. *PP* (1839). XLII, 159, 20
25. *PP* (1854), LXIX, 205, 24, 50
26. Bremner. *Industries*, 193
27. Gala Manuf Corp Minute Book (page unnumbered); *Hawick Textile Congress Souvenir* (1912), 8
28. *Glasgow Herald* (28 Aug 1913)
29. Edin Univ Lib MSS Gen 921 Wage Books (1850-1906); Layton, W. T. *An Introduction to the Study of Prices* (1912), 150
30. Ibid
31. Royal Commission on Labour 1891, *PP* (1892), XXXV c 6708, evidence of C. J. Wilson, paras 7,568-9
32. Wilson. *Chartism in Scotland* (Manchester 1970), 127-8
33. R.C. on Labour, paras 7,647 9
34. Tariff Comm. ii, pt ii, para 1,834
35. Clapham J. H. *Woollen & Worsted Industries*, 204
36. See *PP* (1841), X, 294, 29
37. See Gulvin, C. 'Wages and Conditions in the Border Woollen Industry', *THAS* (1967), 45-6
38. See *PP* (1890), LXVIII, 176, 73; R.C. on Labour (1891), para 7,676
39. *Hawick Express* (9 and 26 Apr 1887); Marwick W. H. *A Short*

     History of Labour in Scotland (Edinburgh 1967), 54

40. Allan. *Crombies*, 97
41. R.C. on Labour (1891), paras 7,582-4; 7,594-5
42. Allan. *Crombies*, 97
43. Rept of Asst Handloom Comm, *PP* (1839), XLII, 159, Rept of Dr Harding
44. *Kelso Mail* (7 and 14 May 1849)
45. *Border Advertiser* (20 May 1874)
46. Bremner. *Industries*, 168-9. Cf Edin Univ Lib MSS Gen 921 Invoice Books; Allan. *Crombies*, 54-8; and Inventory Ledgers, *Johnston Archives*, for gradual nature of the introduction of weaving machinery
47. Robt Gill to Jas Johnston, 30 Jan 1855. 'In-Letters' (1854-6), *Johnston Archives*
48. Tariff Comm, ii, pt ii, para 1,825

REFERENCES TO THE EPILOGUE

1. Returns of the Census of Production, *PP* (1909), CII, 655
2. Crammond, E. 'The Economic Position of Scotland', *JRSS*, LXXV (1911-12), 161
3. *Census of Scotland*. i, pt ii, 2060-61 (1911)
4. Cf Perkin, H. *The Origins of Modern English Society 1780-1880* (1969), 91 ff
5. *Scottish Digest of Statistics* (Scottish Statistical Office, 1970)
6. Bremner. *Industries*, 157

Appendix

The Value of Output of the Scottish Woollen Cloth Industry, c 1884
The figures given on p96 are mainly contemporary estimates incapable of firm verification. My own estimates for the early 1880s of about £5 million appears to 'fit' the picture of steady expansion on trend through the 1870s. This figure is based on spinning capacity in the industry. The total spinning capacity of the UK in 1885 was divided into estimates of the value of final product for the period 1880-84 to give a figure for output per spindle. This sum was then multiplied by the number of spindles in the Scottish branch of the industry (excluding doubling spindles, which do not add to output). This method assumes that the average value of product of Scottish spindles per unit of time was the same as in the whole UK. This was not the case, in all probability, given the high grade of Scottish production, so that this final figure of around £5 million may be conservative. It excludes hosiery and carpet production, and it is possible that the amount of £1 million I allowed for these branches may be too small.

The estimate of UK output was taken from P. Deane and W. A. Cole. *British Economic Growth 1688-1959* (Cambridge 1967), 196, Table 47. Figures for spinning capacity were taken from *Board of Trade 13th Abstract of Statistics*, Cmd 5041 (1910).

Bibliography

MANUSCRIPT SOURCES

(a) *Official Documents*

Census of Tarred Wool Production, 1708 (Berwickshire), SRO (uncat)

Records of the Board of Trustees for Fisheries, Manufactures and Improvements, 1727-1830 (NG 1), SRO

Report of the Special Committee on Premiums for Woollen Cloths 1830, SRO

A Collection of Petitions to the Barons of the Exchequer, Laing MSS, no 488, Div ii, Edinburgh University Library

Customs, 14, PRO

(b) *Private Papers*

Clerk of Penicuik Muniments (GD 18), SRO

Craig-Brown, T. *Private Letter Book*

(c) *Business records*

James Dickson's Ledger, 1805-25 (some omissions). In care of Arthur Dickson & Co, Galashiels

Account Book of Henry Brown, in library of Scottish College of Textiles, Galashiels

Ballantyne Archives, Edinburgh University Library, MSS Gen 921-1215. A useful set of records covering most of the nineteenth century after 1828, belonging to H. Ballantyne & Sons, Walkerburn. Wage and Day books predominate, but also ledgers and batch books. Includes early account book of David Ballantyne of Innerleithen

Johnston Archives. A fairly comprehensive collection of business documents belonging to Jas Johnston & Co Ltd of Elgin, dating from 1808 to about 1911

Watson Records, Edinburgh University Library (catalogued with *Ballantyne Archives* above). Fragmentary business data dating from 1847 to c 1930 belonging to William Watson & Sons, Hawick

Miscellaneous extracts from records, J. & J. Crombie & Co, Aberdeen, given to the author

Miscellaneous data, Paton & Baldwin's, Alloa

Fire Insurance Policy Book, 1805, Caledonian Insurance Company, Edinburgh

Wilson's of Bannockburn, Letters, Queen St. Museum, Edinburgh

PAMPHLETS

Anon. *A Scheme of Scotland's Product and Manufactories* (nd), NLS

Anon. *A Letter to a Member of Parliament Concerning Manufacture and Trade* (1704), NLS

Anon. *A Memorial Concerning the State of Manufactures Before and Since the year 1700* (nd), NLS

Anon. *A Speech in Parliament Concerning the Exportation of Wool* (1704), NLS

Anon. *A Speech Without Doors Concerning the Exportation of Wool* (nd), NLS

Anon. *Eight Sets of Queries by a Peer of the Realm* (1775), NLS

Anon. *Souvenir of Hawick Textile Congress* (1912), HRL

Anon. *The Galashiels Manufacturers' Corporation* (Galashiels 1956)

Black, D. *Essay on Trade* (1706), NLS

Christie, D. *Scotch Tweeds: Four Hundred Years in Fashion* (1952)

Craig-Brown, T. *Tariff Reform* (Hawick 1903)

Craig-Brown, T. *The French Tariff on Woollen Goods* (Hawick 1881)

Scott, R. *One Hundred Years of Commercial History & Progress* (Hawick 1960)

Sinclair, J. *Address to the Society for the Improvement of British*

Wool (Edinburgh 1791), NLS
SSCC. *The Scottish Woollen Trade & Foreign Tariffs* (Hawick 1903)
Wilson, C. *Lecture on Trade* (Hawick 1903), HRL

PARLIAMENTARY PAPERS

(a)   *The Scottish Parliament*
Acts of the Parliaments of Scotland, vols iv-xi, 1593-1707, SRO
Supplementary Parliamentary Papers, vols i-xxi, SRO
Register of the Privy Council of Scotland (17th c), SRO
(b)   *The British Parliament*
*Report of the Select Committee . . . [on] the State of the Woollen
   Manufacture in England* (1806)
Report of the House of Lords Committee on the British Wool Trade
   (1828)
Report on the Select Committee on Hand-loom Weavers (1834)
Reports of the Assistant Hand-loom Weavers' Commissioners
   (1839)
Report on the Arrestment of Wages in Scotland (1854)
Report (2nd) on the Employment of Children in Factories (1864)
*Report (2nd) of the Royal Commission on the Depression of Trade
   and Industry* (1886)
*Report of the Board of Trade on the Relation of Wages to the Cost
   of Production* (1891)
*Report of the Board of Trade on the Cost of Living of the Working-
   classes* (1908)
Returns of Wages, 1830-86 (1887)
Royal Commission on Labour Report (1891)
The Factory Returns and the reports of the Factory Inspectorate,
and Census Returns for Scotland have been consulted where indi-
cated in the text.

DIRECTORIES AND GAZETTEERS

Border Almanac, Kelso, 1868-1912, HRL
Chambers, R. W. *The Gazetteer of Scotland* (1883)
Groome, F. H. *Ordnance Gazetteer of Scotland* (1883)
Pigot & Co. *New Commercial Dictionary of Scotland* (1826)

Pigot & Co. *National Commercial Dictionary of Scotland* (1837)
Wilson, J. M. (ed). *Fullarton's Imperial Gazetteer of Scotland*, 2nd ed (Edinburgh, post-1859)

THESES AND DISSERTATIONS

Haque, A. B. M. Some Geographical Aspects of the Evolution of the Textile Industries of Scotland (MSc Edinburgh 1965)
Hartwell, R. M. The Yorkshire Woollen and Worsted Industry 1800-50 (D.Phil Oxford 1955)
Johnston, W. N. A Study of the Galashiels Fancy Woollen Trade (Scottish College of Textiles, Galashiels)
Philpott, B. P. Wool Prices, 1870-1950 (PhD Leeds 1953)

NEWSPAPERS AND PERIODICALS

Border Advertiser, 1848-1906, GRL
Border Magazine, The, Edinburgh, especially 1897-1914, HRL
Border Telegraph, 1906-1914, GRL
Glasgow Herald, especially c 1890-1914
Hawick Advertiser, 1857-1914, HRL
Hawick Express, 1883 (?)-1914, HRL
Hawick News, 1882-1914, HRL
Hawick Observer, 1842, in private hands
Scotch Tweed, Galashiels, 1923-38
Textile Manufacturer, Manchester, 1874-1914
Textile Mercury, Manchester, 1888-1914
Textile Recorder, Manchester, 1883-1914

ARTICLES

Bowley, A. L. 'Wages in the Woollen and Worsted Manufactures of the West Riding of Yorkshire', *JRSS*, vol LXV (1902)
Campbell, R. H. 'The Economic Consequences of the Anglo-Scottish Union,' *EcHR*, vol 16 (1964)
Carstairs, A. M. 'Some Economic Aspects of the Union of Parliaments', *SJPE* (1955)
Clapham, J. H. 'Industrial Organisation in the Woollen & Worsted Industries of Yorkshire', *EJ* (1906)

Clapham, J. H. 'The Transference of the Worsted Industry from Norfolk to the West Riding', *EJ* (1910)

Cochrane, A. 'The Scotch Tweed Trade', *TNAPSS* (1863)

Crammond, E. 'The Economic Position of Scotland', *JRSS* vol 75 (1911-12)

Gulvin, C. 'The Foundation of the Scotch Tweed Industry', *Wool Record & Textile World*, Scottish Supp (Nov 1966)

Gulvin, C. 'Wages and Conditions in the Border Woollen Industry about 1890', *THAS* (1967)

Gulvin, C. 'The Treaty of Union and the Scottish Woollen Industry, 1700-1760' *SHR, L* 2, no 150 (Oct 1971)

Hamilton, H. 'Economic Growth in Scotland 1720-77'. *SJPE* (1959)

Pankhurst, K. 'Investment in the West Riding Wool Textile Industry in the 19th Century,' *YBESR* (June 1955)

Ryder, M. L. 'The History of Sheep in Scotland', *JBTS* (1967-8)

Ryder, M. L. 'The Evolution of Scottish Breeds of Sheep', *Scot Stud*, vol 12 (1968)

Sinclair, W. P. H. 'The Economic Background of the Tweed Valley Woollen Industry', *Galashiels Woollen Technical College Year Book* (1950)

Smout, T. C. 'The Anglo-Scottish Union of 1707: The Economic Background', *EcHR*, vol 16 (1964)

Turner, W. H. K. 'Wool Textile Manufacture in Scotland', *Scottish Geographical Magazine* (Sept 1964)

Wilson, W. 'The Rise and Progress of Manufactures at Hawick', *TNAPSS* (1863)

BOOKS

Allan, J. R. (ed). *Crombies of Grandholm & Cothal, 1805-1960* (Aberdeen 1960). A privately circulated company history

Anderson, J. *Observations on the Means of Exciting a Spirit of National Industry etc* (Edinburgh 1777)

Anderson, J. *General View of the Agriculture and Rural Economy of the County of Aberdeen, etc* (Edinburgh 1794)

Anon. *Border Tour* (Edinburgh 1826)

Ashley, P. *Modern Tariff History* (1904)

Bischoff, J. *Woollen and Worsted Manufacture*, 2 vols (1842)

Bremner, D. *The Industries of Scotland* (Edinburgh 1869)

Buchan, J. W. (ed). *History of Peeblesshire*, 3 vols (Glasgow 1925)

Campbell, R. H. *Scotland since 1707* (Oxford 1965)

Chalmers, C. *Caledonia*, new ed (Paisley 1889)

Clapham, J. H. *The Woollen and Worsted Industries* (1907)

Clapham, J. H. *An Economic History of Modern Britain*, 3 vols (1932-9)

Craig-Brown, T. *History of Selkirkshire*, 2 vols (Edinburgh 1886)

Curtis, H. P. *Glossary of Textile Terms* (Manchester 1921)

Davidson, J. & Gray, A. *The Scottish Staple at Veere* (1909)

Dawson, J. H. *An Abridged Statistical History of Scotland* (Edinburgh 1853)

Dawson, J. H. *The Abridged Statistical History of the Scottish Counties* (Edinburgh 1862)

Defoe, D. *The History of the Union between England and Scotland* (1786-7)

Dodd, G. *The Textile Manufactures of Great Britain* (1844)

Douglas, R. *General View of the Agriculture of Roxburgh and Selkirk* (Edinburgh 1798)

Edgar, J. *Hawick in the Early Sixties* (Hawick 1913)

Findlater, C. *General View of the Agriculture of Peebles* (Edinburgh 1802)

Franklin, T. D. *A History of Scottish Farming* (Edinburgh 1952)

Graham, H. G. *The Social Life of Scotland in the 18th Century* (1901)

Grant, I. F. *Social & Economic Development of Scotland before 1603* (Edinburgh 1930)

Hall, R. *History of Galashiels* (Galashiels 1898)

Hamilton, H. *An Economic History of Scotland in the 18th Century* (Oxford 1963)

Handley, J. E. *The Agricultural Revolution in Scotland* (Glasgow 1963)

Harrison, E. S. (ed). *Scottish Woollens* (Edinburgh 1956)

Heaton, H. *The Yorkshire Woollen and Worsted Industries*, 2nd ed (Oxford 1965)

Jeffrey, A. *The History & Antiquities of Roxburghshire*, 4 vols (Edinburgh and Jedburgh 1855-64)

Keith, T. *Commercial Relations of England and Scotland 1603-1707* (Cambridge 1910)

Lindsay, P. *The Interest of Scotland Considered, etc* (Edinburgh 1733)

Lipson, E. *A History of Wool and Wool Manufacture* (1953)

Loch, D. *Curious and Entertaining Letters Concerning the Trade & Manufactures of Scotland* (Edinburgh 1774)

Loch, D. *A Tour through most of the Trading Towns & Villages of Scotland etc* (Edinburgh 1778)

Loch, D. *Essays on the Trade, Commerce, Manufactures and Fisheries of Scotland* (Edinburgh 1778-9)

Lythe, S. G. E. *The Economy of Scotland, 1550-1625* (Edinburgh 1960)

Macdonald, D. F. *Scotland's Shifting Population, 1770-1850* (Glasgow 1937)

McLaren, M. *Sanderson and Murray, 1844-1954* (Galashiels 1954?)

Marwick, W. H. *Economic Developments in Victorian Scotland* (1936)

Marwick, W. H. *A Short History of Labour in Scotland* (Edinburgh 1967)

Murray, R. *History of Hawick* (Hawick 1901)

Naismith, J. *Thoughts on Various Objects of Industry pursued in Scotland* (Edinburgh 1790)

Pennant, T. *A Tour in Scotland in 1772* (1790)

Plant, M. *The Domestic Life of Scotland in the 18th Century* (Edinburgh 1952)

Postlethwayt, M. *The Universal Dictionary of Trade and Commerce*, 2 vols (1766)

Pryde, G. S. *The Treaty of Union of Scotland and England* (1950)

Pryde, G. S. *Scotland from 1603 to the Present Day* (1962)

Pryde, G. S. *Report of the Tariff Commission*, vol ii (1905)

Scott, W. R. (ed). *The Records of the New Mills Cloth Manufactory, 1681-1703* SHS, vol 45 (Edinburgh 1905)

Scott, W. R. *Constitution and Finance of English, Scottish and Irish Joint-Stock Companies to 1720*, 3 vols (New York 1951)

Sigsworth, E. M. *Black Dyke Mills* (Liverpool 1958)

Sinclair, J. (ed). *The Statistical Account of Scotland*, 21 vols (Edinburgh 1791-9)

Sinclair, J. *Analysis of the Statistical Account of Scotland* (Edinburgh 1823)

Sinclair, J. *Agriculture of the Northern Counties of Scotland* (1795)

Sinclair, J. *General Report of the Agricultural State & Political Circumstances of Scotland* (Edinburgh 1814)

Smout, T. C. *Scottish Trade on the Eve of Union* (Edinburgh 1963)

Taussig, F. W. *Tariff History of the United States* (New York? 1931)

Ure, A. *General View of the Agriculture of Roxburgh* (1794)

Willis, R. L. *Tour in Scotland* (Edinburgh 1897)

Wilson, J. *Annals of Hawick* (Edinburgh 1858)

Wilson, R. *History of Hawick* (Hawick 1825)

Acknowledgements

This book is based on research carried out between 1965 and 1969 in the Department of Economic History of the University of Edinburgh. I owe a great debt of gratitude to the members of that Department, especially to Professor S. B. Saul for his careful supervision and criticism, and to Professor T. C. Smout who, in addition to extending to me his help and supervision at the research stage, also kindly read this manuscript carefully and critically and helped me avoid some glaring inaccuracies and other shortcomings. In this connection I am also grateful to Dr John Butt of the University of Strathclyde, and to Kenneth Ponting who also kindly read this book in manuscript and made many helpful suggestions.

Many members of the National Association of Scottish Woollen Manufacturers, and its secretary Mr Aglen, showed much interest in my work and gave me the benefit of their knowledge and experience wherever they could. Some kindly allowed me to clamber around in their mills looking for business records and gave me access to them. I am especially indebted in this respect to the late W. Ballantyne, E. S. Harrison, R. A. Lindsay Watson, G. Smith, Ian Brown and H. Dobson. I am particularly grateful to the managements of Messrs Henry Ballantyne & Sons of Walkerburn; W. Watson & Sons, Hawick; Jas Johnston & Co, Elgin; J. & J. Crombie, Aberdeen; and Paton & Baldwin's, Alloa; for granting me access to their business records and allowing me to quote from them. I was also helped by Messrs G. Harrison, woollen merchants in Edinburgh, and by Messrs Sanderson & Murray, wool brokers in Gala-shiels. The Galashiels Manufacturers' Corporation permitted me to quote from its original minute book. I thank the directors of the Company of Scottish History Ltd for letting me quote extensively from my article 'The Union and the Scottish Woollen Industry, 1707-1760', published in the *Scottish Historical Review*, vol L, 2, No 150 (Oct 1971).

The author and publisher would also like to thank the following for permission to reproduce the illustrations used in this book: the *Hawick News* for plates on pp 66 and 84; *The Scotsman Publications* for the plate on p133; the Librarian, Galashiels Public Library for plates on pp 83 and 134; Dr J. G. Martindale for the plate on p 65, and also for his help in tracking down an important document and for giving me access to his college library.

Several other persons not directly connected with the woollen trade gave me invaluable help, including J. Chisholm, who introduced me to the 'Gala folk' early in my researches, and Miss Craig-Brown, who let me see and use important family papers. R. Scott, Curator of the Wilton Museum, Hawick, talked with me a lot and gave me the benefit of his deep local knowledge. Dr M. L. Ryder gave me valuable help concerning the technicalities of wool and sheep. The staff of Register House, Edinburgh, offered me friendly assistance at all times.

It remains for me to thank Jill Armstrong for typing what was often an almost undecipherable manuscript, and my dear wife, who has kept me sane by reminding me that I am not married to the tweed industry but who, nonetheless, has had to endure many long silent evenings and a fearfully untidy sitting-room in the past few years.

Index

Page numbers of illustrations are in *italic* type.